COUNSELLING COUPLES
IN RELATIONSHIPS

WILEY SERIES

in

BRIEF THERAPY AND COUNSELLING

Editor

Windy Dryden

Brief Rational Emotive Behaviour Therapy
Windy Dryden

Brief Therapeutic Consultations
An approach to systemic counselling
Eddy Street and Jim Downey

Brief Therapy with Couples
Maria Gilbert and Diane Shmukler

Counselling Couples in Relationships
An introduction to the RELATE Approach
Christopher Butler and Victoria Joyce

Further titles in preparation

COUNSELLING COUPLES IN RELATIONSHIPS

An introduction to the RELATE Approach

Christopher Butler and Victoria Joyce

JOHN WILEY & SONS

Chichester · New York · Weinheim · Brisbane · Singapore · Toronto

Copyright © 1998   John Wiley & Sons Ltd, The Atrium, Southern Gate, Chichester,
West Sussex PO19 8SQ, England

Telephone   (+44) 1243 779777

Email (for orders and customer service enquiries): cs-books@wiley.co.uk
Visit our Home Page on www.wileyeurope.com or www.wiley.co.uk

Reprinted July 1998, February 2000, November 2001, October 2003

All Rights Reserved. No part of this publication may be reproduced, stored in a retrieval system or transmitted in any form or by any means, electronic, mechanical, photocopying, recording, scanning or otherwise, except under the terms of the Copyright, Designs and Patents Act 1988 or under the terms of a licence issued by the Copyright Licensing Agency Ltd, 90 Tottenham Court Road, London W1T 4LP, UK, without the permission in writing of the Publisher. Requests to the Publisher should be addressed to the Permissions Department, John Wiley & Sons Ltd, The Atrium, Southern Gate, Chichester, West Sussex PO19 8SQ, England, or emailed to permreq@wiley.co.uk, or faxed to (+44) 1243 770571.

This publication is designed to provide accurate and authoritative information in regard to the subject matter covered. It is sold on the understanding that the Publisher is not engaged in rendering professional services. If professional advice or other expert assistance is required, the services of a competent professional should be sought.

Other Wiley Editorial Offices

John Wiley & Sons Inc., 111 River Street, Hoboken, NJ 07030, USA

Jossey-Bass, 989 Market Street, San Francisco, CA 94103-1741, USA

Wiley-VCH Verlag GmbH, Boschstr. 12, D-69469 Weinheim, Germany

John Wiley & Sons Australia Ltd, 33 Park Road, Milton, Queensland 4064, Australia

John Wiley & Sons (Asia) Pte Ltd, 2 Clementi Loop #02-01, Jin Xing Distripark, Singapore 129809

John Wiley & Sons Canada Ltd, 22 Worcester Road, Etobicoke, Ontario, Canada M9W 1L1

British Library Cataloguing in Publication Data

A catalogue record for this book is available from the British Library

ISBN 0-471-97778-0

Typeset in 10/12pt Palatino by Saxon Graphics Limited, Derby
Printed and bound in Great Britain by TJ International Ltd, Padstow, Cornwall
This book is printed on acid-free paper responsibly manufactured from sustainable forestry in which at least two trees are planted for each one used for paper production.

CONTENTS

About the Authors vii

Series Preface viii

Preface – RELATE and its Work with Couples ix

Acknowledgements xvii

Introduction – Couple Counselling 1

1   An Overview 13

2   Stage One – Exploration 27

3   Stage Two – Understanding 52

4   Stage Three – Action 81

5   Sex and Couples 110

6   Problems in the Work 130

7   Clients Requiring Work Elsewhere 152

8   Endings 167

Bibliography 185

References 187

Index 189

TO BOTH OUR FAMILIES

ABOUT THE AUTHORS

Christopher Butler is a BAC Accredited Counsellor. He joined RELATE in 1989 and then worked as a senior officer in RELATE's South Region where he was responsible for overseeing 60,000 hours of counselling a year, delivered by over 400 counsellors in 22 Centres. He has specialised in the development of effective casework supervision and in promoting the take up of RELATE's services by all sections of the population. He is currently head of student counselling services at Royal Holloway, University of London.

Christopher first trained in counselling in 1983. He also has qualifications in teaching and management and worked in the building industry and in education before joining RELATE.

Christopher and his partner Morag have been happily together for eighteen years and have three children.

Victoria Joyce is a Certified RELATE Counsellor and has worked for RELATE for the past thirteen years, firstly as a counsellor and then as a supervisor. In addition to supervising a team of RELATE counsellors, she devises and leads both basic and advanced counsellor training for RELATE's East Region. Victoria's particular interest is developing and adapting counselling practices to best meet individual couples' differing needs.

Victoria also has qualifications in the medical field and managed the staffing side of a medical agency. Her experience in both these fields allowed her to observe how poor personal relationships can reverberate through the work place.

Victoria has been married for over twenty years and has two sons and two stepsons.

Christopher and Victoria have collaborated together for the last five years, and have a shared interest in single session and short-term focused work with couples.

SERIES PREFACE

In recent years, the field of counselling and psychotherapy has become preoccupied with brief forms of intervention. While some of this interest has been motivated by expediency – reducing the amount of help that is offered to clients to make the best use of diminishing resources – there has also developed the view that brief therapy may be the treatment of choice for many people seeking therapeutic help. It is with the latter view in mind that the Wiley Series in Brief Therapy and Counselling was developed.

This series of practical texts considers different forms of brief therapy and counselling as they are practised in different settings and with different client groups. While no book can substitute for vigorous training and supervision, the purpose of the books in the present series is to provide clear guides for the practice of brief therapy and counselling, which is here defined as lasting 25 sessions or less.

Windy Dryden

Series Editor

PREFACE
RELATE AND ITS WORK WITH COUPLES

If we are a metaphor of the universe, the human couple is the metaphor par excellence, *the point of intersection of all forces and the seed of all forms. The couple is time recaptured, the return to the time before time.*

Octavio Paz, 1967

This is the first book that has been written with the explicit aim of trying to capture the whole of the RELATE Approach to couple counselling. This is despite the fact that RELATE, under its present name and its former title of the National Marriage Guidance Council, has been one of the single foremost providers of couple counselling for over 50 years in England, Wales and Northern Ireland, and probably one of the leading providers of such services in the whole world. The reason for this apparent omission is that it has always been a pivotal tenet of RELATE's philosophy to put the clients' needs first. Therefore practice, research and development has always been subordinated to service delivery. This priority has led RELATE in the past to choose to rely on a combination of oral tradition, internal training materials and a carefully selected reading list of texts by others to define its practice, rather than to document it.

This does not mean that RELATE does not have a distinctive and co-ordinated practice. Indeed, the opposite is the case. RELATE's counsellors are all painstakingly selected and carefully trained by the Agency according to a moderately closely defined set of practices. The training lasts for over two years, and leads to a Certificate in Couple and Marital Counselling. RELATE currently has well over 2000 practising counsellors delivering couple counselling using the RELATE Approach, and has trained more than twice this number in its history. The work of these counsellors is monitored and developed by a team of in-house supervisors who are also selected and trained by the Agency. All these counsellors meet with the supervisors for a minimum of thirty hours a year, individually and in groups, in a structure which allows comments and criticisms about the counselling approach to be fed back to the appropriate committees. This provision ensures that RELATE's practice is a largely uniform, co-ordinated and up-to-date one.

In trying to write a book which captures the essence of this practice the authors have a large amount of personal experience at their disposal. We have both been trained by RELATE; we both have a substantial amount of counselling experience with RELATE; we have both supervised the work of other counsellors in RELATE for several years. One of us has been a marker for the RELATE Certificate and so has read case-studies written by counsellors in all parts of the organisation, and has in addition been involved with developing RELATE counsellor and supervisor training; the other trains a full range of Regional Certificate units. As further research for this book we have been involved in an immense amount of discussion with a range of colleagues concerning the RELATE Approach and have read the entire range of RELATE's training materials. Colleagues have been endlessly patient in reading numerous drafts of different sections and giving helpful feedback.

At the end of this research, we are both acutely aware of the vast range of work which is conducted in RELATE. Although every counsellor receives the same training and works broadly with the same method, each counsellor holds firm and valid opinions on such questions as the nature of the unconscious; the importance of active interventions; the precise details of the management of cases. These opinions invariably differ in detail and this richness is the strength of the organisation.

However, the task of writing this comparatively brief book, which we hope will be accessible to a reader who is new to the organisation, has demanded that we order this material into a coherent whole and impose upon it a definite structure. Windy Dryden has been most helpful in encouraging us to do this. In order to do so we have simplified complex theories and omitted qualifications. We have summarised in bullet points discussions which may have taken several hours. We have drawn a definite map of the Approach, although conscious of the wisdom of the dictum that 'the map is *not* the terrain'.

We are aware, therefore, that many workers in RELATE may question some emphases or feel that important elements of their practice have not been fully represented. Even between the two of us many such debates have taken place – usually the result has been a consensus, but sometimes it has been a compromise. We hope that the book will be received in the spirit in which it is offered – a map of a rich and fruitful terrain which will hopefully be the first of many.

PREFACE

Like the first dictionary, this book is intended to be descriptive, not prescriptive. We trust it will be seen as a stimulus for future debate rather than as a constricting rule-book written in stone.

The chance to document this practice, which is offered by the commissioning of this book, is most welcome to the Agency, not least because it has challenged the authors, working in close collaboration with Derek Hill, RELATE's Head of Practioner Training, to firmly define the RELATE Approach to Couple Counselling. As part of this work, Derek Hill has produced a brief descriptive outline of RELATE's practice which has served as a most valuable guideline to the authors. Rather than restate this in a different form, we are pleased to reproduce below this description as a way of introducing the reader to RELATE's current definition of its Approach.

> RELATE's marital and couple counselling practice has evolved over more than fifty years and as a result of work done with hundreds of thousands of couples and individuals involved in disrupted intimate relationships.
>
> 'Fundamental to that practice is an acknowledgement of the uniqueness of individual clients and of their couple and family relationships. Their need to find their own particular balance between autonomy and interdependence is respected, as are the cultural, religious and other influences which affect their thinking and choices.
>
> That stance meshes with an approach to clients which acknowledges that each constructs his or her own set of realities and that they attribute their own meanings to the situations in which they find themselves. There is a commitment to engage with clients with empathy, genuineness and warmth and thereby to create a containing and supportive environment within which clients may address the causes of disruption in their relationships and, through counselling, find shared solutions to the problems being faced.
>
> RELATE's counsellors acquire and employ a focus on clients' couple relationships. They use a repertoire of skills specific to the conduct of interviews with couples, or with lone partners. That work is structured by a three-stage model of counselling (exploration, understanding, action). The focus, structure and skills used are together responsible for the particular characteristics of RELATE's couples counselling and its direct engagement with clients' intimate relationships.
>
> Counsellors' work with disrupted intimate relationships makes them acutely aware of the powerful influence of clients' developmental histories on their adult relationships. This is commonly seen in predispositions to re-enact the dynamics of early significant relationships in adult life. Those processes, the unconscious quality of many of them, and the empirical evidence that by making them conscious and understood they may be modified and made more adaptive, adds a psychodynamic orientation to the practice. Many of the concepts developed by Klein, Winnicott, Guntrip and Fairbairn are used to describe and discuss those influences on adult relationships and to build working hypotheses about inter- and intra-personal

dynamics. Berne's approach to understanding the workings of interpersonal relations is commonly found to be accessible and helpful to clients.

In similar ways, RELATE's couple work has drawn attention to the pervasive influence of early attachment experiences on clients' adult relationships. Bowlby's writings inform work done with clients for whom attachment, separation and loss present particular problems.

Marital and couples work confronts the counsellor with clients' differing capacities to handle dyadic and triangular relationships. Theoretical treatments of the Oedipus myth provide powerful tools when addressing these issues and when seeking to help clients find the origins and meanings of the patterning of their relationships.

Couples casework provides strong evidence that intimate relationships are particularly vulnerable at times when the partners are making the transition from one phase of adult life to another, e.g. single adult–partner, partner–co-parent. The research findings of those who have studied individual and family life-stages are used by counsellors to assist in identifying the issues being faced by clients and the pressures they are experiencing. They commonly assist clients to find answers to the question, 'Why is this happening to us now?

Clients bring their struggles to establish their gender identity, and to find ways to give expression to their sexuality, into counselling. RELATE's counsellors use the insights offered by contemporary writing on gender issues and some of the strategies developed by leading psychosexual therapists when working with clients on those aspects of their relationships. This aspect of the counsellors' work is facilitated by the attention given to the development in them of a capacity to talk comfortably and in an informed and frank way about gender and sexual matters.

The ever-changing characteristic of family life is a constant focus of attention in couples counselling. Concepts drawn from family therapy and systemic theory are used by counsellors to assist clients to explore the complex dynamics of the family settings within which their couple relationships are lived out. Insights drawn from the work of family therapists also assist when clients are faced with the unexpected responses of family members to their own efforts to change patterns of behaviour and modify long-established roles.

The various conceptual frameworks referred to above are available to RELATE's couples counsellors through their initial training and their continuing personal professional development. They are used, selectively, by the counsellors to develop working hypotheses about the nature of clients' couple relationships and the causes of their disruption.

During the first, exploratory, stage of counselling conceptual frameworks assist the counsellors to work with clients to gain a shared, coherent and comprehensive description of the relationship and to identify the features needing specific attention.

The second stage of the work has, as its purpose, the clients' developing understanding of the ways in which their behaviour towards one another responds to the many internal and external influences to which the partners

PREFACE

are subject. The counsellor's constantly refined working hypothesis informs that discourse and prompts a search for meanings which offer the clients a view of the ways in which they can shape their interaction with each other and of the options thus available to them. This work involves the clients in thinking in more depth and in a more structured way about their relationship than most have ever done before. The counsellor's role is to present the clients to themselves and to offer them new perspectives which have their origins in one or other of the conceptual frameworks being used. The language used in these discourses is often full of metaphor and frequently reflects a significant growth in the clients' capacity to inter-relate and make sense of emotions, thoughts and action in themselves and their partners.

In the third stage of counselling clients and counsellor work together to bring chosen options into operation. Roles may be modified, habitual patterns of behaviour may need to be abandoned and replaced by more adaptive interactions, forms of communication which respond better to the partners' needs may be required. Strategies used in behavioural therapy may be employed to support the clients' efforts to free themselves from problematic dynamics and find better ways to meet each other's needs.

RELATE's clients seek help because they find themselves in a relationship crisis, or because chronic problems have been exacerbated by events and no longer feel tolerable. A minority seek help at an earlier stage and with a view to preventing present discomforts becoming major causes of distress and disruption. Most clients attend ten or fewer hour long sessions. The counselling offered is thus shaped to address specific problems and to provide the clients with the understandings and the capacities to work with each other to deal with their differences and the causes of conflict which they face. The purposes of the counselling are thus to deal with the clients' immediate concerns and to help equip them to deal themselves with problems that may arise in the future. The latter purpose is an expression of the notion that an adult intimate relationship can itself be a therapeutic relationship for both partners.

It will be evident that it is not easy to encapsulate the RELATE Approach to couples counselling in a few words. Pragmatism has played a great part in its evolution. It has borrowed from many therapeutic schools. It attunes itself to each new client couple. It is grounded in ethical practice (BAC Code of Ethics and Practice for Counsellors, 1993) yet it is kept free of all but the most basic of rules of practice so as to be able to use the ideas and strategies which are best suited to the clients' needs and capacities. In the hands of an experienced counsellor the Approach has been shown to be able to respond effectively to a great diversity of relationship problems and to cope with the complexities of contemporary family life.

(Derek Hill, RELATE, 1996, reproduced by permission).

Although the RELATE Approach frequently leads to work involving more than six sessions, which is sometimes considered a definition of brief therapy, it undoubtedly falls within the parameters of this Wiley series of books, where 'brief' is defined as requiring less than 25 weekly sessions. Few clients are seen for longer than 15 sessions in the RELATE setting. Chapter 8 deals with the indicators that might suggest where a longer contract could be valuable. However, such work is undertaken with less than 5% of the clients who engage with the RELATE Approach.

We have assumed that the readers of this book will be aware of the field of counselling, and therefore will have an understanding of what counselling is and of some of the techniques of active listening which a counsellor uses. This assumption has allowed us to make use of the book to explore RELATE's particular Approach and not to duplicate much of the more basic material on counselling skills which is already available from a wide variety of sources.

Conversely, however, we have assumed that the reader will not necessarily have any familiarity with psychological theory. Therefore, where we introduce the theoretical underpinning to RELATE's work, we do so assuming no prior knowledge. We expect that these introductions, cast as they are in RELATE's own language with particular examples drawn from our practice experience, will be of interest to all readers irrespective of their backgrounds.

We are aware that there is a wealth of material to include in order to offer an overview of the RELATE Approach. This means that each chapter introduces a variety of concepts briefly and can give only limited space to explaining how these interlink. In the RELATE setting, continued group and individual supervision is offered together with ongoing professional development to allow practitioners to profit from the richness of these separate items and to form them into an integrated whole. Now that this material is presented in book form, we hope the reader will feel able to bear in mind that this is only intended to be an introduction to the Approach and its theoretical underpinnings. A full bibliography based on RELATE's reading list is included at the end of the book to allow for further study.

This book offers a similar approach to that of RELATE's own training. It assumes a grasp of the concept of empathic listening from the outset, together with an interest in and sympathy for the concept of the couple, but with no other prior knowledge. It aims to stimulate thought and exploration within a firm framework, rather than to offer a completely cross-referenced paradigm. The RELATE training requires the active and energetic participation of the trainee counsellor in order to build a holistic approach which is integrated as a counselling model. The aim is to allow each practitioner room to define his or her own distinctive place set firmly within the core material.

We conclude with a brief explaination of how we have attributed gender to the counsellors hereafter and whence we have obtained our casework examples.

When referring to the counsellor, the authors have decided not to use either *he* or *she* exclusively. We believe that exclusive reference to either gender casts a particular slant over all of the text. Equally, the alternative of using the compound pronoun *he/she* and *his/her* has drawbacks. The most significant of these is that it is depersonalising and so makes identification with the text harder for the reader. It is also somewhat cumbersome.

Therefore, we have decided to refer to the counsellor as *he* on some occasions, and as *she* on other more frequent ones. By doing this, we intend to indicate that all aspects of the RELATE Approach are accessible to counsellors of both genders. However, we are aware that the majority of RELATE's counsellors and other workers are female, as is the case in many of the other agencies linked to the caring and teaching professions. There is not an agreed view upon the effect this has on RELATE's work, although the matter has been much discussed within the Agency and care is taken to redress obvious bias. Anyone who accepts that unconscious and systemic processes influence human interactions – and this is one of the premises from which the authors work – must be aware that this imbalance of gender may contribute significantly to the distinctive features of the Approach. We have not sought to disguise this possibility and shall return to this discussion later in the book. However, we do not believe that the gender balance of the practitioners within the Agency undermines the RELATE Approach in any significant way or invalidates its use in a variety of settings. We have therefore set out to reflect this circumstance honestly and unapologetically in our writing.

RELATE places a very high value on the confidentiality of the counselling it offers. We believe that this duty of confidentiality outweighs almost all other needs. The authors feel, therefore, that to compromise this duty by publishing details of actual casework – however disguised – would not be correct. Even if this were done with clients' later consent it would violate the spirit of the agreement in which the work had originally been conducted.

Instead, we have invented the case-studies that appear in this book, taking care to ensure that they bear no close similarity to any of the clients the authors have counselled, or any other clients whose counselling within RELATE the authors have supervised or otherwise learned about. We have endeavoured to make these examples representative of the range of clients seen by RELATE, and to construct them carefully and realistically to ensure they are consistent and credible in the way that convincing fictional characters are normally drawn. In addition we have tried to indicate the different ranges of relationships which exist between the counsellor and clients – hopefully always warm and supportive, but also unique and dynamic personal interactions, each with its own blend of such qualities as kindness, interest, humour and challenge. Should readers feel that they have noticed any resemblance to themselves or to others who might have been clients of RELATE, we can assure them that such resemblance is entirely coincidental and totally unintentional.

It has been a privilege and a pleasure for us to be able to write this introduction to the RELATE Approach to Couple Counselling. Our desire to do so has come from our sense of the central importance of a couple relationship to so many people, and from the satisfaction that springs from better understanding of such relationships. We hope readers will find the RELATE Approach stimulating. It is undoubtedly too complex to be learned from one book alone, and requires a journey through appropriate training, experience and supervision before it can be successfully put into practice. Nonetheless, we hope that this book will serve as a significant signpost along that route and that those who follow it, together with their future clients, will be able to share in the satisfaction that has led us to write this book.

ACKNOWLEDGEMENTS

The authors would like to thank all those who have made this book possible – especially the clients of RELATE who have briefly shared their lives with us, and the counsellors, supervisors and senior officers of the Agency who have offered us thoughts and ideas, support and encouragement.

In particular, may we thank Derek Hill for his patience in reading and commenting on innumerable versions, Marianne de Groot for her help with Chapter 5, Jo Millard for her detailed commentary on the text, Sid Short for her meticulous proof-reading and our families for their unflagging support. Our especial thanks to Victoria's husband Barry for providing both plain English and fancy computing when it was needed and to Colin Murray Parkes for his very helpful and detailed suggestions following the first draft.

Finally, we would like to thank Windy Dryden for suggesting the book initially and then for honing it into shape.

INTRODUCTION – COUPLE COUNSELLING

Counsel woven in the fabric of real life is wisdom.
Walter Benjamin

This Introduction is intended as a prelude to the identification of some of the key elements of RELATE's Approach to couple counselling, by explaining some of the assumptions made by the authors in the preparation of this book.

First, we will explore and clarify our definition of a 'couple' and consider the current context of couple life. Next, we will investigate why counselling is a suitable medium for the solution of the problems that couples experience. We will then attempt to position the RELATE Approach within the context of the many other forms of counselling and therapy that are available. We shall then look at what constitutes a couple problem. Finally, with these established, we will go on to consider the implications for different groups among the potential client base, and discuss how the RELATE Approach operates to combat discriminatory practice.

THE NATURE OF THE COUPLE

The Agency has repeatedly been called upon to define its focus sharply, and to be clear on which of its potential clients can be included, and whom it would exclude from help. We have outlined below what the term 'couple' means within the RELATE Approach.

The RELATE Approach does not make any assumptions about the legal status of the partnership. Married and unmarried couples are equally able to benefit. So are gay and lesbian couples. The couple do not necessarily need to be living together; however, there are assumptions made about commitment to the relationship. The Approach is aimed at relationships which are considered primary. By this we mean that it is the main relationship for each of the partners involved which, even if it is not viewed as permanent, is long-term.

It is assumed that the partners will be seeking to maintain a high degree of sexual exclusivity in their relationship. Therefore, although there is an acceptance that certain couples may involve other sexual partners at certain stages, the Approach is not equipped to deal with the complexities of permanently triangular or multiple relationships.

Whether the relationship need invariably include a sexual component is a slightly more complex question. The vast majority of the couples to which this Approach is applied do have a sexual relationship. Working to help both partners express their sexuality together is frequently an important part of the work. However, most experienced couple counsellors will have met relationships where the partners have chosen to forgo shared sexual activity. Although this choice would undoubtedly be explored as part of the work, it does not in itself exclude the couple from work which follows the RELATE Approach.

Relationships which exist for some other specific or limited purpose, for example business partnerships or house-shares, do not fall within the parameters of the Approach. Even though they might benefit from certain aspects of the work, there are underlying assumptions about intimacy which would preclude these relationships. For similar reasons, relationships that spring from the same family, for instance mother and daughter or between siblings, are also excluded.

Certain degrees of exploitative behaviour or abuse might place the relationship outside the boundaries of the RELATE Approach, even though the precise boundaries are most difficult to define. Broadly, each member of the partnership should have the right to find and pursue his or her own life goals. Inevitably partners are called upon to voluntarily give up on some of the desires which might lead to personal satisfaction, but which will undermine the couple relationship. However, this must be a voluntary relinquishment. Relationships that are clearly coercive fall outside RELATE's Approach. The existence of violence or coercion will not initially exclude a couple from this Approach, since it may well be an expression of the couple's inability to find a more suitable way of resolving differences and meeting their goals. However, if the duress is an expression of the fact that one or both partners rejects the idea of mutuality and believes that the other partner exists primarily to serve his or her needs, then the relationship will fall outside the RELATE Approach.

To summarise, the Approach is designed for couple relationships between two adults with no direct blood links, which is formed with a view to the long term and with an intention of exclusivity. This will typically be characterised by a desire for intimacy, for shared sexual fulfilment and for the achievement of some of the tasks of family formation. These may involve conceiving or raising children, forming a shared household or some other joint enterprise. The relationship will not be maintained by coercion. Individual autonomy and growth are an essential constituent part of the relationship, as is the modification of purely personal goals in favour of joint ones.

In Britain at the end of the twentieth century, the economic and social pressures which buttress a partnership, in particular that of marriage, are considerably less than they have been in earlier times. The potential for earning is more available to women than it has been at any other time in the past. The stigma and difficulty attached to raising children outside a conventional couple relationship has lessened. There is more control over fertility than has ever been the case previously. Marriage is no longer an indissoluble union. Divorce is an accepted concept in the vast majority of areas of public life. Finally, advances in welfare have lessened the necessity of a firm family structure as the main method of surviving ill-health or old age.

Now that the extraneous forces which held couples together have diminished, relationships are dependent on the partners' intrinsic relationship skills and motivation to cement the bond. Although there is a marked decline in the number of couples marrying, there is still a strong sense that a majority of individuals are concerned with the formation of a successful couple relationship. In the words of RELATE's Common Purpose Statement, 'While marriage as the pivotal relationship in a family has come under unprecedented pressure, a happy and lasting partnership remains an ideal to which most couples aspire'. It is to this individual aspiration towards a successful partnership which is so widespread in our society, that the couple counselling approach described in the following pages is devoted.

WHY COUNSELLING?

When the National Marriage Guidance Council was originally formed, counselling was not foreseen as the major component of its work. Its goal was that of education, and there was an expectation that marital problems could be alleviated largely by a didactic approach.

Now, half a century later, the Organisation's principle involvement is in counselling. RELATE's Common Purpose Statement specifically underlines that 'The quality of couple and family relationships can be improved, avoidable breakdown prevented and the new relationships formed with the help of a trained counsellor'. Windy Dryden (1991) notes '...that the very word counsellor was for many years associated mainly with MGC and its work in the field of marital and relationship difficulties'. Currently RELATE can lay claim to being one of the world's largest counselling agencies, with half a million sessions of counselling and sexual therapy being delivered annually in England, Wales and Northern Ireland. Although RELATE still energetically supports its goals by providing a thriving Education Service and a growing library of accessible publications which offer advice on forming successful relationships, counselling remains its key service to couples experiencing relationship problems.

We shall devote a brief space to considering why counselling might be a more appropriate form of help than other methods. The authors would offer three suggestions to explain why this approach has gained pre-eminence over others. These are:

- The uniqueness of each couple's problems.
- The shame attendant on the experience and exploration of relationship problems.
- The helpfulness of a personal relationship in facilitating change and learning.

The Uniqueness of Each Couple's Problems

Tolstoy's famous opening words to his novel *Anna Karenina* are frequently quoted in this connection: 'All happy families resemble one another, but each unhappy family is unhappy in its own way'. Couple problems are usually composed of a complex mixture of ingredients which make up a whole that is individual and idiosyncratic. The component parts include each partner's own personal history and character, the character and history of the relationship and the attendant circumstances at the time of presentation.

Most couples, by the time they seek counselling, are aware of the existence of a problem in their relationship, and may have had recourse to various forms of assistance. They have often tapped their own problem-solving skills. The specific advice of relatives and of other professionals, especially general practitioners, has commonly been sought – a recent study of RELATE clients reveals that the couple are twice as likely to have visited their doctor in the previous fortnight than the rest of the population (McCarthy, 1996). They may have read the general advice of newspaper columnists and other authors. The existence of the problem may well have made the couple receptive to this advice and keen to experiment with a variety of solutions.

There is no particular reason to doubt that the advice offered will be full of good sense and practical value. It may differ little from the solution that the couple find for themselves at the end of successful counselling. However, the critical factor that counselling offers is the sustained focus upon the particular relationship. The solutions arrived at from a course of counselling will be the product of an average of eight hours of energetic interpersonal interaction between the two or three individuals in the counselling room. It will typically be reinforced by at least an equal amount of time spent by each of the individuals reflecting on the process or engaged in related tasks. All this time will have been single-mindedly devoted to dealing with the problems of the couple. Therefore, there is an approximate total of fifty hours being spent in exploring the nature of the problem, understanding its particular dynamic and experimenting with possible solutions. This large-scale investment of time on the particular problem allows for a detailed appreciation of its exact dynamic and for a tailor-made solution to emerge. It is very difficult to produce such an detailed focus through other means such as books, training, group work or interactive media.

The Shame Attendant on the Experience and Exploration of Relationship Problems

We live in an age that is in some ways more accepting of individual failure and less condemnatory of people when they experience problems. In an increasing number of areas, problems are regarded as challenges to be overcome, or as manifestations of past sufferings or neglect, rather than grounds for condemnation. Marital breakdown is viewed in a similar way. It has become less of an arena for the attribution of personal fault or blame. However, welcome though this change of attitude is, we should not let this change of attitude blind us to the deep sense of shame which is commonly attendant upon failure. This shame is well described by Milan Kundera (1991).

> The basis of shame is not some personal mistake of ours, but the ignominy, the humiliation we feel that we must be what we are without any choice in the matter, and that this humiliation is seen by everyone.

Without seeking to increase or validate this sense of shame, RELATE counsellors have a long tradition of respect for the pain felt by couples who are faced by relationship problems. RELATE, like many counselling agencies, places a premium upon the confidentiality of the counselling process. This confidentiality guarantees that the matters that the couple discuss will always be treated with immense respect and that, except in the most extreme of circumstances, considerable steps will be taken to ensure that nothing they say can be linked back to them. It also ensures that the couple know that all their contacts with the Agency, and indeed the very fact that they are in contact with the Agency, will never become known against their will. This determination is a distinct feature of all aspects of RELATE's practice.

There is a potential that this shame can be intensified when we link our present problems with our past life. The psychodynamic view of relationship problems acknowledges that it can be a necessary and helpful process, albeit a painful one. Windy Dryden (1993) has drawn our attention to the fact that many in our culture find this process difficult. George Bernard Shaw went further: 'We are ashamed of everything that is real about us; ashamed of ourselves, of our relatives... of our opinions, of our experience, just as we are ashamed of our naked skins'.

The authors would not wish to suggest that this sense of shame is universal. Neither would we oppose a general move in society to lessen it, although there are disadvantages as well as gains to be had from a more confessional culture. We would, however, say that avoidance of shame is a significant determinant in the choice of help for a vast number of couples. There is a distinct advantage in a confidential counselling approach which can, far more easily, guarantee privacy and a safe arena for the exploration of personal issues than other methods.

The Helpfulness of a Personal Relationship in Facilitating Change and Learning

The importance of an interpersonal relationship to aid learning has been long recognised. Educational establishments place emphasis on the importance of a personal relationship with a tutor to produce more creative work. In the world of management, it has been accepted that more than simple training is needed to allow change to take place. The use of consultants and mentors abound, and an increasing emphasis is being placed upon the importance of a close interpersonal element in managerial relationships. In the counselling world, stress is placed upon the interpersonal relationship with the supervisor as a most important support for a counsellor's learning. One of the present authors has conducted research into this area and concluded from a detailed review of relevant literature that: '...it has emerged that a close personal relationship is helpful in ensuring the transfer of knowledge.' (Butler, 1995).

Learning rarely comes easily to adults; this is particularly true when the situation is exacerbated by the existence of a problem. An industrial psychologist expressed it thus:

> Insight is often difficult to achieve and when we cannot solve a problem because it is too complex we become frustrated and anxious. To avoid [this] we deny the problem or simplify it, even if that means distorting the problem, or project the problem onto someone else, or in various other defensive ways manage not to learn... Unlearning is emotionally difficult because the old way ... has become embedded... For habit and skill learning to take hold, we need opportunities to practise and make errors (Schein, 1993).

A management consultant succinctly summarises the role of a third party at such a time, who...

> ...confirms that the client's difficulty and concerns are understandable, that the situation can be examined to see what might be done, and that the client need not condemn himself, immobilise himself with guilt, or act impetuously out of anxiety. This is an extremely important role but is often overlooked (Zand, 1993).

The RELATE Approach places strong emphasis upon the quality of the personal relationship which the clients form with their individual counsellor and which thus facilitates the process of learning and change. As befits a methodology that works in a brief time-scale, allowing the focus to remain with the couple and their struggle, the relationship with the counsellor is seen as a transitional one rather than a central one. It is nonetheless critical to the success of the Approach.

THE RELATE APPROACH AND OTHER COUNSELLING AND PSYCHOTHERAPEUTIC DISCIPLINES

We have ranged far wider than the counselling and psychotherapeutic field in order to explain the RELATE Approach, and have quoted from writers from a variety of disciplines as an expression of our desire to normalise the experience of having a problem. It is not helpful to unnecessarily *pathologise* the clients' problems or, in other words, to see them as expressions of personal defect or psychological weakness.

The ability to form and nurture a successful couple relationship is not developed in everyone. Indeed, current divorce statistics tend to suggest that the absence of this ability is more common than its presence. To nurse a couple relationship successfully through the changes of life requires the dynamic and ongoing exercise of a whole range of awarenesses and interpersonal skills. The amount of these skills needed will differ, depending on the exact circumstances of the couple and the nature of the problems facing them. Research has suggested that the skills that are present in healthy relationships are concerned with flexibility in problem solving, ability to communicate effectively and capacity for mutual empathy (Crowe and Ridley, 1996). These skills are usually learned through experience, and many couples facing crisis are, in fact, merely being required by circumstances to ascend a steep learning curve.

Therefore, couples are encouraged to view the encounter with their specific problems as an opportunity to examine their usual patterns and solutions, and to experiment with new ways of acting. This process is well described by Derek Hill in the Preface to this book. There is no suggestion that because these skills have not been learned in the past, that it is a sign of pathology. It is merely a deficit that now needs to be addressed if the couple are to proceed along their desired path.

In working with couples, many signs of the defensiveness in the face of change noted by Schein will be met. This is a normal human phenomenon, and usually the signs can be understood by reference to the clients' earlier life experiences and to the effects of change. Once resistance is understood, behaviour patterns can be modified. This occurs in the vast majority of RELATE contracts, where the process is normally achieved in a brief number of sessions, typically falling between six and sixteen. Within this time-scale, it is normal for the couple to both solve specific problems and generalise the learning in order to equip themselves to deal better with problems in the future. In a few instances, which are discussed later, the process follows this pattern, but requires a longer time-scale for the desired change to occur.

In a minority of cases this is not possible, and clients find themselves unable to modify the thought process or the behaviour which is causing them problems, or are unable even to agree on the area of modification needed. Usually this is either because there is too great a degree of emotional disturbance or else because the problems are too deeply entrenched. In such cases, depending on the exact situation, one or both clients might be directed towards psychiatric help – usually via a referral to their GP – or towards some other form of therapy. This may be of a psychodynamic type (such as psychoanalytic psychotherapy), of a behavioural nature (such as cognitive–behavioural therapy) or of a systemic type (such as family therapy). None of these therapies are included as such within the RELATE Approach although, as Derek Hill has stated, learning from the schools of these therapies has contributed greatly to the RELATE Approach. Neither are any of these therapies offered to clients within RELATE apart from RELATE Psychosexual Therapy, a highly successful integration of couple counselling and specifically focused behavioural sexual therapy.

RELATE accepts that there is a distinction between counselling and psychotherapy. RELATE considers that this distinction springs from the fact that in most counselling there is a limit to the degree of disturbance or resistance that can be tackled. Most psychotherapies offer the chance of more structure and specificity of approach and greater intimacy in the contact with clients in a suitably safe setting. RELATE certainly accepts the possibility of some clients requiring such therapy to help them further than the RELATE Approach can do. However, we do not accept the suggestion sometimes offered that counselling only works at a lesser 'depth'. RELATE's experience is that the majority of clients with relationship problems are able to mobilise their own resources and heal their own hurts – or more usually turn their couple relationship into a vehicle for this healing – with the help of a brief counselling intervention, rather that being in need of longer therapeutic engagement to aid their progress, and that this process can lead to the most profound changes and the most significant relief of distress.

DEFINING THE COUPLE PROBLEM

Crowe and Ridley (1996), in their useful discussion of factors affecting suitability for couple therapy, note the lack of research into this question and the inhibiting effect of a dogmatic approach. They also helpfully cover many of the main problems in answering this question.

Where a couple present with a problem which they regard as common, or where one partner presents with a problem which he or she wishes to work on as a couple problem, the situation is comparatively simple. The only factor that might inhibit exploratory work would be if some aspects of one individual's behaviour or pathology suggested to the counsellor that it would be irresponsible to begin couple work, without first ensuring that the immediate symptoms were addressed. For example, one partner may be clearly suffering from acute mental illness, or actively suicidal or threatening to severely harm others. In the most extreme cases, severe individual pathology might prevent couple counselling ever being possible. However, such cases are very rare.

A more common difficulty occurs when one individual is apparently the major symptom bearer. Assuming the symptoms do not fall into the categories described above, and assuming also that the client or clients are content to regard the problem as a joint one, couple work can be usefully begun for several reasons.

Firstly, even if the symptom is clearly affecting one partner more than the other, exploration may help mobilise both partners' helping capacity. It clarifies the joint aspects to the problem and to what extent it may be an individual one. It may also allow the partner who is less affected to explore whether his or her remedial actions are truly helpful. Partners can often perpetuate rather than help an individual problem. Both partners may also find it helpful to explore the impact of the problem on the relationship and to vent some of their feelings, for example frustration or sadness, which the existence of the problem may cause.

More importantly, as will be seen from later chapters, the client who carries the overt symptoms may often only be the visible harbinger of a problem which in fact belongs to them both. For example, a client who initially appears over-anxious about his partner's fidelity may well be testifying to the couple's shared agenda of concern about the continuance of the relationship. Many of the models used by RELATE counsellors suggest that it is unwise to unthinkingly attribute the problem to one individual. The counsellor should hesitate and reflect, just as one might initially resist the card that is being forced upon one by a conjuror. In addition, it is the authors' experience that most individuals have a good sense of what form of help they require. Therefore, someone presenting and requesting couple counselling may well be indicating a firm sense of having a couple problem, even if natural defensiveness and anxiety when in counselling appears to initially discount or exaggerate how this problem is shared.

There is, however, little evidence to suggest that couple problems cannot also be helped by individual action to remove one set of symptoms. Indeed, such evidence as there is, seems to point in the opposite direction. So, even if a counsellor considers, for example, that one partner expresses all the distress over the relationship problems by becoming severely depressed, the removal of this depression by appropriate and sympathetic individual treatment would certainly benefit that individual, and may well place the couple in a better position to address the underlying issues.

Overall, the RELATE Approach encourages the clients' desire to present their problem as a joint one, unless this is clearly contra-indicated. This is because we see the couple dynamic as a joint unique construction deriving from the interaction of the hopes and fears of each individual. The Approach is very open to the exploration of a large variety of problems. However, it allows a client to seek other support for severe individual symptoms, especially when this can be done without that individual feeling obliged to take responsibility for all the couple's problems that are not directly related to these symptoms.

We will return to these issues frequently in the ensuing chapters. They may seem initially daunting and complex, but the couple counsellor must be able to address them with competence. It is one of the most fundamental and valuable skills.

MAKING THE COUNSELLING ACCESSIBLE TO EVERYONE

We have included a short summary of the work that has been done to make this Approach generally and uniformly available so that the reader may gauge the accessibility of the RELATE Approach.

RELATE has a long and proud history of striving to make couple counselling accessible to all the population of England, Wales and Northern Ireland. (Since London Marriage Guidance established itself as a separate organisation in 1993, RELATE does not have a centre in Inner London, although many couples working or living in the vicinity travel to centres in the suburbs.) Patricia Hunt (1985) noted in her research in Manchester that her sample indicated that the counselling reached 'a much wider range of people than the professional middle-class clientele that is commonly attributed to the MG Agency'. The results of the survey carried out more recently by the RELATE Centre for Family Studies at Newcastle University, based on a much larger sample of 943 in the Midlands, concluded that:

> RELATE clients were more likely to be in employment than the average members of the population, but this may simply reflect a lower age distribution among RELATE clients. The clientele of RELATE is clearly not confined to people with jobs and able to pay for services... RELATE serves members of all occupational groups, albeit that there is a suggestion of some bias in the direction of higher-status occupations (Walker, 1995).

RELATE works hard to ensure that its counselling is accessible to all its potential clients. Counselling centres are located within easy travelling time of population centres. They are generally easily accessible by public transport and arrangements are made to ensure that access to our services is made available to those who have physical disabilities. A substantial proportion of the counselling is offered out of normal working hours, and a sliding scale of charges is normally operated with the intention that no-one should be required to pay more than 0.1% of their gross annual income towards a counselling session. Additionally, there is a commitment that no-one who could benefit from counselling should be denied it for financial reasons. Research has been conducted (Butler, 1993) to see whether the need to make regular pre-booked appointments is a deterrent to certain groups but is inconclusive as yet; however, several centres offer drop-in single-session counselling for clients who may not want to make the longer commitment initially or feel that they are in a crisis and need to explore their options immediately.

Research into the ethnic balance of the client base suggests that RELATE counselling is most significantly under-used by the Asian sections of the community. Although several initiatives are currently under way to address this, the causes are not yet clear. There appears to be a significant general engagement in counselling by lesbian couples, and a more local engagement by gay couples. Overall, significantly more women approach RELATE than men. Work is equally distributed between partners attending alone and as couples.

RELATE does not make a practice of matching counsellors with clients – by sex, race or other criteria. The occasional exceptions occur when strongly supported by clinical indicators, or when use of a language other than English is required. The organisation does, however, strive to ensure that the overall counselling work force is representative of the community as a whole. The most noticeable imbalance to date is that of gender, with the vast majority of the counsellors and other workers being female.

In attempting to ensure that its counselling does not carry an overt or covert bias against any group, RELATE has sought to embed an awareness of questions of equality of access into all aspects of its work. This has also been the approach adopted by the authors of this book. The reader will find that this diversity is reflected in the examples selected for the main body of the book.

There has not yet been a survey linking the outcome of counselling to employment status or ethnic balance. Local centres monitor their own performance and account to local authorities; the current sense from these reports is that the RELATE Approach generally serves local communities equally, with the exception of some bias towards higher-status professions and away from the Asian communities.

We shall return to the question of equality of access in Chapter 6.

1

AN OVERVIEW

The world can doubtless never be well known by theory: practice is absolutely necessary; but surely it is of great use to ... have at least a general map of it.
Lord Chesterfield

The purpose of this initial chapter is to give the reader a sense of the overall structure of the RELATE Approach to Couple Counselling. Much attention has been given in recent times to the evolution of different counselling approaches. Some, often coming from an academic tradition, have stressed the value of theoretical consistency and pointed to the mediocrity and sometimes even danger that can arise from ill-informed assembling of a variety of different elements. Others, often in the public and voluntary sectors, have taken a catholic approach and have valued evidence of successful outcome without being concerned with the precise theoretical provenance of the method, arguing that over-emphasis on theory can lead to rigid models which are divorced from the everyday world of the client and the counsellor.

RELATE can identify itself with both sides of the debate. As has been mentioned, RELATE is a major service provider in the area of couple counselling. RELATE has over 100 independent counselling centres, delivering over 300 000 hours counselling a year in England, Wales and Northern Ireland. All this work is done using the Approach we are describing. These Centres survive by attracting funding from a variety of sources – Central Government, Local Authorities, Health and Social Services and charitable bodies, as well as clients themselves. Given that most funders require detailed evidence of effectiveness before committing any funds, RELATE is consistently challenged to prove that its Approach is effective, competitive and accessible. This leads to an openness – indeed a continual search – for new methods which can be usefully incorporated into our Approach.

However, RELATE has also developed a complete training and supervisory structure. All RELATE couple counsellors are trained in the RELATE Approach over a period of two years, and all the training and supervision of the work is carried out by staff employed and trained by the National

Organisation working to an approved and closely defined syllabus. This structure gives the RELATE Approach wide dissemination and allows the Agency to refine the Approach continually in response to counsellors' experiences with the clients. Therefore, RELATE is ideally placed to exploit the value of a consistency of approach where this is helpful.

The RELATE Approach has evolved pragmatically, taking and adapting elements from other disciplines to build an integrated whole. In helping the reader understand what has influenced this pragmatism, it may be helpful to outline the particular determinants which have shaped the growth of the RELATE Approach:

- *RELATE's clear and acknowledged goal is helping clients to improve their adult couple relationships.* Different elements have been evaluated according to the degree in which they directly achieve this goal.
- *RELATE's intention is to engage with as broad a client base as is possible.* Firstly, this means that elements are favoured which are cost-effective. Models that require very extensive training or particularly intensive supervision have been passed over in favour of ones which are more easily grasped by trainees and which can be safely put into practice without extensive supervision. Secondly, elements have been sought and developed which are accessible to a broad range of clients. Those which are distinctly linked to particular cultural assumptions, which require a high degree of articulacy or psychological-mindedness or which call for particularly high motivation on the part of clients have been rejected or adapted in favour of those which are accessible to a broad client base.
- *RELATE's placing of a premium upon client safety.* Although initially this may sound an obvious point, it needs to be underlined that RELATE offers an approach which will be taken and used by a large work force – currently over 2000 counsellors – in many different areas. The majority of clients approach RELATE not on personal recommendation as they might an individual therapist, but rather because they have confidence in the Agency. So that RELATE can be sure of honouring this trust, concern with client safety is central to the RELATE Approach and leads to many of its distinctive features. In particular, it causes RELATE to favour elements that are amenable to clear contracting and that enhance client autonomy. It excludes elements that cannot be used safely without closer supervision, more detailed investigation of the competence of individual counsellors or closer involvement with the client than is possible within the RELATE setting. Where cases appear to call for such elements, the supervisory system is used to carefully assess the indicators of deeper disturbance with a view to carefully limited work and referral to other help where appropriate – usually via GPs.

AN OVERVIEW

The RELATE Approach has been arrived at by a process lasting 50 years and which has in that time combined many elements. Therefore, a little time needs to be taken to build up an overall map so that the reader will be able to see the structure that underlies the surface complexity. The subsequent chapters of this book then follow this same plan, so the map will also serve the reader as a guide through the book.

The underlying strategy behind the RELATE Approach to clients is that of the three-stage model of counselling, which is well known and has been articulated by writers such as Carkhuff, Nelson-Jones and Egan. These three stages give an initial outline for our map (Figure 1.1). We shall now take each stage in turn so that we can begin to place some specific items within this outline.

Stage One – Exploration
Stage Two – Understanding
Stage Three – Action

Figure 1.1   The three-stage model

STAGE ONE – EXPLORATION

We have stressed in the Introduction that RELATE seeks to offer a non-pathologising approach to the clients it receives, utilising wherever possible the resources the clients have in themselves to deal with their own problems with minimal help from the counsellor. Much evidence has been gathered in the field of counselling to suggest that the chance to discuss a problem with another person in a setting that aids reflection is of itself a helpful process. Certainly RELATE has gathered much evidence that suggests that even a single initial session can greatly relieve distress and can help clients find their own direction. For instance, one client who had attended only a single RELATE intake interview said, when interviewed for research purposes:

> I found it helpful that blame was not discussed. Whose fault it was became irrelevant. This gave me the confidence to move on, and build on the more positive elements of my relationship (McCarthy *et al.*, 1996).

RELATE has always approached its exploration sessions with a sense that they need to be a valid helping experience in their own right, and not merely the introductory stage of a longer piece of work. We have found that this is best achieved by a non-judgemental empathetic approach and by use of the techniques of active listening, and so these skills are carefully taught and their importance emphasised. However, there are a number of tasks which do need to be addressed in the exploration phase.

Firstly, the client needs to be informed broadly of the nature of the service on offer, the limits of confidentiality and the general approach. An initial contract needs to be made. Some basic information needs to be taken and a brief summary of the problem gained. This is termed an 'intake procedure'.

Once this has been done, any clear signs that have become apparent to indicate that the clients have other pressing therapeutic needs are addressed. An *assessment* of appropriate depth is used and possibly a referral made. Some counsellors express the fear that clients who are so assessed and redirected may feel judged or rejected. However, this is not RELATE's experience – assuming, of course, that the process is handled sensitively.

> I was most impressed with the way in which the counsellor picked up on, and described, my mental state. I have since been able to seek medical attention for this, as I had not been aware of this condition (client feedback quoted by McCarthy et al., 1996).

Where clients are clearly not demonstrating any pronounced degree of specific disturbance, counselling begins and assessment progresses gradually during the *initial exploration* as the *presenting problem* is discussed. This time gives the counsellor and the clients more chance to examine the problem and to experience the reality of working together. During this process, the counsellor will be using her skills to promote the formation of a *therapeutic alliance* with the clients.

This process will typically take from two to six weeks, depending on the complexity of the clients' situation and the ease of engagement with the counsellor. When this process is well under way, there will be an opportunity for more detailed *contracting* with a view of conducting a longer piece of work.

Therefore, the first area outlined on our map now contains the features set out in Figure 1.2. For many clients, this phase alone is adequate. The opportunity to take time to consider and detail their problems can lead to a resolution. Clients that wish for further counselling move into the second stage, the understanding stage.

STAGE TWO – UNDERSTANDING

National Marriage Guidance counsellors initially relied heavily in the understanding stage upon the clients' own innate sense of where the

Stage One – Exploration

    (a) Intake and assessment
        (i) usually general
        (ii) detailed where necessary
    (b) Initial exploration
    (c) Formation of therapeutic alliance
    (d) Ongoing examination of presenting problem
    (e) Contracting for further work

Figure 1.2   Detailed map of the Exploration stage of the RELATE Approach

problem lay. By taking time, by carefully staying alongside the client and by refining the insights which arose during the counselling, many successful outcomes were achieved. However, there were several major drawbacks to this approach. The first was that there was a large element of reinventing the wheel with each set of clients; insights gained with one couple could not easily be generalised and used with subsequent clients. Secondly, the reliance on material being gained from the clients alone meant the counselling was denied the insights into couple behaviour which had been derived by a variety of other therapists working in different areas. Finally, without any detailed theoretical models to explain clients' problems and so to suggest strategies for advancing the work, counsellors were not able to challenge clients or to help them modify their actions in any systematic way. These problems led to frustration for both clients and counsellors, and so to a search to add to the broad counselling approach sound and useful theoretical models of couple interaction.

The results of this search led to an interesting and valuable amalgamation. Elements were brought into the RELATE Approach from the fields of psychoanalytic psychotherapy, child psychiatry, systemic family therapy and from social and developmental psychology. However, once brought into the RELATE Approach, they were adapted so that they fitted with the need of the counsellors and the clients to have models which were appropriate for use within a time-limited counselling model.

From the psychoanalytic tradition, RELATE has developed models of unconscious interaction. These are originally derived from the theories of Freud, Klein, Fairbairn, Winnicott and others and are often refreshed by referring to those currently working in this tradition. They are mainly used in RELATE to help clients explore material which is accessible to them, although not presently conscious, and to understand why their behaviour tends to follow certain patterns which, although previously partially seen by clients, are not fully understood or yet under conscious control. RELATE's models differ significantly in use from the models used by psychotherapists and psychoanalysts. In its understanding stage

RELATE uses an awareness of unconscious processes in the concepts of *transference*, and then has models based on *splitting and projection* (derived from Object Relations Theory) and *triangular relationships* (derived from aspects of theories concerning Oedipal interactions).

RELATE has also utilised theory which originally stems from the field of child psychiatry, and in particular from the works of John Bowlby. Thus has been developed the model of *attachment*, for use when couples experience difficulty in establishing and maintaining a bond. Again, RELATE has added its own insights to this model, concentrating on the effect of attachment patterns on the ongoing adult couple relationship, rather than on child–parent relationships or on other attachments and losses.

In a separate field, family therapists have developed a theoretical approach based upon a consideration of families as *systems*. Some of these concepts have been incorporated into the RELATE Approach, especially when working with clients whose problems are linked less with them as a couple, and more with others around the couple – especially those in their own present family, their families from previous relationships and their families of origin.

Finally, counsellors are aware of the particular transitions the adult couple has to make during their lives. The conflicts inherent in these had tended to be overlooked by the many researchers who had looked mainly at the psychological developments of the young. However, developmental psychologists, and in particular Erikson, had offered definitions of the different later *life-stages*. A model derived from this definition, and dealing particularly with the conflicts of adolescence, young adulthood and mid-life, completes the range of theoretical models that has been developed to support the understanding stage of the RELATE Approach. Not only does this model help the counsellor to understand the transitions in the clients' present, it also gives an idea of the different developmental stages that the clients will have had to pass through in their own development.

All of these theoretical models have one unifying feature when they are used in RELATE. They all explore the fact that there is more going on in the couple's problem than the individuals involved are aware of. These extra elements might come from clients' past experiences, from deeper conflicts within clients personally or from unacknowledged struggles in the immediate groups of which clients are members. This is RELATE's sense of the *unconscious* – the factors which affect the clients' behaviour and situation, but of which they are not conscious. However, these factors are not so deeply buried or repressed that they cannot quickly and comparatively easily be made conscious and brought under the client's control. Therefore, the theoretical models RELATE uses in its understanding stage are accessible to the everyday experiences of counsellors and clients alike. The concepts of transference and counter-transference have been broadened and simplified so that they too can apply to all the theoretical models. In addition, care has been taken to integrate the use of the models so that clients can benefit from the insights gained from one or more of them in the same piece of work.

Therefore it will be seen that RELATE's idea of the unconscious does not require the exploration of deeply buried or repressed material. RELATE does not particularly deny the existence of this, or question those who wish to go on as counsellors or clients to explore this area. Indeed, we have greatly benefited from the researches conducted in this area. However, as an Agency we do not necessarily subscribe to the theories of the unconscious beyond those elements we have chosen to borrow and use. Neither do we try to create in the counselling room the atmosphere of the consulting room. The fact that RELATE has adapted these concepts to its own use needs to be kept clear in the reader's mind in order to avoid confusion between the RELATE Approach and that of other disciplines; however, RELATE remains close enough to these roots for the term 'psychodynamic' – describing approaches which emphasise the importance of the formation of emotional responses by past experiences – still to be generally applied to its work.

Therefore, the detailed map of this second area, Understanding, now appears as shown in Figure 1.3.

Stage Two – Understanding

(a) Overall use of a simplified and accessible concept of the unconscious, including transference
(b) Use of specific models of adult couple interaction based upon this concept
   (i) Splitting and Projection model
   (ii) Attachment model
   (iii) Triangular Relationship model
   (iv) Systems model
   (v) Life-stage model

Figure 1.3 Detailed map of the Understanding stage of the RELATE Approach

STAGE THREE – ACTION

For many clients, an understanding of their problem is enough – they then feel able to modify their behaviour appropriately. Others need to engage actively in new behaviours to consolidate the understanding and to allow change to take place. Therefore, this stage of the counselling is concerned with the actions that will be taken as a result of the understanding gained by the counsellor and the clients in the previous stage. Some of these actions are for the clients to use in order to begin to develop a new way of looking at themselves and their relationships. Others represent new ways of interacting which, it is hoped, will be of lasting use to the couple. These active techniques have been selected from a large range of different counselling disciplines. Those that have become a permanent part of the RELATE Approach have been retained because they fit well with the models of unconscious processes described in the understanding stage, yet are also memorable and easily accessible to clients. The use of active techniques as an alternative to complete reliance on discussion in counselling is an essential feature of the RELATE Approach, and one that contributes to its characteristic energy and its accessibility to a broad range of clients.

As explained previously, the models of unconscious interaction used in the Understanding stage are predicated on the belief that none of us responds to another person in a way that is fully involved and rooted in the present reality. Rather, we allow unexamined expectations from our past experiences and assumptions, based upon our own idiosyncratic perceptions, to affect our behaviour. Often we bring about the very outcome we have come to expect solely because we are unintentionally sticking to familiar patterns of behaviour. Relationships reach a crisis point when this tendency has become so marked that neither partner is engaging with the needs of the present situation adequately.

Each of the models of unconscious interaction which has been described in the previous section naturally gives rise to a *course of action linked to the model*, designed to allow the clients to experience a new way of relating and to challenge their previous automatic assumptions. To put these into operation the counsellor has to be familiar with the skills of *challenging*, *reframing* and *behaviour modification*.

However, the goal of the RELATE Approach is to bring about a deeper change, so that clients are more able to solve their own problems in the future. Therefore, the counsellor needs to have an *understanding of the process of change* in order to know what he is trying to achieve and to be able to evaluate the possible pitfalls.

All of RELATE's active interventions are aimed at encouraging clients to see how the present reality differs from their assumptions about it. This allows them to form a more objective and agreed view of the situation and so to channel their energies into creating new patterns of relating which take into realistic account the factors that are present in the situation.

One of RELATE's commonly used active techniques is that of the *communications exercise*. When a relationship has become problematic and partners have become distanced from one another, clear communication is one of the first casualties. Once good communication is lost, the potential for each partner to attribute to the other feelings which belong elsewhere is greatly increased. The encouragement of active communication is an extremely effective way by which this problem can be reversed, and each partner can be encouraged to begin to re-engage with the other and re-examine the unconscious preconceptions which have replaced active interaction.

Another distinctive tool RELATE uses is the *genogram*. This is like a family tree of the couple, including their parents, their siblings, previous relationships and their children. However, on this family tree significant events and interactions are written. As we have explained in the Understanding phase, the RELATE Approach believes that the attitudes, experiences and beliefs which have been with us since birth influence our understanding of the present situation in ways of which we are not consciously aware. The careful and sympathetic exploration of a genogram with clients allows them to take account of these factors.

Sculpting is a further development of the genogram, which allows a visual representation of a family system to be made using simple objects – stones, coins or buttons, for example. The clients' choice of how to represent particular individuals and how to depict their closeness or distance from each other provides a powerful visual tool for representing a situation, and almost invariably leads clients to become conscious of influences or assumptions of which they were previously unaware. It is also remarkably effective in allowing clients to see the difference between their perception of the situation and their partner's perception.

One other discipline has yielded tools which fit particularly well with the RELATE Approach and so are regularly used. This is *Transactional Analysis* (TA). In particular, the Ego State Model from TA allows clients to distinguish between their tendencies to act as a child, an adult or a parent. The child and parent roles are both linked to the clients' past; only the adult role is entirely concerned with dealing with the present reality. This fits closely with the RELATE Approach's intention of encouraging clients to distinguish between what is part of the present situation and what predates it. A great part of the value of this tool (as with many TA models) is its accessibility to clients.

The detailed map of the Action stage is now as set out in Figure 1.4.

SEXUALITY

When considering the various areas of the couple relationship, sexuality is clearly an important part. Sexuality is as amenable to the three-stage

Stage Three – Action

   (a) Actions deriving from the models in Stage Two (b) (Figure 1.3) and requiring:
      (i) Challenge
      (ii) Reframing
      (iii) Behaviour modification
   (b) An understanding of the process of permanent change leading to the additional use of the following tools:
      (i) Communication exercises
      (ii) Genograms
      (iii) Sculpting
      (iv) Tools from TA

Figure 1.4 Detailed map of the Action stage of the RELATE Approach

model of exploration as any other aspect of couple life. However, because of the unique importance of this area in any couple relationship and the tendency for it to be inadequately dealt with, owing to embarrassment on the part of either the couple or the counsellor, the RELATE Approach trains counsellors to consider the couple's sexual interaction in particular depth, and to develop an ease in asking about it. This is reflected in this book by the fact that a separate chapter is devoted to sexuality. This chapter is aimed to ease the exploration of sexuality, to aid understanding and to suggest various actions that couples can take to deal with difficulties that do not require specialised therapy.

DEALING WITH PARTICULAR PROBLEMS THAT MIGHT ARISE IN THE COUNSELLING

Counselling is a complex human activity and is rarely as straightforward as any book might like to suggest. A large degree of simplification has been employed when making this Introduction to allow the essential overall features of the Approach to show without being disguised by specific case problems. However, once this has been done in the next few chapters, Chapter 6 is devoted to more detailed discussion of how counsellors should proceed when specific problems appear to impede the counselling – for example, when only one partner wishes to attend or when sessions are missed or the work seems to have stalled for other reasons. It also includes an introduction to the concept of *counter-transference.*

As we have touched on before, certain details may emerge in the counselling which may suggest that one or both of the clients are in need of more urgent help elsewhere, or that careful thought needs to be given to how safely to proceed. The possibility of suicide, evidence of mental illness or the emergence of other evidence of severe distress or disturbance demand more specific assessment, which may be followed by work in consultation with other agencies or by sensitive referral elsewhere. Chapter 7 deals with these situations.

ENDING

Finally, ending the work with clients brings many issues to the fore and the RELATE Approach lays particular stress on the importance of making a considered ending wherever possible. The ending may be made more complex by the fact that one partner has decided that he or she wishes to end the relationship. Alternatively, the counsellor may feel that the clients have not been suited to the RELATE Approach and so wishes to suggest a referral elsewhere. Clients each have their own way of making an ending and the counsellor will need to be sensitive to these possibilities. The final chapter of the book has been devoted to the issues that need to be considered when the counselling work with the couple finally comes to an end.

CONCLUSION

This brings to an end this overview of the RELATE Approach, which has been concerned with giving the reader an overall map of the terrain which will be traversed in this book. Figure 1.5, at the end of this chapter, sets out the complete map which has been built up, with the references to subsequent chapters upon it.

It will no doubt be clear to the reader now that the RELATE Approach has been built from many elements with the intention of fulfilling a particular need. Different readers will no doubt react to this in different ways. Those who are comfortable with eclecticism and borrowing may welcome the variety of influences that have been combined in the Approach and indeed may find the fact that the Approach is quite a defined one seems in some ways proscriptive. Others who prefer homogeneity andtheoretical unity may be more attracted by the underlying structure of the three-stage model and the consistent reference to RELATE's idea of the importance of the unconscious, and may wish for more consistency yet. Before ending this consideration let us take the discussion further, firstly by using a metaphor derived from another profession, and secondly by briefly reviewing the research evidence about the effectiveness of the RELATE Approach.

By way of a useful metaphor which may help to illuminate this discussion in a different way, let us look at the different styles of building which can be seen around us.

At one extreme is the vernacular style which is seen in many settings. Various bits and pieces are combined as and when they are needed. Houses and schools, hospitals and factories grow, with the addition of an outhouse here, a prefabricated cabin there. Occasionally an old railway carriage appears pressed into a new use or a garage is converted into a usable room. The style is rarely tidy and orderly and sometimes additions can be positively unsafe or dangerous. To the newcomer the impression is one of confusion. However, the scale is very human; and the cost is economical. Building may have been done very cheaply; there have probably been several changes of use and modifications can be made by people with little formal training.

At the other extreme stands a modern purpose-built structure, possibly in concrete or steel and glass. Its purpose is clear and its elements all match. It has been designed from scratch to occupy a new site where all previous buildings have been demolished. To the newcomer the impression is one of order and clear purpose. Comparatively few contractors will have been involved in its construction, and they will have been specialists who have a long and disciplined training in their work. Building tolerances may have been small and the work hazardous, but once the work is completed successfully the building is safe and well adapted to its purpose. It has, however, been very expensive to build, and if the demands made on it change it may well prove difficult to adapt.

Between these two stands a new, traditionally built building. It could be a small or large house, a shop or a light industrial unit. Most of the methods used in its construction have a long history. The materials are comparatively easy to handle and flexible and the building will probably have been largely adapted from a standard plan to the needs of those who intend to occupy it. Although there is a mixture of materials to joint – bricks and slate, glass and wood – the methods of joining these are well-known and reliable. Those who have built it will have served full apprenticeships in their trades and will be confident in handling their materials, but they are more likely to be generalists than specialists. They will have used the same materials again and again in many settings, and will be familiar with the care that is needed at the critical points. To the newcomer the building will have familiar elements, yet each building will also have a distinctive design which is closely allied to its purpose. The building process will be safe and generous margins of error will have been built into it. In the future it can be comparatively easily adapted to changing use. The cost of building will have been reasonable – neither very cheap, nor prohibitively expensive.

Our sense is that the RELATE Approach is closely comparable to the traditional building. It is constructed from different elements, but these have been adapted to complement one another. Few of its elements are original, but the design gains more from being familiar than it loses. The methods used are tried and tested, and many of the possible problems which could arise have been met in the past and are now anticipated and catered for. Those who work on it need to have served a proper apprenticeship and to have mastered their craft, but they do not need to be highly trained specialists. Therefore, the method is commonly available and economical; it is not, however, universally available or cost-free. Margins of safety are broad and the adaptability of the method is large; however, the method does have definite limitations and where very particular and difficult problems exist to be solved, another more specialised approach may well be better.

Anecdotal evidence has long suggested that the RELATE Approach is capable of repeatedly achieving good outcomes. The RELATE training has won much respect, and RELATE counsellors are working in many settings and are often keenly sought after. However, we now fortunately have access to more detailed and reliable research than this in the form of the study which has been conducted by the RELATE Centre for Family Studies at Newcastle. This unit has tracked a total of 2000 users of the service over the last three years. This report has shown a high degree of satisfaction with the service provided by the RELATE Approach. Over 60% of those who complete a course of RELATE counselling feel it has met all or most of their needs. The majority of clients who attend an initial interview choose to go into counselling, and of those who opt out during the process, many have received all they had hoped for. Eighty per cent of those who have attended counselling using the RELATE Approach, irrespective of how brief the contact, indicate that they would definitely or probably return should they need further help. Over 90% of clients would willingly recommend the service to others seeking help with similar problems. We quote in full the final conclusion:

> Our evaluation of RELATE counselling points to benefits available to people who use it. Most clients, irrespective of the degree of their involvement, were satisfied with the service they received and felt that many of their needs had been met. Most of them would go back again in the event of further problems. Our research was able to identify problem areas, however, and suggest areas for further research. This research is at present continuing, with a view to examining long-term outcomes six months and a year after clients terminate contact with RELATE (McCarthy *et al.*, 1996).

Stage One – Exploration
This stage is dealt with in Chapter 2

    (a) Intake and Assessment
        (i) Usually general
        (ii) Detailed where necessary
    (b) Initial exploration
    (c) Formation of therapeutic alliance
    (d) Ongoing examination of presenting problem
    (e) Contracting for further work

The exploration stage for couple sexuality is dealt with in Chapter 5
Problems in the exploration stage are dealt with in Chapter 6
Detailed assessment for particular problems is dealt with in Chapter 7

Stage Two – Understanding

    (a) Overall use of a simplified and accessible concept of the unconscious, including transference
    (b) Use of specific models of adult couple interaction based upon this concept
        (i) Splitting and Projection model
        (ii) Attachment model
        (iii) Triangular Relationship model
        (iv) Systems model
        (v) Life-stage model

The understanding stage for couple sexuality is dealt with in Chapter 5
Problems in the understanding stage are dealt with in Chapter 6
Detailed understanding for particular problems is dealt with in Chapter 7

Stage Three – Action

    (a) Actions deriving from the models in Stage Two (b) above and requiring:
        (i) Challenge
        (ii) Reframing
        (iii) Behaviour modification
    (b) An understanding of the process of permanent change leading to the additional use of the following tools:
        (i) Communication exercises
        (ii) Genograms
        (iii) Sculpting
        (iv) Tools from TA

The action stage for couple sexuality is dealt with in Chapter 5
Problems in the action stage are dealt with in Chapter 6
Endings are dealt with in Chapter 8

Figure 1.5 An overall map of the RELATE Approach including chapter references

2

STAGE ONE – EXPLORATION

When we turn to one another for counsel we reduce the number of our enemies.
Kahil Gilbran

In the previous chapter we have drawn a map of the RELATE Approach. It is our intention in this chapter to explore the first part of this map – the exploration stage.

INTAKE AND ASSESSMENT

Clients will approach a couple counselling service with different understandings of what may be on offer and how this may fit their needs. How accurate these understandings will be depends largely on the route the clients have taken. They will also be in a variety of circumstances and may have other problems and be in other helping relationships. Before we look at a specific recommended intake and assessment process, let us consider the question in more general terms. There are three possible approaches that a counselling service or an individual counsellor can take, either separately or together:

- Clients can be given more detailed information about the approach offered and allowed to make an informed choice.
- Clients can be assessed for suitability and a decision made.
- Clients can be offered counselling and they and the counsellor can review the situation in time.

Each approach has its strengths and weaknesses. Let us examine them in slightly more detail.

Giving Potential Clients Information

This has several advantages. The clients will be greatly empowered to understand what is on offer and, if they proceed, their relationship with the counsellor will be strengthened by the relative lack of ignorance and uncertainty on the clients' part. Much information could be given comparatively cheaply and easily by leaflets or by partially trained assistants. Clients who realise they will not benefit from the service will be able to make a decision not to participate, saving time and energy on both sides.

The disadvantages include the fact that it may be very difficult and time-consuming to try and give a detailed picture of what a counselling session would be like for clients without actually involving the clients in counselling. There is also the danger that the anxiety raised by the emphasis on the choosing process may put clients off making a definite choice. Some clients may choose to continue while unaware of reasons that mean they could not benefit from the service. This system also discriminates against those whose personal preference is to try something to see if they like it.

Assessing Potential Clients

There are many reasons for operating some form of initial assessment. Many assessment criteria exist to measure suitability for counselling. If assessment indicated signs of a serious problem that could be better treated elsewhere, one could advise the client or make a referral. A detailed history-taking and diagnosis of the clients' problems might be beneficial to the ongoing work and could allow referral to workers with specific skills or levels of experience. One could make provision for clients exhibiting signs of serious mental illnesses at this stage, who might otherwise involve the counsellor in inappropriate work for which he or she has not been trained. The investment of time and emotion implicit in a course of counselling could be saved in the case of clients who appeared to be unsuitable for counselling by not offering them the service. Finally, assessment is an accepted part of the psychodynamic approach to counselling.

The disadvantages of this process are that, firstly, there is little agreement on factors that make clients suitable for counselling, especially where the model that is employed contains a client-centred element. Indeed, some research into the RELATE Approach shows considerable success with clients who would have been rejected as unsuitable for counselling had common criteria been used. Further, there is a risk that any criterion used, especially the more subjective ones like 'psychological mindedness', may inadvertently reject clients because of discriminatory reasons linked with intelligence, gender, class or culture. One is assessing clients whose capacity for insight may be limited because they are in crisis and the method could rule out clients who might respond quickly and change their demeanour once they were offered the support of a counselling relationship. Assessing is a skilled task requiring an experienced counsellor, and so a large amount of both client and counsellor time that could otherwise be spent offering counselling might be devoted to the assessment procedure. There is a distinct shift of emphasis onto the counsellor as the expert and the client as the passive recipient, which may in itself be anti-therapeutic for ongoing clients and leave clients who have not been offered counselling with increased distress. Finally, it is less in harmony with a client-centred approach.

Engaging in Initial Work with all Potential Clients

This system has several advantages. Firstly, the use of resources associated with any other form of intake procedure are avoided. Clients are given a chance to experience the counselling process and find their place in it without prejudgement. With the use of explicit contracts that allow for a review, both counsellor and clients can comment on the helpfulness of the counselling from a basis of real experience of working with each other. Counsellors' assessments will not be based on opinions formed initially but rather on those gained from deeper knowledge. The danger of clients feeling prematurely judged is lessened and the procedure is much more client-centred.

The disadvantage of such a system include the fact that counsellors may become engaged with clients whom they are not in a position to help. Danger may arise for clients and counsellor if serious contra-indications are not acted upon immediately. The service may be diluted by being offered to both suitable and unsuitable clients, and counsellors' expertise may be slower in developing if they are seeing a broad range of clients, some with couple problems and others without. The chance of a second opinion is lost, as is the chance of referring clients to counsellors with particular expertise in a shared practice setting.

As can be seen from the above discussion, there is no single approach that has a preponderance of advantages. In addition, the choice of client intake procedure raises some profound questions about the underlying philosophy being employed and to what extent the client is seen as a customer or a patient. It will come as no surprise to the reader, in view of what we have said before about the pragmatism of the RELATE Approach, that the recommended intake procedure combines elements of all models:

1. *An information exchange.* Information is made available to the client about the counselling offered and how it might fit their circumstances.

This allows an informed choice by the client of whether to proceed further under an initial contract.
2. *A broad assessment is made* based on a brief summary of the clients' situation. The very small number of clients who clearly are not appropriate for the service are referred elsewhere, possibly after more detailed assessment. Where several services are on offer, clients may be advised of other possibilities so that they can make a more detailed choice. Where particular needs are highlighted (language needs or expertise with a particular presenting problem, for example), clients may be directed to a specific counsellor.
3. *A period of firmly contracted work is engaged in* (usually of up to 4–6 weeks) to allow clients to experience the RELATE Approach and for counsellors to make a more detailed assessment of their needs. This initial contact also involves active use of the Approach and so can be expected to resolve a significant number of cases.

Answering General Enquiries about the Approach

We shall now give an overview of the RELATE Approach by answering some of the questions a client might ask at the initial information session.

How long are the sessions and how frequent are they?
Sessions are between 50 and 60 minutes in length and take place weekly.

Does this have to be the case?
Experience suggests that generally one session a week gives the right balance between the counselling and giving the client time to digest the session and put what was decided into action.

You mean there's homework?
The counsellor and you may well agree that you will perform some simple tasks between sessions.

What if my partner doesn't want to come?
You can certainly start counselling alone. If your partner definitely decides not to come, this might limit how much work can be done but doesn't make doing any work impossible.

Could you help me with other problems, such as my relationship with my mother or my workmates?
No, the Approach is only designed to deal with intimate adult couple relationships. Therefore, the only help you will get with family or work problems is that which arises from improvements to that relationship.

STAGE ONE – EXPLORATION

Can we bring our children to participate in the sessions?
No. The Approach is designed only for the adult couple themselves, although improving this relationship will hopefully benefit your children.

Do I have to be heterosexual and married to benefit?
No. The Approach is designed for any committed adult couple relationship.

What do you mean committed?
The Approach assumes couples, whether homosexual or heterosexual, to be in regular contact, to be working towards an exclusive relationship and to be open to the long-term continuation of that relationship. If one or more of these does not apply the Approach may not be so helpful.

Part of our problem is to do with our sex life. Can you help with this?
Yes, the Approach can definitely help with general sexual problems.

Our only worry is a specific sexual problem. Otherwise we get on fine. Will the Approach deal with this?
No, you will need to be referred to sexual therapy for a specific dysfunction.

Will the Approach help us if we decide to separate?
The Approach will help you understand your relationship. This may help you decide to stay together; it may help you understand why you have decided to separate and deal with some of the emotional problems that arise during this process. It is not, however, a substitute for mediation.

Is the counselling confidential?
Yes, all information learned from counselling is kept within the Agency. The only time counsellors would break confidentiality would be if they learned something that made them believe someone was at serious risk of harm. Even then, your counsellor would try to discuss the matter with you first if this was practical.

Can I use this Approach if I or my partner is already in counselling elsewhere?
Certainly, as long as the two forms of counselling do not conflict or overlap too greatly.

Can I come if I am suffering from a mental illness?
Yes, unless your illness is of such severity to make couple counselling impractical or inadvisable.

How long does the counselling take?
This varies from client to client. For clients who work to a planned ending, a typical contract is between 6 and 16 sessions.

Am I likely to find this Approach useful?
Yes. Recent research into the Approach shows over two-thirds of couples

who stay with counselling until a planned ending find most or all of their needs are met (Walker, 1995).

What about the ones that dropped out?
The main reason was because they felt there had already been sufficient improvement; 90% of all clients surveyed indicated they would recommend the Approach to others.

There are obviously many more specific questions clients might want to ask about charges and arrangements, but the answers to these would be specific to the setting in which the counselling is delivered. We have included some details about such matters as confidentiality and relationship to other services, even though it may not apply to all settings, to inform the reader of some of the assumptions the authors are making about the context in which the work is carried out.

Assessing Potential Clients for Suitability

There are very few clients who would be considered clearly unsuitable for couple counselling using the RELATE Approach. Indeed, one of the strengths of the method is that it is applicable to a very broad range of clients, and seems equally effective irrespective of the social and psychological background of the clients. However, there are some clients for whom it would be unsuitable.

Clients who Are Currently Suffering from a Severe Mental Illness or Disturbance – either Acute or Chronic

It can sometimes be inadvisable to offer counselling to such clients and they may well have pressing prior needs. If such clients present themselves, careful assessment should be made, probably in consultation with those responsible for the treatment of the other illnesses. Such clients are further considered in Chapter 7.

Clients without a Couple Relationship – Present, Past or Potential

It is possible to use the RELATE Approach to offer a degree of help to those who are hoping to embark upon a relationship. It is certainly possible to do a significant amount of useful work with those wishing to reflect on a recently ended relationship. However, separation or divorce

STAGE ONE – EXPLORATION

work requires a separate speciality (although one that couple counsellors often have, as is the case at RELATE). It is unlikely that the Approach will be of much use for those who have never successfully formed any enduring couple relationship at all. For further consideration of working with clients whose partner does not attend, see Chapter 6.

Clients Seeking Counselling for a Primary Sexual Dysfunction

Such clients should initially be referred to a specialist sexual therapist.

Clients who Are Completely Closed to the Idea of Personal Change

Many clients will present reluctantly, or expressing the feeling that the problem is solely with their partner. Other clients will have been recommended to attend, by a GP or Social Worker for example, and might show marked unwillingness to participate. This is normal defensive behaviour, not a contra-indication. However, if clients display a total unwillingness to be present, express an absolute refusal to consider their own part in the situation or desire solely to use counselling for an extrinsic gain, for example to satisfy an external authority such as a Court, they are unlikely to benefit from the Approach.

Clients Unable to Make a Negotiated Time Commitment

Accommodation can be made for those with irregular life patterns – see Chapter 6. However, there does need to be a commitment to regular attendance, once the pattern of sessions is agreed, and the couple usually need to make time available for work together between sessions.

Clients Unable to Control Harming Behaviour

Sometimes clients request counselling who are involved in relationships where severe physical violence between partners, serious self-harming behaviour or physically or sexually abusive behaviour toward others is either present or is threatened. The occurrence or threat of such behaviour can act as a powerful motive for clients to seek and make good use of help. However, before engaging such clients in counselling using the RELATE Approach, the counsellor should be satisfied that the client is able to give a realistic and unconditional assurance that they will refrain from such behaviour, irrespective of the progress of the counselling. If clients are not able to do this, or if the counsellor severely doubts that such an undertaking will be kept, clients are not suitable for work using this Approach. What other action the counsellor takes, or what help they offer, will depend on their own particular work policy and the referral network and skills available to them.

It will be seen that the number of clients who could be reliably predicted to be unsuitable for this Approach is very small. The authors would suggest that this is as it should be, and any method of counselling that is offered generally for improving couple relationships should be adaptable for use with nearly all that are able to form such relationships. However, there is a larger category of potential clients who may have difficulty in engaging with the work, and with whom the work will need to be disciplined and closely monitored, with the focus firmly held on the couple rather than on the individual. Examples are those who have survived severe early psychological trauma or those suffering from moderately severe mental illness. Working with such clients is dealt with in more depth in Chapters 6 and 7.

This stage of the work will be concluded by the making of an initial contract for further exploration.

THE INITIAL EXPLORATION

In the first few sessions the counsellor will largely be concentrating on putting each client at ease, allowing them to feel that they are being given time to express the story as they see it and to describe the problem in their own terms. The counsellor needs to form a relationship with each client before work can concentrate purely on the relationship, as is shown in Figure 2.1.

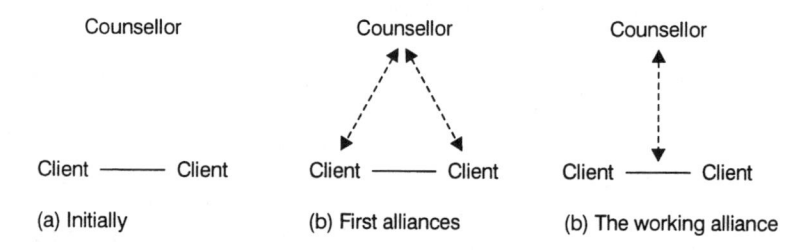

```
         Counsellor                    Counsellor                    Counsellor
                                          ↗ ↖                            ↑
                                         ↙   ↘                           ↓
Client ──── Client              Client ──── Client              Client ──── Client

  (a) Initially                 (b) First alliances             (b) The working alliance
```

Figure 2.1 Moving to the relationship focus in the work

The RELATE Approach would hold that this period is critical to the success of the counselling and in many cases can resolve the problem of itself. If clients feel that their way of seeing the world is understood and remembered in the counselling room, that their hopes and fears are listened to and taken into account by the counsellor and that their perspective is not going to be dismissed in the hope of grasping a short-term solution, then the chance of helping them solve the problem is greatly increased. This happens for several reasons.

Firstly, only if the individuals are listened to and given time to express their perspective can they themselves begin to understand it. As long as the clients feel besieged and under attack, they will not be able to expose their basic beliefs to scrutiny – not even their own scrutiny. Therefore, knowledge of the clients' situation can only emerge if the clients feel safe enough to explore it.

Secondly, only if this relatively relaxed explanation has taken place will the counsellor have those authentic facts that are the fundamental basis of forming an hypothesis of what problem is afflicting the clients. As will be seen in the next chapter, we have a number of models to enable useful work to be done on the problems clients present. The choice of model is made by matching it with the essential part of the problem that is worrying the client.

Thirdly, when clients are at ease their own problem-solving ability is greatly heightened. Therefore, instead of the counsellor working against the clients, or the client couple working against one another, all the resources of the three people in the room can be focused on the essentially fascinating task of using human ingenuity to resolve life's problems.

We shall return to this theme in more detail later. At the moment it is our intention to look at the different areas of information that the counsellor is working to investigate in this initial stage. The importance of the empathetic aspect of this stage is emphasised to indicate that the initial sessions are by no means solely for information-gathering. However, the information-gathering process is an extremely important one and we shall now look at what the counsellor is seeking to learn about the couple in the first few sessions.

The initial enquiries usually tend to be around the specific problem.

The Problem that Has Brought the Clients to Counselling

This is referred to as the 'presenting problem'. Later in this chapter we consider in more depth how the counsellor decides whether this problem is the main area to work on, or whether it is a symptom of a deeper difficulty. However, it is extremely important that the initial problem, as perceived by the clients, is carefully heard and recorded. It will be the key to measuring progress, and clients are not likely to feel heard and accepted if their problem is quickly redefined.

The Help the Clients Want with Their Problem

The clients might be hoping for active interventions. Alternatively, they may just require a safe and controlled area in which to discuss matters. It is important for the counsellor to know whether they are looking for a definite outcome and for their sense of what length and depth they wish to work at. The final counselling contract may not precisely fit the clients' initial hopes, but they certainly need to have been listened to and taken into account.

How Long the Problem Has Persisted

The history of the problem in the relationship will be important in assessing the type of work. If the problem has always been present and existed in previous relationships, the counsellor is more likely to be considering theories of personal development in each of the individuals in the couple. If the problem has suddenly arisen, it is more likely to be linked to a current life change.

Factors Perpetuating the Problem

Often the initial presenting problem seems to be something that could be simply changed. However, were there not a deeper significance, the partners would undoubtedly have solved it for themselves. Similarly, when the problem is apparently linked to an isolated event, there will probably be a deeper significance for the couple, otherwise they would have resolved the situation and moved on. Finally, when the problem seems to lie with just one partner, there are significant questions about the purposes the behaviour may be serving for the other party.

There is then the setting of the relationship to be considered.

Current Major Life Issues

The counsellor needs to have a good understanding of the pressures on the couple at the present moment. Otherwise there is a danger of seeing as abnormal what may just be normal adjustment reactions. For example, a degree of exhaustion and anxiety is quite normal in a couple with a first baby, and little more than reassurance and support from the counsellor may be needed. However, if this anxiety has persisted unchanged for most of an older child's life, the anxieties are unlikely to be solely linked to the arrival of the baby. One is not just looking at family events. Major incidents in the life of each individual in the relationship, such as the death of parents, work or health problems, often precipitate a relationship crisis.

How the Partners Interact Together

The counsellor needs a good understanding of the dynamic between the couple. What are their shared fears and fantasies? It is most important for a couple counsellor using the RELATE Approach to form as strong a sense of the couple's shared dynamic as they do of the individuals in the couple. This will include a consideration of the couple's sexual relationship if this has not been mentioned in detail as part of the presenting problem.

The Couples' Social and Cultural Context

It is important for the counsellor to understand what social influences are important in the couple's life. These will very strongly affect the couple's way of looking at things and will determine the pressures on them. A couple who are in the army and move regularly may well have a different attitude to change and loss than a couple who grew up together and live close to their families of origin. The couple's sexual orientation may well have a marked effect on their social context. Similarly, the counsellor must have some understanding of the influence of racial and ethnic identity and of religion and culture. Counselling which implicitly challenges clients' social or cultural context will soon run into difficulties, unless the nature and validity of this challenge have been carefully considered. It is also important that counsellors use this information to allow them to begin to identify and work with their own areas of prejudice.

There are then questions which relate to the individuals in the relationship.

Each Partner's Physical and Mental Health, both Now and in the Past

Although counsellors do not require a detailed medical history, it is important that they are aware of significant factors. It is certainly necessary that they are aware of past and current episodes of mental illness. If a client has a significant mental illness, this is not a bar to couple work, but it will certainly affect the scope of that work. This is dealt with in more detail in Chapters 6 and 7. Similarly, physical illness can affect couple interactions – a couple in which a partner has suffered a heart attack may well be more concerned not to disagree and argue, for example. Prescribed medication can also be a factor in altering an individual's behaviour, especially in altering emotional response and sexual interest.

Each Partner's Family Experience

It is most helpful to know at an early stage the broad relationship patterns in each client's family of origin. The reasons for this will be apparent in the next chapter.

There are then some general questions concerning factors that will affect the overall progress of the counselling.

Legal Proceedings in Hand

The counsellor needs to know whether there are injunctions in place, current legal proceedings or pending court appearances, as these will place constraints upon the work.

Other Helpers or Agencies Involved

A couple-worker's role will be changed and limited if one member of the couple is already receiving individual therapy. Liaison with other workers is dealt with in Chapter 7. It is also helpful to know whether the couple is being supported by other agencies, such as the Social Services, or by voluntary groups such as Victim Support.

Significant Interactions Concerning the Couple that Are Not Apparent

Often when there is violence, threats of suicide, drug or alcohol abuse or other distressing circumstances, couples will not mention them automatically to the counsellor. Obviously, this is largely the couple's choice. However, it is well worth the counsellor asking, when they feel they have an understanding of the problem, 'Are there any other major factors affecting your relationship that it might be helpful for me to know?', rather than proceeding to work in ignorance of a significant factor.

Significant Third Parties Involved in the Relationship

It is helpful for the counsellor to know, at an early stage, whether a family member or other individual plays a significant role in the couple's life.

Finally, the counsellor needs to have a sense of how the couple will most likely want to use the counselling relationship. If the couple clearly enjoy intellectual discussion, they may well initially feel at ease with an approach that includes some of this. If they enjoy action-based learning, they will probably appreciate being offered some tasks to perform. The counsellor should not feel constrained to work only within the couple's area of preference, as this might well limit what can be achieved. However, it is important not to disregard a couple's preferences lightly or to alienate them through ignorance. Therefore, the counsellor might wish at an early stage to offer some alternative interventions – gentle challenges, possible explanations of responses, references to feelings, questions about past events, simple tasks – to gauge the areas in which the couple feel comfortable or uncomfortable. The counsellor will also be gathering information about how the couple interact and about the counsellor's own reaction to the couple, which will be of great importance.

Case Notes

Considering the amount of information which has been asked above raises the question of how this is to be recorded. Counsellors working in RELATE are assisted by a detailed set of Agency forms which allow space for all the above information to be recorded systematically. These are useful both as a prompt and a record. Subsequently, a brief record of the factual details of each session is kept, and an additional form is used to record details of separate parts of the counselling contract. In addition, most counsellors use some form of genogram (see Chapter 4) for recording family details. RELATE clients are entitled to ask to see these records. Irrespective of whether the client is likely to see them, it is important that formal case records contain objective information that is factual and non-judgemental. Consideration of whether the counsellor would feel able to justify what was written to the clients is often a good test of this objectivity (as long as relevant facts are not omitted in an attempt to keep the notes uncontroversial). Routine note-keeping is rarely a popular part of any job; however, both authors have a strong sense from their work as supervisors that the keeping of adequate brief case notes aids counsellors in giving a case adequate reflection. Clients should be made aware of the fact that case notes are kept.

We shall now look at the process from the point where the clients have decided to start counselling. They will have mixed feelings about the work, based on past issues with the helping professions, real or imagined. The counsellor will need to help the clients engage in a trusting relationship to form a *therapeutic alliance*.

THE THERAPEUTIC ALLIANCE

Forming a therapeutic alliance with the clients is essential and cannot be cut short, however brief the counselling. The counsellor brings her own humanity – her individual character, tempered by her life experiences, along with all the counselling skills that she has learned. The clients bring their individual humanity, their interaction with each other and the destructive forces endemic in the breakdown in their couple relationship. It is a potential minefield that is further complicated in that all participants will not be consciously aware of all the elements.

Figure 2.2. shows this graphically. The two boxes on the left of the diagram are open or conscious. The two boxes on the right are unknown or unconscious. Box 1 shows the characteristics that are known to yourself and obvious to others as well, the *public self*. Box 2 shows the characteristics that are known to yourself but you would prefer others not to know about, the *hidden self*. Box 3 shows characteristics that others see in you, that you are unaware of in yourself, defined here as the *blind self*. Box 4 shows the unconscious, of which neither you nor others are aware, but which might account for some of the unexplained feelings that emerge in the counselling room. This is the *unknown self*. The dotted arrows illustrate how counselling interventions and the closer examination of the couple interaction can help give clients a better understanding of how they relate and communicate with each other. The blind part of the couple interaction can be made more available by accurate empathy and by challenging inconsistency in thought and behaviour to one another. The part that is hidden from one another can be examined and discussed in the safer atmosphere of the counselling, once trust has been established. The collusive fit that often underpins an intimate relationship, good or bad, is unknown to the couple, but insight and accurate interpretations can allow the information to emerge. The clients have to explore their feelings in their blind and hidden selves to gain the understanding that will be a cornerstone for change. Gaston Bachelard, the

STAGE ONE – EXPLORATION

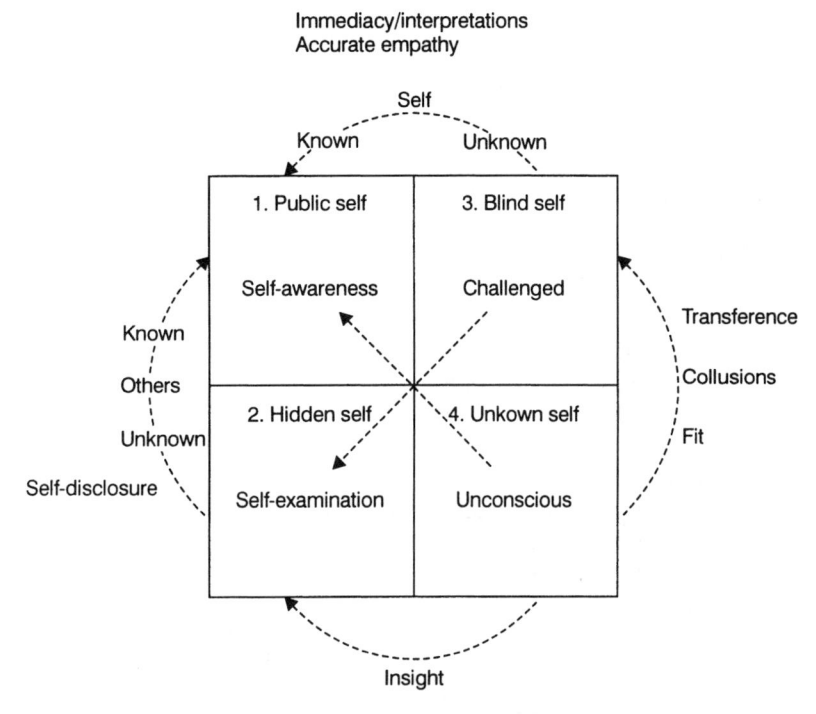

Figure 2.2 Joharri window: communications by self/others

French philosopher, was referring to this area – although under another name – when he wrote:

> The subconscious is ceaselessly murmuring, and it is by listening to these murmurs that one hears the truth.

It is possible in the counselling setting to start looking at feelings that are trapped in these different aspects of self. Self-disclosure and examination can give clients new insights to themselves. This in turn allows them to question the interactions they experience with their partners. Clarifying and managing all this, without being overwhelmed by it, is of enormous importance. The depth and quality of this engagement is crucial to the later stages, and ultimately to the possibility of a successful conclusion.

Good empathetic listening is the first step to forming the therapeutic relationship. Empathy is the power of understanding and imaginatively entering into another person's feelings. 'Imaginatively' is a key word, as the counsellor needs to make an intuitive mental leap in order to capture the exact nuance of what the client is feeling. It is not what the counsellor would feel in the clients' place. That is sympathy. Basic empathy is a response that demonstrates that the counsellor has perceived accurately what the client is feeling now, and perhaps the source of that feeling.

In person-centred counselling there is a basic requirement that the counsellor must be non-judgemental. RELATE has adapted this to a degree, preferring what may be better described as suspending judgement and taking a neutral stance with our clients. During the first exploration stage of the counselling, judgements are made as to what approach would make most sense to these particular clients. This is a clinical or diagnostic judgement and important for our work. It has to be separated from any personal judgements about the clients and client material. For instance, a couple may present with a relationship that openly condones extra-marital affairs. The counsellor may wonder if there are attachment issues underlying this case. This is a clinical assessment, rather than a moral judgement, and may require further exploration. The counsellor may find the concept of such an open relationship personally abhorrent. This is a personal judgement and will hinder any emerging alliance with the clients. The latter has to be suspended and worked through in personal supervision.

Empathetic listening requires interaction. The counsellor may be listening yet remain mute. Being mute can make the clients uncomfortable, seeing the counsellor as powerful and withholding, so that the fragile beginnings of the alliance are hindered. However, being too active in responses can crowd the clients and paralyse their thought processes, and so also stop or hinder the alliance. Thus, a continuing and evolving balance has to be struck. Each alliance could be described as being made-to-measure for the individual couple, much as a bespoke tailor might make a set of garments. A rapport will develop between the clients and the counsellor and the trust will deepen. This has to be consolidated because painful issues will have to be addressed during the work. The clients' natural response is to blame the process or the counsellor for these often frightening feelings. If enough trust and rapport have been built into the therapeutic relationship, the counselling will survive and contain the problem so that it can be worked upon. If the therapeutic alliance is not good enough, the clients may leave prematurely and in a worse state than they started. Their anxieties will be heightened, linked to a feeling of impotence that nothing can be done.

One of the most challenging aspects of forming an alliance is to engage with a couple each of whom has very different responses and expectations of the counselling. Initial findings from research carried out by the RELATE Centre for Family Studies at Newcastle University (Walker, 1995) suggest that men and women have different approaches to issues concerned with feelings and therefore want different things from counselling. More women wanted to confront and understand their feelings, while

STAGE ONE – EXPLORATION

men were more comfortable with the notions of problem-solving. Being understood by their counsellor was less important to men than it was to women. An understanding of these differences can release the couple from what appears to be bickering over trivial items but is actually a different way of thought processing. Each is valid and needs to be heard with respect and not dismissed out of hand. Let us look at an example of a case where the couple had a shared problem but their ways of dealing with the feelings around it were divisive and destructive, highlighting the gender difference. This was reflected in how they approached the counselling and what they expected of the counsellor.

> Jane and Martin presented their problem of complete breakdown in communication. Jane was resentful that Martin 'ran back to his family', rather than talk to her on any kind of intimate or emotional level. She had nursed their baby for six months and he had finally died from a rare genetic disorder a year before. It was a terrible time for them both and for their respective families, who were all grieving. The counsellor could see a number of ways of starting to work but the big block was Jane's overwhelming grief and anger. Martin's grief was much more understated, albeit just as intense. Jane had spent the intervening year learning all about their genetic problems, as they wanted to plan another pregnancy. The counsellor could see that Jane used all her energies into proving what fools the doctors were. She antagonised them rather than ask for the help that she desperately needed. This carried on with Martin and his family. In a very short space of time Jane was challenging the counsellor 'to put Martin right'. Counselling was 'useless' unless, basically, it was all done Jane's way. The counsellor pulled back from the overt confrontations, reflecting that it sounded as though Jane did not feel heard. It was the first stage of empathy – understanding how Jane felt but not siding with all the blaming. Martin needed to listen to what she said rather than immediately defend what he perceived as attacks on him and his family. Jane's attacks became less vicious and Martin slowly began to talk about his grief and anxieties for the future, rather than withdraw into himself.
>
> This took many sessions, but the core of destructive behaviour was the misunderstanding of how they dealt with their joint grief. Martin saw Jane's confrontation with the medical profession as very embarrassing and withdrew. Jane saw Martin's withdrawal as a betrayal of both her and their son that made her even more angry.

This example shows how precarious the start of counselling can be. The counsellor could see many ways to proceed with the work, but first needed to get beyond the anger that was being directed at the doctors, Martin, his family and finally the counsellor.

When clients truly trust the counsellor, the rapport will suffer when there are set-backs, but it will not be lost. When some of the set-backs and anxieties are worked with, then the rapport is strengthened ready to face deeper work. Gradually a picture of the clients' world will begin to emerge. It is like trying to see through the obvious flat images on a page to a hidden three-dimensional image. Sometimes it will appear quickly, but at other times it can be frustratingly difficult to engage. This process is essential, not only to enable the counsellor to start making a full assessment, but also for the individuals in the couple relationship to begin to explore their familiar territory from a new perspective. For clients, who are often dispirited and suffering from low self-esteem, it starts the process of trusting themselves and underlines the uniqueness of what they both bring to the relationship. Nelson-Jones (1993) quotes Lao Tzu in this context:

> It is as he listened
> and such listening as his enfolds us in a silence
> in which at last we begin to hear
> what we are meant to be.

Each client will have their separate truth and this will need to be heard and understood.

THE PRESENTING PROBLEM

It is vital that this should be carefully recorded, because it is of central importance to the assessment the counsellor will make over the next few sessions. The presenting problem could be just the tip of the iceberg, or it could be the deeper conflict in one or both partners that brings them into counselling. Whatever it is, although its importance to the client should never be underestimated, it may not be the subject of the subsequent work. For example, the crisis may be the discovery of an affair, but the work may be about the disappointments in the marriage, the affair being a symptom of this rather than the cause of the problem. The tip of the iceberg may be the interference of one partner's mother, but the work may be about attachment issues between the couple. Thus, what the couple present simply provides the focus from which an assessment will be made during the period of exploration.

Clients are usually bewildered and vulnerable about not being able to resolve their problems. They have often exhausted all their normal coping strategies, and feel powerless to do more. The clients' position is analogous to being lost in the middle of a forest. There are numerous paths to try but some are entirely unsuitable for one or both of the clients. The skill of the counsellor lies in helping the clients to find a usable path, one they both can negotiate. It is the choice of path that is difficult.

Let us look at some presenting problems, and how a focus and assessment is made over the first few sessions, assuming that the broad basic assessment that counselling can help the couple has already been done.

STAGE ONE – EXPLORATION

Robert and Jill presented with a very clear idea of what their problem was. Approximately 18 months earlier they had stopped having sex. They had been married for four years and sex had been dwindling for some time, although it had been very satisfactory for both in the early years. Jill was the one who had withdrawn from sex in the marriage. Thus, she had come to counselling as the one with the problem, and Robert was merely there to support her.

The immediate overt focus the couple wanted to work with was, therefore, Jill's withdrawal from sexual intimacy. However, Jill made it plain that she did not wish to deal with the problem by means of direct sexual therapy. It was agreed at the first session that the next four weeks would be dedicated to exploring the problem.

The counsellor had a sense from the initial session that both clients seemed comfortable to allow Jill to be the one who 'had the problem'. The next few sessions would confirm whether this observation might be of use to the counselling. At this stage, it was important to stay with the clients' agenda before broadening it out. The couple had come to make changes, but if the counsellor explored areas that made no sense to them, it would hinder or even stop the counselling. Equally, the counsellor needed to know when to start gently challenging some of the assumptions that this couple were bringing. During the next four weeks, the counsellor's engagement both with the clients and with the work progressed well. She took a detailed history of both families and the couple's past. A picture of this couple and of their expectations of each other gradually emerged more clearly. The counsellor's idea of the interaction was accurate to the extent that Robert was a strong, caring man bought up in the services, where such a role was expected. Jill came from a chaotic family. Her father had left the family home after a series of affairs with other women. However, from these very deprived social and financial beginnings, through a combination of a good education and hard work, she had become very successful, to the point of being her husband's equal in the workplace. She therefore had many strengths and a recognised equality in this partnership. The couple found this exploration helpful and interesting. After four sessions the counsellor gently challenged the couple to look at their perceived notion that Jill needed Robert to look after her, despite her strengths. It seemed only in the sexual area that she needed Robert to look after her. The counsellor and the couple wanted to look behind this apparent inconsistency, and the couple agreed to a further contract – this time more open-ended and with regular reviews. This approach led to an understanding on Jill's part of the way she used helplessness as a way of forming relationships, and on Robert's of how he was nervous of his wife's independence.

Clients come into counselling for all sorts of reasons and in couple counselling, as we have already seen, each partner can have different expectations and responses to the work. The Brief Therapy Group at Palo Alto makes a useful division of potential clients:

- *Customers.* These are clients who want to engage in counselling, believe in the usefulness of the service and are prepared to work towards the goal of resolving some of their problems.

- *Complainants.* These are clients who are not happy with the relationship but expect the partner and the counsellor to do something about it, preferably without having to engage in much change of themselves.
- *Window-shoppers.* These are clients who are very hesitant about committing themselves to the counselling, but are prepared to come and look and see. They may have been directed by their doctor or other authority figure.

It is useful to use these categories to help adapt the counselling techniques. Complainants and window-shoppers may be very hostile initially to the notion that they may have to be responsible for any change. Part of the initial work in the counselling will be to acknowledge their ambivalence and their position, rather than assuming that they are deliberately resisting the work.

In the case of Robert and Jill, the initial contract was to look at Jill's withdrawal from sex, but subsequent contracts were used to address the intimacy in emotional and sexual terms. It had become a joint problem and the contracts were of longer duration. If the counsellor had tried too early to steer them to looking at the underlying problem, then engagement could have been lost and Robert and Jill may not have taken up further contracts. Jill was the committed customer; Robert was the complainant – to him, his wife and marriage seemed faulty. There was also an air of window-shopper about him, in that he preferred just to observe. The skill of the counsellor is to turn the complainant and the window shopper into customers. Whoever is initially perceived as holding the main problem, many aspects are a shared problem for the partnership.

In the above example, the couple had both agreed on the presenting problem. However, many couples come to counselling with a totally different perception of what their problem is, and merely wish to negate their partners' view. This is often referred to as a *split agenda.*

> Sandra and David had been married for seven years and Sandra had returned to work when their youngest child started school. She had a brief affair with a man she met through work, but that had now finished. David found out about it by chance some time later and was absolutely devastated. Sandra appeared to be totally dismissive about David's hurt. She felt it was a gross over-reaction to something that she had finished, regretted, but from which she now wanted to move on. David was unsure whether they could go on, since he did not believe that he would ever be able to trust her again. They arrived into counselling with Sandra determined not to 'wallow' in the past and David desperate to have some kind of understanding of how it had happened. Where could this couple even begin to focus?
>
> The counsellor could see that the more dismissive Sandra was, the more bewildered David became. If David could understand some of what had happened he might be able to think about some kind of future together.

However, something was clearly stopping Sandra discussing the matter. The counsellor hoped that by encouraging further dialogue he might learn more about what each partner was denying. This proved to be the case. Sandra found the affair difficult to talk about because of the guilt she felt, not because she had any feelings left for the other man. David had all sorts of fantasies about whom she really wanted, and needed to know that she had some definite commitment to him. Her dismissiveness had made him doubt it. Over the weeks Sandra was able to explain how she had been feeling at that time. She had been excited about going back to work and flattered by the attention that the other man gave her. She had completely separated her work from her home life. She had not seen the affair as a rejection of David and had, in fact, finished it after a few weeks. David became less bewildered as he understood more. This allowed Sandra to be less defensive and feel less guilty.

This couple came into counselling in totally polarised positions. David was sitting on one end of the see-saw with hurt and bewilderment, very unsure if he could go on with it. Sandra was sitting at the other end with guilt expressed as dismissal, frightened that her past behaviour might have jeopardised the marriage that she wanted to save. Both were stuck in those positions. They starting edging towards the middle and a more balanced position by working with the counsellor. The couple were not only split but in different time-scales. Sandra had processed some of her feelings about the affair and had placed the details behind her. David had only just found out about it and was shocked by many aspects, which were like a mountain in front of him. The skill of the counsellor was first to recognise this and then to help David and Sandra recognise their different positions.

Contracting

Firm and clear contracting is an important aspect of the RELATE Approach to engagement with the clients. Clients are usually offered weekly sessions of 50 minutes to an hour. Clients are usually highly anxious when entering the Agency, so that this very practical process also acts as a measure to contain that anxiety. The knowledge that each session will be at the same time, on the same day, and with the same counsellor provides an easily remembered structure and commitment. The session is allotted 50 minutes. A time limit is considered essential, since there is a limit to how much the clients and counsellor can absorb at one time, and 50 minutes seems a suitable period. A 10-minute pause between sessions offers room to make a suitable ending to one session without fear of eroding the time of subsequent clients. The 10 minutes between clients allows the counsellor to reflect on what has happened in session, and maybe record some key feelings for later reference and contemplation. Immediate thoughts and processed thoughts are both parts of the assessment process. New counsellors sometimes have a fear that their clients might feel cheated, losing 10 minutes of the hour they thought they had paid for. However, the whole hour is in fact being devoted to the clients, and they would be far more seriously cheated if the counsellor's mind was still partly reflecting on what happened during the last session or worrying about finishing in time for the next one. Explaining the practicality of the arrangement usually dispels such fears.

It is important that the counsellor clearly states the length and frequency of the session at the beginning of counselling. This pre-empts problems, and the certainty further helps to contain anxiety. Where possible, flexibility can be built in for those clients who work shifts and irregular hours. This requires good management and communication skills on the part of the counsellor because it will have to be arranged around the existing appointment system.

Towards the end of the first session the counsellor will summarise what appears to be the presenting problem. If this is agreed by both clients, the counsellor will offer a short contract to see how this problem can be looked at. It is essential that it is made very clear that this period is to be used to explore the problem in order to try and make sense of what is going on. Clients sometimes hear this as, 'In four to six weeks this problem will be solved or the counselling will end', but we have already seen that presenting problems can be red herrings, and this initial contract may simply be the springboard to further contracts. Hesitant clients may be undecided about committing themselves to counselling and so the contract may only be from one week to another initially. A good counsellor will tailor the contract to suit the clients in the same way as she will seek the most appropriate way to engage in the counselling. Thus, the three-stage model of exploration, understanding and action can usefully be applied to discrete parts of the work as well as to the whole.

Contracting in blocks of sessions also makes the counselling more manageable for both clients and counsellor. The first contract provides a means of focusing, one agreed by all parties. Depending on how the clients engage, it can be adapted or amplified after review. It allows time for other aspects to be considered and perhaps for a fresh new focus to be agreed. Although the counsellor holds the ultimate authority in the room, the clients can start getting in touch with their own competence and begin to challenge what may arise during the sessions. Each review allows the clients to summarise what they are feeling now, to consider whether they have moved on, and generally to review their expectations and disappointments.

STAGE ONE – EXPLORATION

We have looked at the practical and management aspects of contracting. How the clients behave during the period of the contract can give further clues as to how their behaviour may influence other aspects of their lives. For instance, clients that never manage to arrive on time may be displaying their ambivalence in attending. Exploring and understanding hurt feelings, now and in the past, can be very painful. They may have appeared to understand that this would be part of the process but nevertheless want to avoid it. When this happens they may try and change the times and days of the sessions, citing a variety of reasons. All experienced counsellors can quote numerous cases where they have tried hard to accommodate these changes, only to find the clients have decided to withdraw. It is a better strategy to work in less depth initially until there is greater trust.

Breaks have to be carefully planned because of the effect they can have on the engagement and the work with clients. Weekly sessions are designed usually to give clients time to reflect but not to lose the thread of the work. It is easy to lose clients if interruptions are handled in an off-hand or thoughtless fashion. The clients should be informed of any planned holiday arrangements or absences in the near future. Giving the clients only one week's notice puts severe strain on the therapeutic alliance, and the anger it can engender may negate some of the work already achieved. It is better to give time to allow anxieties to be addressed, and coping strategies worked out with the clients. Clients' responses vary enormously, and here again the counsellor must use her understanding of unconscious issues in order to respond appropriately.

Normally, counsellors will be expected to honour all the times contracted for, but inevitably there will be times when they have to cancel a session due to illness or some other unforeseen event. This can have positive and negative effects on the clients. Some clients may feel very let down and hurt. They may show their anger and disappointment by cancelling or not turning up for the next session. On the other hand, it can be a moving-on point. Clients often realise that they managed very well despite the missed session, and had dealt with their difficulties just as if they were discussing it in session. In other words, they are internalising their counsellor and are moving on to independence from counselling.

Other clients may fill a session with seemingly trivial occurrences and then disclose a major problem just as they leave. The counsellor has to be firm and should immediately put it on to the agenda for the next session. This enforces the session boundary, but also states clearly that the problem can be tolerated for a further week. This 'doorknob disclosure' can also be a sign of testing out to see if the counsellor can tolerate it and be trusted.

Professional Boundaries

The contract with clients provides a contained structure to enable the problem areas to be explored. Clear boundaries of behaviour must also be established to ensure the safety of both clients and the counsellor. There is a tension between the depth of the alliance growing between clients and counsellor and the professional distance that is required for sound evaluation and work. The counsellor must be responsible for these boundaries and should be most chary of succumbing to any temptation to modify her role. For example, it is wise to question the natural desire to comfort distressed clients in a physical way. Most clients feel perfectly well contained by quiet listening in a comfortable and supportive setting, rather than needing physical contact which may well reflect the counsellor's anxiety rather than problems that the clients are having. Contact with clients outside sessions should be similarly considered. Counsellors using the RELATE Approach normally have no contact with clients between sessions apart from exceptional circumstances. Whenever possible these are conducted by letter or through a third party. At accidental meetings it is always left to the clients as to whether they wish to acknowledge the counsellor or not. Close contact with clients outside the counselling raises the most profound ethical questions, whether counselling is finished or not. The power differential between clients and counsellor does not cease at the end of counselling and it can be a misuse of the professional relationship to extend it without careful consideration or to transform it into any kind of social or intimate one. The RELATE Approach would generally strongly advise against such a transformation, and would always expect counsellors contemplating such a step to make use of detailed supervision.

Payment

This is a thorny issue for both counsellor and clients. If handled poorly, it can damage the emerging therapeutic alliance. A good counselling service has to be paid for, and in most counselling settings some or all of this expense has to be met by client payments. The counsellor has to be aware of her own anxieties and prejudices surrounding the asking and getting of money before starting this part of the contract. Some counsellors absolve themselves from this issue by handing it over to office staff, but in doing so they deprive themselves of the opportunity of addressing the feelings surrounding this important part of the therapeutic relationship. The caring, nurturing side of the counsellor may feel threatened by asking for money at a time when her clients are in great distress – perhaps out of fear of making money out of misery. However, there is a therapeutic benefit

STAGE ONE – EXPLORATION

for the clients in their ability to own some resources. Anecdotal evidence has also shown that clients seem to have a greater commitment to a service they are paying for. A balance has to be struck when an agency can offer a sliding scale of payments, as RELATE does, to ensure the clients are paying enough to support the service and to encourage them to value it but not so much that it becomes a worry or a reason to stop.

It is important to strike an appropriate balance between firmness and compassion. A tough negotiating stance over money negates the relationship between counsellor and clients. A counsellor who seems to say, 'If you value your marriage you would pay' is giving an underlying message of judgement. At the opposite end of the scale, a counsellor who negotiates in a very apologetic style builds a false therapeutic alliance. She seems to say, 'You are in such an awful situation I can quite see you cannot possibly pay'. The underlying message that the situation is so bad increases the clients' dependency and helplessness. Counsellors need to state the position simply and allow the clients to respond in an adult way. The counsellor and the clients are inevitably going to have to face discomfort if the work is going to progress. Showing a willingness to do this within a principled framework from the beginning is a good model.

We hope that in this chapter we have shown how in this RELATE Approach it is necessary to name the presenting problem, and then to start looking at the underlying processes. Different problems will lead naturally to the use of a different aspect of theory. The theory underpins the understanding of the work, but must not itself lead the work. The counsellor therefore must have a sound theoretical base and the ability to adapt it to the needs of the clients. We have begun to outline how this happens, and will continue to define this in greater depth in the next chapter.

We have looked at the importance of empathy in order to engage with clients to explore the overt and underlying problems presented. Counsellors must have a high degree of awareness, not only of what the clients are bringing, but also of themselves. How else is the counsellor going to know whether the emerging thoughts and feelings belong to herself or to the clients? It is an essential part of RELATE selection and the training programme to foster counsellor self-awareness to help the counsellor to correctly define and attribute feelings that arise during counselling and as a result of the training. This is a process that continually evolves throughout the working life of a counsellor.

3

STAGE TWO – UNDERSTANDING

Happy is the person who knows why things happen.
                                                        Virgil

INTRODUCTION

In this chapter we shall deal with the concepts and models which underlie the second stage of the counselling – the understanding stage. These have been detailed as shown in Figure 3.1.

Many clients are helped by the process of exploration alone to form a clear idea of their problems and to solve them themselves. Where this has not been possible, RELATE has found that the counselling work needs to go deeper and to be supported by models of couple interaction to allow it to progress. As explained in Chapter 1, RELATE has assembled a body of theory to allow it to understand the influences which may be leading clients to experience problems that they cannot understand. Broadly, RELATE applies the term 'unconscious processes' to these influences, although we are aware that our engagement with the unconscious may differ from that of other disciplines which use the same word, dealing as it does with influences which can comparatively easily be raised to the clients' consciousness.

Stage Two – Understanding

    (a) Overall use of a simplified and accessible concept of the unconscious, including transference
    (b) Use of specific models of adult couple interaction based upon this concept
        (i) Splitting and Projection model
        (ii) Attachment model
        (iii) Triangular Relationship model
        (iv) Systems model
        (v) Life-stage model

Figure 3.1 Detailed map of the Understanding stage of the RELATE Approach

STAGE TWO – UNDERSTANDING

In this area, the RELATE Approach seeks to be both client-centred and psychodynamic. The RELATE Approach has an agreed theoretical base. This postulates that there are important processes going on for every client that contribute to their ability to form an intimate couple relationship. These processes condition the feelings that are brought to the relationship and influence how the couple interact. Particular patterns and struggles that a couple are having can be illuminated in part by looking back to earlier relationships and how these were experienced. In this, the RELATE Approach is close to the psychodynamic position.

However, the RELATE theoretical base is a broad one. There are several different strands and elaborations which we will refer to as *models* in this book. They are a codification of different areas of theory that clearly overlap. Nevertheless, they are regarded as largely discrete within RELATE, and it is in the application of these models that the more client-centred element of the integration is apparent. Counsellors will work to match one or more of the models to the problem that the clients bring, rather than match the clients to a model. In this way, an overall approach is possible which accords with the clients' chosen presentation of their circumstances. The couple will work with the details that seem important to them and towards the desired outcome that they have articulated.

RELATE offers a rich theoretical background to the counsellor to inform her use of the *understanding* phase of the work. This background is concerned with the development of our interpersonal skills. It illuminates the processes which have taken place in early relationships in the families and places of origin of the clients. It does not concern itself with the development of the individual alone. It focuses on the development of patterns of relating to others.

THE UNCONSCIOUS AND TRANSFERENCE

Belief in unconscious motivation is an important and central part of the RELATE Approach. We believe that relationships that conform to certain patterns do so not only out of conscious choice, but also due to the unexamined attitudes that experiences to date have given the couple. Notions of what behaviour is acceptable and unacceptable, what roles are proper and improper, what emotions are to be welcomed or avoided will all have been the product of unexamined assumptions formed on the evidence of previous experience. Therefore, when we speak of the unconscious process of couple attraction, we are looking at the choice of partner each individual makes, without being consciously aware of what led to that choice. When we speak of a denied emotion, we are speaking of an appropriate and likely feeling about an event which the clients did not express at the time, and which they may need encouragement to express now.

The term 'the unconscious' is in many ways a metaphor. We do not know whether the memories and feelings that apparently dwell there actually exist. It is possible that when clients in counselling make a seemingly new recollection about their past, they may be expressing facts that were never in reality lost to memory. Rather, they may have previously seemed to have had little significance or interest. They may have been left dormant because there seemed little purpose in recalling memories that had only negative feelings attached to them. However, the RELATE Approach does believe that these disjointed memories and elusive feelings are central to the understanding of the people we now are and the patterns that affect our relationships.

It will be seen, then, that in the RELATE Approach we expect our clients to be able to recall, albeit with gentle encouragement, the significant details that may illuminate the history of their problems. We do not ever pressurise clients to access these details, or create situations in which deeply repressed feelings may be likely to emerge. If the clients cannot offer us, after adequate respectful enquiry into a particular area, insights which are mutually useful we move to another line of enquiry and possibly to another model of unconscious interaction altogether. Therefore, although we are dealing with matters hidden from conscious knowledge, in this counselling we are not trying to access deeply repressed material.

The word 'unconscious' will occur frequently henceforth. So will references to linked concepts, such as repression and defence mechanisms. These terms will sometimes be linked to models which do not spring from the psychoanalytic tradition, such as systemic models. It is hoped that they will be read in terms of the explanation delivered above – as a metaphor about latent, unretrieved memories and ideas which are invaluable and central to RELATE's Approach to couple counselling.

Transference carries the underlying theory of the unconscious one step further, and explains how thoughts and feelings that are not conscious can influence our new relationships. Instead of reacting to each person we meet for the first time as a totally fresh individual and thus being open to experiencing him or her without prejudice, we *transfer* onto him or her the conscious and unconscious expectations we have formulated during our lifetime. The person encountered in this way is offered one or more templates, to which his or her behaviour is expected to conform. For example, someone who has been consistently bullied in the past may approach another with a timid demeanour, expecting to be hurt. In some cases there is no correspondence, and either no relationship ensues or one is formed which breaks the patterns of past relationships. More often than not, however, the person encountered adapts his or her behaviour to somehow fit one of the templates that they are being offered. Clients frequently produce similar reactions in a counsellor, who finds that she feels a pressure to adapt her behaviour and thinking. It is a powerful and significant process. Where couple relationships are involved, the process will be happening on both sides and the resulting relationship will be all the more powerful, since each person corresponds to the other's conscious and unconscious expectation.

For example, the timid person mentioned above may meet a partner whose past relationships have led him or her to expect to dominate others. The two patterns will fit. The one who is bullied will not be too surprised, as past history has led him or her to expect such treatment. Similarly, the one who is dominant will not find the position uncomfortable. Both partners will thus unintentionally repeat past patterns rather than building the relationship from new. These patterns may be produced despite both partners' earnest conscious wish to break this cycle. When there is such an interlocking of transferences in a relationship, the process is entitled a *fit*. Where a couple have fitted together in a way that reinforces each other's feelings over a single issue they can be described as being *in collusion*. This term literally means they are playing a game together, but it is of course an unintentional game. Several points of collusion give rise to a more thorough transferential fit.

We will now consider the five separate models and make a very brief exposition of each one. We will illustrate each model's relevance to couple work and the counselling interventions that are formulated as a result. Finally, we will draw on some examples of couple counselling casework to illustrate how we apply this understanding and how we work with it.

THE SPLITTING AND PROJECTION MODEL – INTRODUCTION

For most people, adult life is a constant turmoil of positive and negative feelings. Much of our energy is spent in pursuing the positive experiences and avoiding the negative ones. The matter is made more difficult by the fact that frequently the positive and the negative feelings are inextricably interlinked. Positive feelings could be described as those linked with gratifying experiences or pleasant emotions; negative feelings as those leading to frustration or uncomfortable emotions. Most positive feelings carry within themselves their opposite. For example, if we cannot conceive of unhappiness, we may not know when we are happy; if we cannot imagine being unloved we may not celebrate being loved, and so on. To truly live in the 'here and now' is a difficult and painful struggle, since having a realistic view of the world involves being conscious of our innumerable negative emotions as well as our positive ones. To live contentedly and fully consciously in such a world requires a distinct sense of optimism – or at least of personal strength and worth – to allow us to feel conviction that we will be able to overcome the negative emotions enough to enjoy a tolerable life. Living fully consciously in such a world can be considered as coping with *ambivalence,* and is a difficult task. The concept of ambivalence – describing the co-existence of opposite emotions towards the same object – is a crucially important part of this concept.

When we find coping with ambivalence difficult, a more comfortable alternative can be to step away from consciously seeing both positive and negative feelings, and instead to *split;* to focus only on the positive or only on the negative. In this situation the painfulness of facing reality is relieved. To split in this way is not a choice of which the individual is consciously aware – it is an unconscious defence.

In stressful situations we all split the positive and the negative and remain conscious only of our positive feelings. So when we lose someone dear, we may only be conscious of our love for them and suppress the negative feelings. This is a natural reaction which passes as we grieve; however, clients for whom this appears to have become a problem habitually keep their emotional world divided, and remain unconscious of negative feelings for a much greater proportion of the time.

Equally common is the reverse, where the clients are aware of their negative feelings, but not conscious of the positive ones. This may seem less instantly explicable – why deny positive feelings? Possibly positive feelings may be too painful – if one has never felt loveable it may be safer to deny the possibility of love in oneself. Possibly the risk of losing the positive might seem too great – better to deny one's feelings of love rather than reveal them, only to suffer rejection. Maybe the familiarity of the feelings makes change undesirable – if one has always lived with anger, giving it up would seem most threatening.

However, when one has split the world in order to discount an area of feeling, whether positive or the negative, one is still confronted by the fact that the denied emotions exist and may well up in one in response to normal stimuli which provoke the denied feelings and threaten to upset the arrangement. These unwelcome feelings have to be attributed elsewhere to keep the split secure. The process of displacing unwanted feelings onto others is called *projection*.

Let us take the example of a man who has a tendency to split and to deny his own negative feelings. He may be in a bad mood for some perfectly natural reason unconnected with his home life. However, rather than accept this he may choose to blame his partner for the mood he is in, accusing *her* of being grumpy and explaining his mood as a response to hers. In many cases she may simply realise that he is in a bad mood, avoid taking any responsibility and keep out of his way. However, let us imagine she too tends to split, and has a negative view of her inner emotional world. She may then rise to the bait – and genuinely believe she was entirely responsible for the situation. An argument may ensue, at the end of which the man has had his belief that he is a placid soul afflicted by an irritable wife confirmed, and she ends up feeling again that she is a habitually bad-tempered woman lucky enough to have a saintly husband whom she does not deserve. Thus, both individuals' split view of the world is confirmed, and the scene is set for further unresolvable arguments.

When two individuals become locked into responding to the denied and projected emotions of the other and regarding this as their own in this way, the process is called *projective identification*.

This model originates from the works of Melanie Klein, although it has been greatly simplified and lifted to the accessible areas of the unconscious in the adaptation. Much of Klein's work is developmental and deals with the stages of emerging consciousness of emotional separateness in children. We do not, however, need to involve ourselves with this debate in order to use the concept with adult couples, except to note the words of one later commentator. Winnicott (1964) referred to the mothers who help their babies move away from splitting and to tolerate *ambivalence* – by being neither unduly neglectful nor over-protective – as '*good enough*', i.e. able to give enough nourishment and support so that the child can tolerate living in the emotional world as it really is. If the counsellor shows a similar ability to support the clients just enough, the clients can be helped to re-integrate the positive and negative in their conscious world.

SPLITTING AND PROJECTION MODEL – RELEVANCE TO COUPLE RELATIONSHIPS

The great majority of our clients have much capacity to tolerate intense feelings and to understand ambivalence. However, when their relationship becomes strongly conflictual they take refuge in a split position, denying the full range of feelings in both themselves and their partners.

As we have explained, when splitting takes place in an individual, the 'good' feelings of love and desire for attachment can be conscious and the 'bad' feelings of anger and rejection can be unconscious or *vice versa*. We have enclosed good and bad in inverted commas to indicate that these values are not necessarily absolute. It is because the subject is choosing to split feelings into good and bad ones that value judgements then attach themselves to certain emotions. Partnership or marriage then becomes an arena in which this conflict can be externalised. There are three possible collusive combinations and RELATE uses the classification of couples initially proposed by Mattinson and Sinclair (1979).

1. Babes in the Wood

In this case the couple are both conscious of positive feelings of love and desire for attachment. All 'bad' feelings of anger, rejection and destructiveness are seen to belong to the world outside, hence the name of the syndrome. Such couples will probably be idealistic and likeable, making the counsellor feel destructive as she urges them to take note of their negative feelings. Often such couples do not find their way to counselling as they consider the problems not to be their own. However, they may present with sexual problems, as having a successful sexual relationship involves being able to integrate the more dangerous 'bad' desires into their life scheme.

2. Cat and Dog

In this case both partners express anger, rejection and other destructive emotions, yet they stay together. As both are conscious only of the bad in themselves and their partner, all the good is projected on the world outside. They cannot conceive that they themselves have the ability to behave positively. Although each can see the other's faults all too clearly, they do not part since neither can imagine themselves being able to form a relationship with anyone better. The counsellor, like the outside world, is idealised, which may mean that the couple feel they cannot attain anything the counsellor suggests to them.

In both of these cases the work of the counsellor is to help the couples to appreciate the side of themselves that they are denying. There are several ways of doing this, which will be dealt with when we have explored the third category.

3. Net and Sword

In this case the split between good and bad is held within the relationship, with one partner showing all the love and yearning, and the other all the anger and rejection. In other words, one partner accepts and displays the denied emotions which the other partner seeks to project elsewhere. The

STAGE TWO – UNDERSTANDING

technique for dealing with such clients is similar, except that the counsellor must beware of the tendency to be drawn into taking sides with one or other of the clients.

The *Splitting and Projection model* can be appropriate when some of the following indicators are present in the interaction:

- Strong 'primitive' emotions.
- A sense that the couple are bound together.
- Simple notions of good and bad are spoken about.
- Words such as 'ought' and 'should' abound in describing preferred actions.

The way forward is for the counsellor to resist the attempt to split things into good and bad and to help the clients move towards a position where more complex emotions are allowed. The following methods are helpful:

- *Modelling coping with ambivalence.* The counsellor demonstrates that she does not need to split the world into good and bad, but can accept that she has mixed feelings about many things.
- *Encouraging open communication.* It is much harder to maintain a simplified view of the world if one allows others free expression and listens instead of interpreting. Therefore, communication exercises that encourage open, non-stereotyped dialogue are helpful.
- *Containing destructive arguments.* It is most useful if the counsellor can stop the familiar repetition of litanies of faults and manages instead to encourage new ways of looking at these matters.
- *Allowing clients to become conscious of the denied parts of themselves.* The counsellor makes it possible for the partner who is in touch only with his positive feelings to safely own the negative ones, such as anger or destructive impulses. Similarly, the partner who is conscious only of these negative feelings is put in touch with her positive ones.
- *Demonstrating the possibility of not being drawn into the conflict.* The counsellor needs to offer the clients a different way of relating, so it is important not to side with the clients' view, which may be that the world is a terrible place, or that they themselves are awful, or that one partner is far worse than the other.

SPLITTING AND PROJECTION MODEL – CASEWORK EXAMPLE

When George and May first approached RELATE, the counsellor thought of them as the 'couple from hell'. They systematically belittled each other – as far as May was concerned George was one of life's failures. He had not made much of himself – he should have seen that engineering was a dying trade before he was made redundant, he should have spent more time with the children before they left home – 'They despise him too, you know' – and his personal habits left much to be desired. The counsellor would have felt sorry for George was it not for the fact that he could clearly give as good as he got. He told the counsellor that May had smothered the children and turned them against him; he said their marital home was like a prison with innumerable petty rules and he was most scathing and bitter about her sexual attractiveness, saying he could not see now why he had remained faithful all these years.

In thinking about the case after the first session, the counsellor realised that this was a 'Cat and Dog' couple. There was certainly intense and primitive emotion in the room. The couple did seem bound together. Despite all their vilification of each other they had remained married and faithful for nearly 30 years. Things were clearly seen in terms of good and bad, with each partner and the marriage being a total and irredeemable failure, while other couples were held up as 'so happy'. Shoulds and oughts abounded – May had been vehement about what George should have done and George had responded by letting her know how a wife 'ought to treat her husband'. The counsellor realised that her thought about them being 'a couple from hell' was a reflection of how nothing that was good or tender was spoken of in the whole session. She was also aware that she had herself almost been drawn into the conflict a couple of times when she began to find the level of bitterness upsetting.

Working on this, she decided to begin to model ambivalence herself and look for the positive side and the gentler emotions that the couple were denying. For the next three sessions, she found herself making general comments like, 'It is difficult to know what work to choose nowadays' and 'It is hard to run a house efficiently without any rules isn't it, yet you don't want to be too strict'. At times she felt she was being merely platitudinous in the face of the couple's scornful disparagement of one another, but a calmer atmosphere did begin to enter the sessions. Once, when George was dismissing the fact that he had lost contact with his children, she ventured, 'That must have been sad' and was rewarded with a thoughtful look. After four sessions a calmer atmosphere prevailed, and she decided to make use of a communication exercise. When May was bemoaning that they never went out, she asked if she had ever suggested this to George. 'What's the point?' said May, but the counsellor persisted (this exercise with George and May is described in more detail in Chapter 4) and was rewarded by a more reasonable discussion, in which both partners began to address their own uncertain feelings about wanting to please the other which had not previously been shown. Two sessions later, the counsellor asked each partner to describe their family history using a genogram (see Chapter 4). This exercise helped them see how they had both been brought up to see the worst in themselves and their families – probably because their parents had little faith in their own ability to bring up children successfully.

The work continued on this basis until the couple decided to leave counselling on the twelfth session.

STAGE TWO – UNDERSTANDING

This is only the briefest of introductions to the use of a model drawn from Object Relations Theory. Work based on projective identification in particular can form the basis of more sustained work.[1]

The anger expressed in the George and May case study is an example of a predominant emotion that would be worked with in the counselling. The use of this model can frequently enable the counsellor to stand back from the dynamic and model a different way of coping with the conflict. Couples can then swiftly change their own interaction.

THE ATTACHMENT MODEL – INTRODUCTION

This is based on the studies of John Bowlby, who carried out much significant research, working particularly with orphaned children. He observed that babies form a strong disposition to attach themselves to key adults in their lives. From the age of about six months, the child becomes able to discriminate between the individuals who people its world. It then seeks to form a firm relationship with a *primary carer*. Once the child is confident that it has a *secure base* it can explore beyond it, although it tends to regress when

---

[1] In this connection, Derek Hill, RELATE's Head of Counselling, has offered us the following useful contribution. 'Object Relations Theory, which makes considerable use of the primitive processes of splitting and projection, is founded on the assumption that humans are driven by a basic motivation to relate to their fellows. It is argued that the motivation exists from birth and results in the infant, the child and the maturing adult passing through a number of developmental phases which are linked to the individual's growing psychic capacities. The consequences of that developmental history are that an adult has memories of important relationships and how they work and, equally significantly but much less accessible (that is, located through the process of repression in the unconscious), the traces of early and profoundly influential relationships that are either too frustrating or too frightening to be tolerated in the conscious mind. Frustration results from gratification being denied, and the repressed relationships linked with that emotion are those that promise ultimate intimacy and security – for example, the ideal mother. Fear is linked with rejecting or annihilating relationships, as might be those between the self and the bad destructive mother – or indeed, father. One of the most significant features of Object Relations Theory is thus that it conceives of the inner world of an individual being made up of consciously and unconsciously retained objects – that is, mums, dads, important people – a sense of the nature of the relationships between the self and those 'internal objects' and memories of the emotions associated with those different relationships. The beauty of this theoretical approach is that it offers a very straightforward mechanism by which transferences are set up. If a relationship with another individual has features which resonate with a past and repressed internalised relationship – like my persecutory infant school teacher – then what happens is that we are disposed to invest the other individual with all that teacher's hated or feared characteristics, and to relate to that individual as if she were that teacher, with all the associated feelings of fear and hate.'

(Derek Hill, RELATE, 1996, reproduced by permission)

it feels itself threatened. This attachment is about emotional security, where the adult mediates the world for the child. When this secure attachment is disrupted the child passes through a process of separation, of which shock, anger, grief and finally acceptance are all a part. If the separation is then ended these emotions must be revisited to allow reattachment. Since this is a painful process, severe or repeated disruption of attachment results in an unwillingness or inability to reattach – *detachment*. Disruption of the attachment to the primary carers can be caused by death, separation or severe illness. In later life, the attachment experience and the associated learned behaviours strongly influence how adults bond closely with another.

Other events, such as the primary carers being inaccessible to the child due to economic or other circumstances, depression, mental illness or their own anxieties, result in an *anxious attachment*. It is important to note that the carer is not necessarily absent; he or she may be present but preoccupied. In this case the child has the attachment, but as it is insecure it cannot be used as a safe base to move away from at will. It has to be continually checked and rechecked. This can produce a tendency to form anxious, insecure attachments in later life.

Sometimes primary carers are so afflicted that they need to be cared for by their own children; for example, if they become alcoholics, invalids or if they are bereaved. In this case a pattern of *reverse attachment* may be formed where the individual becomes a *compulsive carer* and looks to form relationships by seeking others in need of help.

Where there have been attachment problems in the past, the natural expectation of forming firm, secure bonds is lost. The possibility of rejection is always around. One reaction may be to avoid closeness and always be the first to reject. Alternatively, the individual may form a *false self*, a term used by Winnicott, to describe a facade that he presents in order to be acceptable. This facade could be one of caring competence or of helpless vulnerability. However, even if this is successful the individual is aware, on some level, that he is not liked for himself and so is constantly fearful of rejection.

ATTACHMENT MODEL – RELEVANCE TO COUPLE RELATIONSHIPS

Often there are shared attachment problems within a couple, possibly with one partner who is anxiously attached in a relationship with a more detached partner. The partners have become caught in this pattern because of complementary attachment behaviours. The more anxious partner does not find it strange to have to struggle to hold the relationship because it is what he has always done in his past. The detached partner is

STAGE TWO – UNDERSTANDING

used to being pursued because her pattern has always been to stay detached and this feels natural. Any difference in the level of *intimacy* would feel strange to either partner. However, the continual struggle around attachment is exhausting to both and the inherent insecurity makes it difficult for the relationship to progress.

Signs that help the counsellor identify that the Attachment Model may help include:

- Attachment issues as part of presenting problem – separations, affairs, desertion.
- Recurrent pattern of losses in later life – redundancies, separations, moves.
- Involvement of clients in very structured work (e.g. armed forces, nursing), or very lonely work (e.g. long-distance driving).
- Frequent reference by clients to attachment concepts – commitment, rejection and loss.
- A difficulty over partings and meetings.
- Attachment with the counsellor becomes an issue – either anxious attachment shown by notes, phone calls etc. or detachment shown by missed sessions.
- There are feelings of attachment towards the clients or a desire to reject them in the counsellor.

The way forward is for the counsellor to help the couple focus on the issue of attachment. Working on the past may be made more difficult because someone with a history of distant relationships may well find her past hard to recall, but this can be helped by focusing on specific events, anniversaries or festivals. Attachment issues are more easily made conscious than some of the concepts underlying the Splitting and Projection model and so can be explained to clients. The counsellor may find it helpful to do one or more of the following:

- Examine the couple's expectations around bonding.
- Consciously address the effect of past losses and separation.
- Use behavioural tasks to improve partings and meetings.
- Create more realistic scenarios around rejection.
- Uncover and mourn past unacknowledged losses.
- Model security in the arrangement of sessions.

ATTACHMENT MODEL – CASEWORK EXAMPLE

Dionne and Martin were a young couple who had lived together for four years but didn't seem able to settle down together. Although Dionne had definite plans about the future she wanted for them both, Martin would slip away every so often – sometimes drinking with his friends, at other times just going to the cinema, spending evenings with his parents or just riding around the town on buses daydreaming. He didn't turn up for the first session owing to a mix-up and the counsellor spent the time with Dionne, who talked about her plans for the future; her job as a nurse and her hopes of the family they could have if only Martin could be a bit less rootless. At the end of the session she said Martin would probably want to come on his own next week, but she paid for the session in advance and checked very carefully that the counsellor would be there. In fact they turned up together. 'I thought I'd better make sure he came,' Dionne apologised. Martin didn't seem to mind being there and was quite affable. One thing the counsellor had not expected from Dionne's description of him was that he walked with a marked limp. 'I fell down a cliff when I was little and it never seemed to get fixed,' he said airily. 'I don't let it bother me, but I have to hide it at work or they'd sack me.'

The Counsellor went home puzzled. For one thing she could not get them out of her mind. She found herself strongly wanting to make it all right for Dionne, who seemed to have such detailed plans for her future, built on such fragile foundations. There was also something touching about Martin's acceptance of his injury. He was like an orphan, she thought. She wondered why she had thought that since she knew his parents were alive, but then remembered that he had said they had left him in a hospital in the West Indies for his leg to heal when they came to Britain. She made a link with the other attachment issues in the case and decided that the attachment model might suit these clients. She realised it might be difficult to explore their past as Martin seemed so vague about his, while Dionne gave the impression she could talk endlessly about her large family, who she was always rescuing from various scrapes.

The next week the counsellor asked about the mix-ups over who was coming to the first two sessions, and wondered how it had happened. It seemed that when Martin left for work only the vaguest arrangements were made. He was a bus inspector and his work took him all over town, and he would return home as and when circumstance dictated. Dionne was often out by then with one of her sisters. The counsellor asked them if they would consider using a diary so they both knew when the other would be in. She explained that although they might find it strange, it might be helpful for each to know when they could expect to see the other. Most of the session was spent discussing this, as it was clearly a totally novel idea, and by the next week it had been put into practice.

During the next few weeks, they talked about many different aspects of Dionne's and Martin's lives. The diary idea seemed to focus the couple on the idea of routine, and as they described the changes they were making, they began to realise how many things had been left to chance in the past. Whether they shared a meal, whether they met friends together, whether they were both home to spend the night together – all had needed protracted planning and their sex-life had been so haphazard as to leave them both frustrated.

The counsellor had originally made a six-week contract. As the end approached, both clients reacted in a different way. Dionne admitted she was afraid that the counsellor might end the sessions abruptly; Martin had forgotten about the contract and so was not worried at all. A new contract was made and the counsellor suggested they draw up a genogram together to look at attachment issues in their past (Martin and Dionne's genogram is described in detail in Chapter 4). As part of this exercise they focused on specific losses. Martin was much more forthcoming about how desperately upset he now remembered being over his accident, and his sadness and feelings of hopelessness when his parents had left him behind. The session prompted him to talk it over with his parents and in the next week he approached his trade union at work, who told him that his fear of dismissal if the company discovered his injury was groundless, since he was clearly able to do his job. Dionne wondered how much her decision to be a nurse was conditioned by the fact that she had been the oldest child in a large family and had always made herself useful, as both her parents needed to work long hours. 'I was determined no-one would forget I was there,' she laughed in one session and then promptly burst into tears when she realised how genuine that fear had been. The counselling ended by agreement at the end of the third six-week contract, although the counsellor has always received a Christmas card from them in the subsequent years.

There are many additional typical attachment themes in this case which the readers are invited to note for themselves.

THE TRIANGULAR RELATIONSHIP MODEL – INTRODUCTION

Freud first commented upon the sexual tensions that exist in the triangle of two parents and one child in 1897 and coined the term 'Oedipus complex'. The name comes from the Ancient Greek myth of Oedipus who, having been abandoned by his parents as a baby, unknowingly kills his father and marries his mother. This thesis has been much developed and elaborated in psychoanalytic theory. RELATE's Approach to it comes via Fairbairn, who detached the phenomenon from a specific developmental stage and saw it rather as a 'love-hunger' which persists throughout life and can lead to primary personality and emotional problems.

In RELATE's thinking, Oedipal feelings that arise in significant triangular relationships have the following constituents:

- They involve the yearning for a desired object in the presence of a competitor.
- They often have a sexual content, even if the yearning is not primarily sexual.
- The relationship involved is often idealised.
- The roots of the feelings are linked with the formation of our sexuality.
- Clients for whom this model is helpful have often had problems with triangular relationships in their past.

Much of our life is spent in triangular relationships. The baby with two parents, a child and a sibling competing for one parent's love, a child with two siblings. The couple counselling relationship is itself a triangle, and for some clients this is an additional source of difficulty.

RELATE has a theory of healthy triangular interaction derived in particular from the writings of Robin Skynner. Take the example of two parents expecting a child.

Before the child arrives, the relationship may be as shown in Figure 3.2a, in which the double line indicates strong affection between the two partners. Initially, when the baby arrives, the pattern may change to that shown in Figure 3.2b, in which the most intense relationship is between the mother and child, but others remain connected. In time, the primacy of the parental relationship will reassert itself, but the child will remain connected to both (Figure 3.2c). However, in dysfunctional situations, the child may be excluded by the parents (Figure 3.2d) or may form a relationship with one parent from which the other is excluded (Figure 3.2e). Whatever patterns arises, the individual will receive a sense of triangular relationships being competitive ones in which the winner is rewarded by an intense exclusive relationships and the loser is isolated.

TRIANGULAR RELATIONSHIP MODEL – RELEVANCE TO COUPLE RELATIONSHIPS

Clearly these triangles will impact on a couple relationship whenever a third party is involved, whether it is a child inside the relationship or an affair outside. The situation will quite possibly be made more complex by the couples' distrust of the triangular relationship within the counselling room. These situations can also arise where there has been sexual abuse in a client's past. At the root of the problem is that if the *Oedipal Fantasy* were to be achieved, i.e. if the client were to gain a special exclusive relationship with his or her keenly desired other, the reality would probably fall far short of the fantasy. Instinctive knowledge of this often means that desire is kept alive but the final enactment of the fantasy is constantly postponed.

Facts that indicate that the Triangular Relationship model may be useful include:

- Affairs.
- Difficulties over a first child or subsequent child of different gender.
- Competitive relationship between clients.
- Jealousy.

STAGE TWO – UNDERSTANDING

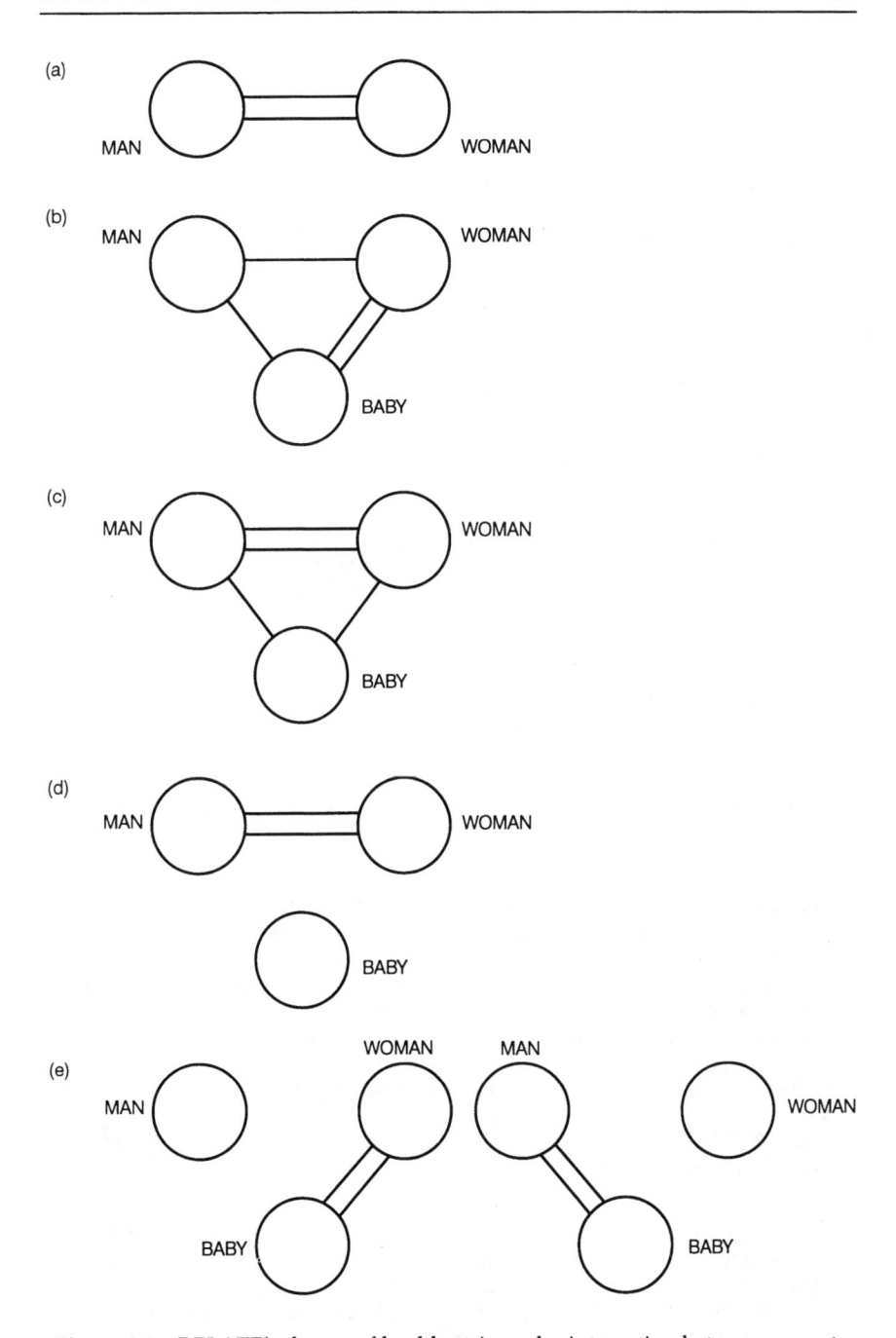

Figure 3.2 RELATE's theory of healthy triangular interaction between parents and their child (single line = bond of affection; double line = a particularly strong bond of affection)

- Past history of client being drawn into close relationship with one parent.
- Significant triangles in clients' past.
- Seductiveness towards counsellor.
- Struggle between clients for counsellor's attention.

Helpful work the counsellor can do includes:

- Modelling and facilitating non-exclusive triangles.
- Addressing trust issues.
- Looking at the ultimate disappointment of enacting the fantasy.
- Examining past experiences of triangular relationships.
- Normalising the feared exclusion.
- Using the triangle in the room to help insight.

TRIANGULAR RELATIONSHIP MODEL – CASEWORK EXAMPLE

Jane and Emma had been in a committed relationship together for several years. Before they met, Jane had been married and had a 10 year-old son, Mark, who now lived with the two of them. Emma had always considered herself a lesbian but her relationships in the past had been non-exclusive. Emma was angry with Jane because she felt the depth of her love was not returned in equal measure, although Jane would always remind her at this point that she had risked losing custody of her son and had given up his maintenance to move in with her. Jane was finding Emma's jealousy hard to handle. 'You've got to remember, I'm just a beginner,' Jane said, winking at the counsellor, 'I was straight for years.' 'Well you're extremely good at it,' Emma replied, turning to the counsellor, 'Isn't she?' The counsellor let the first three sessions pass feeling alternately entranced and bemused. At times she felt one or the other was trying to seduce her; on other occasions she felt both of them were laughing at her. Initially she had thought that maybe Emma had doubts about Jane's sexuality, but this seemed clearly not to be the couples' concern. Yet they continued to come, and there was real distress when they talked about the problems in their relationship. At the end of the fourth session, Jane said, 'We don't seem to be making much progress, do we? I wondered if it would help if we each had a few sessions alone with you?' 'No!' said the counsellor, somewhat abruptly, hastily covering herself by adding that it was her policy to work with couples together wherever possible.

The counsellor decided she had to do some hard thinking about the dynamics in the room and what she was going to do the following week, if only to have something with which to impress Jane! 'That's strange,' she thought, 'I don't usually feel I have to impress my clients.' As she thought further she realised there was a lot of competition in the counselling room, and indeed the clients' preference for witty badinage had prevented her getting to know any significant facts about their lives. 'I don't even think we've mentioned the boy more than in passing,' she thought. Her mind turned to triangles, and suddenly things seemed clearer. 'Emma's fear of losing Jane is being acted out in the counselling,' she thought, 'Yet she must know I wouldn't let Jane seduce me.' It was then she realised that Emma's fears were probably not conscious and rational and resolved to return and ask her clients to examine the influence of triangular relationships in their earlier lives. Also she felt that focusing on the past might take some of the pressure off the difficult dynamic in the room.

Jane started promisingly by stating that she had thought a lot about triangles in the past. She was an only child of a couple who had her late in life. 'I think they were both devoted to me,' she said, rather dully. However, the more she talked, the more the counsellor had the feeling that Jane had been on the outside of a very established relationship which had not been able to find much room for the new child. 'I did always feel a bit in the way.' said Jane 'That's why my husband and I separated, too. I always felt that once I'd had our son he lost interest in me. I was surprised he didn't push for custody. In fact, he went straight into another relationship with a friend of mine when I started expressing my doubts. I think they'd always had their eye on each other when I look back now.'

Emma's experience was different. She had been the youngest of five – and all her elder siblings were boys. She had been very close to her father. They had both had an interest in design – he had worked as a fabric designer and when she was a teenager they used to spend hours together in the evening making new patterns. 'And your mother?' the counsellor asked. 'I can't really remember,' said Emma. 'She was very active in local politics – to be honest I think she was pleased to have Dad off her hands.' The counsellor asked whether there was a sexual edge to this relationship. 'Not on Dad's part,' said Emma, 'Though I do have to say I had quite a crush on him for a bit, until I started getting involved with other women. Neither Mum nor Dad seemed at all surprised or worried when I came out to them, though. I sometimes feel guilty about how easy it all was for me.'

The counsellor shared the thought that neither client has managed to have a successful triangular relationship. There had been special bonds and exclusions in both of their childhoods; in adult life Jane had felt excluded by her husband and son; Jane's husband had gone off with her friend; all Emma's previous relationships had involved third parties and had come to nothing. Jane alluded to the tensions and difficulties that had existed in the counselling room. 'Yes, what were you expecting to happen if you came on your own?' the counsellor asked her. 'I don't know,' Jane replied, 'I just felt really strongly that something special might happen.' In the subsequent weeks, the couple examined their fantasies about what happened between the other two people in triangles when they were not there. The counsellor used the counselling to model that they stood to gain more from the process as a couple than they would individually, since they had their joint memory of the sessions to share afterwards, which was more useful than an illusory specialness.

At the ninth session, Emma said, 'You know, I think a lot of my jealousy was around the fear that because Jane had Mark they could both leave me...' 'And now…?,' prompted the counsellor. '…and now, I'm pretty sure she won't go,' said Emma, 'But if she did, I don't think I'd have the same fear that she and Mark would be having this earth shatteringly good time without me.'

The counselling ended with this session.

THE SYSTEMS MODEL – INTRODUCTION

The other models that are being outlined have all had their origin in the psychoanalytic tradition. Systemic theory addresses the connections between individuals. It forms the theoretical base of Systemic and Family Therapy. RELATE follows a model based on the ideas of Minuchin, a structural family therapist. This model concentrates on relationships between people and does not address unconscious processes, although in the RELATE Approach it is often made compatible with other models which do.

The process of integration of this theory into the RELATE theory base has been as follows. It was noted that the models based on theories of the individual and couple unconscious were more difficult to apply where the couple was part of a significant larger system. Although work could be done to help the couple change their relationship and their attitude to others, it was found that this did not allow the couple to realign themselves with significant others who were not involved in the counselling. This was particularly true in the cases of extended families, reconstituted families and clients who were members of distinct cultural groupings. Systemic theory addresses the relationships and connections between the couple, the wider family system and the social system.

RELATE's theory was already familiar with some concepts that are part of the systemic approach, such as roles and boundaries. What it lacked was a method of appreciating and working with *homeostasis* – the tendency of a system to maintain the status quo in order to maintain the stability of the whole.

All groups operate as systems, with different roles ascribed to different individuals. If a group is healthy and functioning well, these roles will not be too rigid. They will be openly acknowledged and it will be possible for roles to be modified to suit either changes in individuals or the perceived purpose of the group.

The systems operating around individuals in problematic relationships are unlikely to be so healthy or flexible. These systems function as protective devices to ward off the possibility of change, which is seen negatively as a painful experience that is certainly more dangerous than retaining the status quo. When an event impacts on one member, everyone is affected and works to maintain group stability. For example, in a system where attention may be drawn from a problematic parental relationship by a delinquent child, attempts by outside authorities to help may be subtly undermined by the system. If this fails and the child is lost to the system, another member may become the symptom bearer.

Role attribution can be a part of the system – the carer, the rebel, the symptom carrier are all examples of roles found in family systems. Whilst serving to keep the family stable, they can nevertheless be cruelly limiting to the individual. To keep the whole functioning there will be systems of belief that may be passed down through generations. These beliefs may govern what can be talked about (family secrets; don't mention sex); who can talk to whom (not in front of the children; don't worry Dad); they may govern behaviour (no arguing; everyone meets up at Christmas); they will also identify how the group makes decisions (divide and rule; men decide). In addition, every family holds beliefs about the world – how safe or unsafe it is; whether contact with the world outside the family is dangerous or to be welcomed.

The *boundaries* of the system are also important. Maintaining clear boundaries is an important way of keeping the system going. Often systems with weak internal boundaries, an abusive family for example, have strong, almost impenetrable external boundaries.

The above description is applied to a family but could equally apply to other groups. Many religious and political groups make explicit their beliefs of expected behaviour, and have powerful sanctions to use against members who wish to change their relationship to the group. Similarly, many types of occupation have their own culture and expected styles of behaviour. Friendship groups also can quickly ostracise a member who challenges group assumptions.

SYSTEMS MODEL – RELEVANCE TO COUPLE RELATIONSHIPS

A systemic model is helpful when the client couple are also members of other significant groupings. A common instance will be when clients have important roles in their families of origin. The need for the originating family to keep the individual in their set role may conflict with the individual's own desire or partner's wish. Additionally, there may be a 'culture clash' between the beliefs of the new family and those of the original one. It may be very difficult for the individuals to be objective about the beliefs of their family group for, no matter how these beliefs may seem to an outsider, for the person himself it is his passport to being accepted and needed. Additionally, the beliefs inherent in the system he has accepted all his life will not seem like beliefs but self-evident truths. There may also be shared assumptions about the consequences of breaking the beliefs, with strong feelings of guilt and disloyalty. The counsellor's approach is again to try to understand the clients' belief systems and to discuss them openly in session.

A natural tendency, when clients find they have a variety of demands placed upon them by different people, is to try and meet them all. However, this is only possible if the roles in the differing systems are complementary. Where they make opposite demands, the individual or the couple will be caught in *role-conflict*. This is potentially exhausting, since each system will see the individual's failure to fulfil its demands as a personal failing rather than a problem with the system itself.

Indicators which favour this model include:

- Extended family linking, especially cross-generation alliances.
- Network of second or reconstituted families.
- Clients subscribing to strong value systems.
- Tendency of clients to be influenced by others outside the group.
- Clients' attempts at change are resisted or undermined.
- Counsellor has a strong sense of confusion and of only having part of the story.

Useful approaches which help systemic work include:

- Find ways of identifying systems using stones, models or drawings.
- Examine the beliefs of different systems.
- Assess the clients' roles and look for conflict.
- Facilitate definition of preferred system.
- Reassure clients that it is rarely an 'in or out' choice – rather, it is a reordering of priorities.
- Strengthen boundaries of preferred systems.
- Loosen boundaries of secondary systems.

SYSTEMS MODEL – CASEWORK EXAMPLE

Michael and Soulla had been married for four years. They had met at school and continued seeing each other for five years before they decided to marry. Soulla's parents were conventional and would not have countenanced her and Michael cohabiting. Soulla did not want to upset them. Michael's family was well-known in the community and comparatively wealthy, while Soulla's was poor. Soulla's family had also often expressed the wish that she married

STAGE TWO – UNDERSTANDING 73

someone from Cyprus, while Michael's family came from mainland Greece. However, the decision caused less controversy than they had expected. Soulla's family had accepted her decision to marry Michael with sadness, but not with anger or rejection. Michael worked in his family business, wholesaling electrical equipment, which was quite successful and which paid them a good living. Soulla was training to be a schoolteacher. However, instead of settling down in the way that they had hoped, both found their life was strangely unhappy. Although Soulla visited her family frequently, they seemed to need a lot of looking after. Her younger sister had become pregnant by accident a year ago. Her parents had taken her and the baby in. This gesture had touched Soulla, but it meant that a lot more of her time and attention had to be given to her family, as both of her parents found having a baby in a small house very demanding. Michael was having problems at work. Three years ago his uncle had opted out of the family firm. Financially it should not have mattered, but his father had decided to open two new outlets immediately afterwards. Although they were doing very well, there was just too much work to do and he was arriving home exhausted, only to find the 'phone ringing because one of the new store managers was in difficulties. The precipitating problem was that the couple were now arguing because Michael wanted them to start a family and Soulla could not face the thought.

Both clients knew they were under too much stress. They had made several attempts in the counselling to relax and take time for themselves, but somehow it never happened. There was always a crisis that undid their best plans. They had looked at attachment issues and done a family genogram, but none of the insights seemed to help.

The counsellor wondered whether there was some important aspect of Greek family tradition he didn't understand – but when he asked, both clients seemed doubtful.

'Nobody in our families has any more idea how to help us than you have,' they replied.

'People know you are unhappy, then?' the counsellor asked.

'Oh yes, and everyone knows about us coming here,' said Michael, 'My parents say we should have kept it in the family.'

'And mine keep saying I should just have a baby and everything will be better,' said Soulla.

Thinking about boundaries, and wondering whether he fully understood what was going on for this couple, the counsellor indicated a box of stones in the corner of the room and asked the couple if they could each make a representation of their situation as they saw it (there is a detailed description of this exercise with Michael and Soulla in Chapter 4).

The counsellor was surprised to see in each case the large number of groups clustering around the couple, and that several members of the family and even Michael's store managers and Soulla's schoolchildren were placed almost as close to them as they were to each other. Even Michael and Soulla were a bit overwhelmed by these representations. The counsellor drew up the representations on a chart and asked the couple to draw a line around each group. They would take one a week for the next few weeks.

Work started with Soulla's family.

'What are the beliefs?' asked the counsellor.

'No-one gets out!' said Michael, immediately.

'Children can do no wrong.' said Soulla after some thought.

'Do you find those beliefs helpful?' asked the counsellor.

'No, in some ways I wish they'd pushed me out when I married Michael. I'm pleased they're supporting Maria though. Yet they always make me feel my teaching isn't very good because I sometimes have to discipline the kids.'

'I think they live through you and Maria,' said Michael.

In time they came to understand Soulla's family better. It was now more possible for the couple to think of ways in which they would relate to the family – resisting the demands and pressures which they did not feel were justified and supporting the causes which were.

A similar process was carried out with Michael's family and his business, which was almost a subgroup of the family, but with store managers who were Michael's sole responsibility. He realised he was going along with his father's desire for the business to expand, while absorbing alone all the complexities that arose because they now had to employ non-family members in important positions.

'There is a basic belief in our family that you can't trust anyone outside, so you don't give them enough facts to do the job.' he observed, 'And my family's not like Soulla's. Work and home life are one. Once my uncle left the firm there was no place for him.'

'You stopped ringing him up as well, even though we were fond of him,' said Soulla.

Soulla's job was analysed in the same way. She realised that her knowledge that the school had taken her on because she was bilingual had led to her offering some of the Greek speaking children more of her time than she had originally intended. She was the only member of staff who was regularly called at home by pupils.

The couple worked to change their position in the different systems, using small changes. They dealt with some of each other's phone calls, consulted before they made any commitments and stopped discussing their marital problems in their families. Soulla realised some of her aversion to having children was because she had always felt she would have to give in to all their demands and subordinate herself to them. Now she started to see some positive aspects in her niece.

Michael and Soulla saw his family more often socially and he re-established contact with his uncle. Michael took on as much work but he took less responsibility for the store managers, whom he referred to his father. Shortly afterwards, his father announced he was selling the least profitable new outlet.

They offered Maria the chance to bring the baby and live with them, which she was now considering.

'We'd both like to have them in the house and she wants to move. I don't know why I didn't think of it before. Who knows, maybe my parents will take a holiday in Cyprus now,' Soulla said.

Both clients were surprised how quickly others had changed around them when they had made the first small moves.

'I think they knew we'd moved on and that they'd have to change,' Michael said at the final review after the eighteenth session. 'They started to realise it when we stopped telling them what was happening here.'

THE LIFE-STAGE MODEL – INTRODUCTION

Lastly, we come to the Life-stage model. In some senses this is also the starting point of any piece of couple work. What frequently brings couples into counselling is that they have encountered challenges that have tested their normal resources and problem-solving abilities. So in some ways all that has passed before is an exploration of life-stage problems.

However, there is also a more formal theory that attaches to this model, proposed by Erikson (1995). He built on the developmental models of earlier theorists, but also introduced a *psychosocial* element. He observed that the process of development does not stop after the completion of childhood, but continues throughout life. In each stage there is a *conflict* to be resolved and the successful resolution of this is the *task* of that stage. He noted that even when stages are successfully negotiated, individuals can tend to *regress* back through stages when afflicted by difficulties. His eight *life-stages* are summarised in Figure 3.3.

LIFE-STAGE MODEL – RELEVANCE TO COUPLE RELATIONSHIPS

To an individual therapist, the relevance of this model could be to focus on the different life-stages and help the client reconsider ones where the

Stage	Tasks to be achieved
Babyhood	Manage anxiety, develop trust
Toddler	Deal with shame, doubt, frustration
Pre-school	Balance initiative with guilt, learn values
Early school	Learn about independence and work
Adolescence	Develop identity, balance creativity with self-absorption
Adult	Learn to cope with sharing and dependency inherent in relationships
Mid-life	Balancing needs of others and self
Later life	Balancing achievements and disappointments of life

Figure 3.3 Life-stages and tasks to be achieved

transition has been particularly difficult. However, in couple work, the position is slightly more complex. Depending on their age and life circumstances, couples are not only negotiating life-stage changes of their own; they are also being affected by their parents' and elders' passage through more advanced stages, and are coping with their children's passage through earlier stages. All these elements may combine to awaken the conflict of many stages in the clients' lives.

Such conflicts express themselves in the couple relationship through the activation of mistrust, anger, mutual accusations and loss of intimacy. The partners may both respond to the stress by withdrawal, or by repeated unsuccessful attempts to implement the same solution to the problem. Where these responses refer to the treatment of younger family members, they can often be the repetition of responses that were adopted in each partner's family of origin and are an expression of each partner's entrenched value system.

Additionally helpful in Erikson's model is the postponement of adulthood to what others would call early mid-life. A majority of the couples presenting at couple counselling agencies fall within this age group. The recognition of this as a significant developmental phase is a helpful counterbalance to other branches of psychodynamic practice, which tend to link present problems to childhood developmental stages. For many couples the entry into couple counselling is a result of a combination of life-stage transition and changes in circumstance.

Cues that alert the counsellor to the relevance of this model are:

- Specific triggering cause – baby, teenage child, mid-life crisis, death of parent.
- Regression of client to earlier stage.
- Noticeably difficult past life event.
- Shared difficulty of certain stage in both clients' family histories.

Helpful strategies include:

- Recognise the existence of a difficult stage.
- Examine the tasks and conflicts of the stage.
- Compare history of similar transitions.
- Address anxieties aroused by change.

LIFE-STAGE MODEL – CASEWORK EXAMPLE

Darren and Susan present for counselling. They are in their early 30s and have two young children. Their relationship has become more tense since

STAGE TWO – UNDERSTANDING

the arrival of the children, especially their baby son, whom Darren considers 'spoilt'. Their problems have come to a head because Susan has got herself into conflict with the law by sheltering a teenage nephew who was involved with drug dealing. Susan works at a Neighbourhood Advice Centre and is part of a large local family that frequently involves the couple's life. Although Susan is furious at her sister, who has given up on her son, and very disapproving of the boy's lifestyle, she also believes passionately that 'blood is thicker than water'. Darren, on the other hand, is much more of a loner. He is very principled and patient and commands much respect locally. He works on his own as a mechanic and is relied upon by a number of local groups for whom he arranges transport. He has moved away from his family, for whom he has little time – specially his father, whom he sees as a bully. He cannot see why Susan will not make a similar break from her family.

Although initially the couple presented a variety of problems to the counselling, it was their total disagreement over Susan's support of her nephew Keith which was clearly the flashpoint, and had made the other tensions in their relationship pass from being merely irksome to being intolerable. After two sessions of icy politeness between the couple, this came to a head in a heated argument in the third session.

'I just can't believe you've put our whole family, all we've worked to build, at risk, to support that degenerate!' shouted Darren.

'Oh, it's so easy for you,' replied Susan. 'If people make a mistake you just write them off.'

'That's just rubbish and you know it! I'm as involved in charity work as you are. Probably more so, since I don't get paid for it. I just believe in helping those who want to help themselves – not spongers'.

'That's all very fine, but not everyone wants to belong to the Scouts and the Boy's Brigade and go away on parades and do good deeds, do they? What about the others? I see a whole stream of youngsters at my work who can't find jobs and are bitter and angry about it. It's not surprising they turn to crime.'

'They should have more respect for themselves.'

'I sense you're both talking about the difficulties of being a teenager,' said the counsellor – having linked this argument with past issues that had arisen, and being conscious that she sometimes felt her own authority in the room was very closely questioned in a way that reminded her of dealing with teenagers.

'I find it hard to see what that has to do with what we were talking about,' said Darren. 'I'm talking about responsibility.'

The counsellor persisted, saying, 'Last week you both mentioned your own teenage. Darren, you said your father had been very strict about making you leave school and start work. He made it plain he wasn't willing to go on supporting you. I remember the words you said he used. You said he said, "You've been living off us long enough." You said you still hadn't forgiven him – or your mother for not sticking up for you.'

'Well yes...'

'I wonder if some of your anger towards Keith is because Susan is offering him a chance you were denied.'

'So you're saying I'm right and he is being too strict,' said Susan.

'No,' said the counsellor. 'Do you remember what you said about your teenage last week?'

'Yes. I said my family was very free and easy and we were all allowed to do whatever we wanted. If we made mistakes someone put it right for us. You said something about "How did I feel about that?" I'd never thought to question it before. You confused me.'

The counsellor set the couple a task at the end of that session – to go away and spend a quarter of an hour each describing their teenage to each other. They were not to link it to the present, just to describe the good and bad points. Next session, she asked each to report back what they had learned from the other.

The next two sessions were linked to exploring this theme further. Darren had seen his teenage as totally negative; Susan saw hers as very positive. Revisiting them allowed them to see the positive and negative in both experiences. Darren had learned to be responsible from an early age but had been denied any parental support; Susan had total support, but had not ever had to face the consequences of her actions. Over Keith they were both trying to replicate what had happened to them instead of thinking over a fresh joint approach. This discussion then broadened to include firmness and kindness. It was Darren's sense of purpose that had originally attracted Susan, and it was Susan's caring nature that had appealed to Darren. Yet when they argued that was also what they differed about.

'So you reckon this whole thing was because we didn't get ourselves properly sorted when we were teenagers?' Darren suggested at the last session.

'Not exactly,' said the counsellor. 'Adolescence is one of the stages of life, but early mid-life is another. That feels like the one you're preoccupied with now.'

'And what's that one about?'

'Roles beyond work and family. Morality. Finding your own answer as a couple to the sort of things we've talked about.'

CONCLUDING THOUGHTS

In this chapter the attention to each model has necessarily been very brief. Similarly, in the casework examples presented, the clients have all neatly benefited from one model, whereas in reality a counsellor might often combine elements from more than one model. It has also been necessary to give only the briefest summary for each model. In every case there is far more that could be discussed. However, we hope that we have conveyed some of the essential elements of RELATE's theory of unconscious processes, and to have made a start at illustrating how this can be used in couple casework.

One final element to touch on is the impact of this learning on the counsellor. Just as the counsellor learns to understand what underlies her clients' actions, so she learns more about herself in the process. This can be an enriching experience, but also a disturbing one. However, one thing is certain, and that is that the learning is never complete, and an alert counsellor will frequently find herself sharing an area of unawareness with her clients – and then hopefully resolving the question in supervision as a prelude to helping the clients resolve it.

Figure 3.4 summarises the indicators relating to the different models.

Indicators for Different Models of Understanding

Projection and Splitting Model

- Strong 'primitive' emotions.
- A sense that the couple are bound together.
- Simple notions of good and bad are spoken about.
- Words such as 'ought' and 'should' abound in describing preferred actions.
- The counsellor herself feels drawn into the struggle.

Attachment Model

- Attachment issues as part of presenting problem – separations, affairs, desertion.
- Recurrent pattern of losses in later life – redundancies, separations, moves.
- Involvement of clients in very structured work (e.g. armed forces, nursing), or very lonely work (e.g. long-distance driving).
- Frequent reference by clients to attachment concepts – commitment, rejection and loss.
- A difficulty over partings and meetings.
- Attachment with the counsellor becomes an issue – either anxious attachment shown by notes, phone calls etc. or detachment shown by missed sessions.
- There are feelings of attachment towards the clients or a desire to reject them in the counsellor.

Triangular Relationship Model

- Affairs.
- Difficulties over a first child or subsequent child of different gender.
- Competitive relationship between clients.
- Jealousy.
- Past history of client being drawn into close relationship with one parent.
- Significant triangles in clients' past.
- Seductiveness towards counsellor.
- Struggle between clients for counsellor's attention.

Systems Model

- Extended family linking – especially cross-generation alliances.
- Network of second or reconstituted families.
- Clients subscribing to strong value systems.
- Tendency of clients to be influenced by others outside the group.
- Clients' attempts at change are resisted or undermined.
- Counsellor has a strong sense of confusion and of only having part of the story.

Life-stage Model

- Specific triggering cause – baby, teenage child, mid-life crisis, death of parent.
- Regression of client to earlier stage.
- Noticeably difficult past life event.
- Shared difficulty of certain stage in both clients' family history.

Figure 3.4 Indicators to help focusing on different models of Understanding

4

STAGE THREE – ACTION

Talk that does not end in any kind of action is better suppressed altogether.
Thomas Carlyle

This Chapter deals with the final stage of the three-stage model – the Action Stage. Our map is given in Figure 4.1.

By this stage of the work many clients will have resolved their problems. Some will have found that the time and support given to them in the exploration phase has been enough to allow them to mobilise their own resources and to resolve the problems that brought them to counselling. Others will have found that the additional insights offered by the focus on unconscious processes in the understanding phase have allowed them to see their problem in a different light and now they can find their own way forward. However, many will find that insight alone is not enough. They need help in actually bringing about change.

In the last chapter the description of the clues to the usefulness of each model were followed by some simple suggestions for further action. Most of these need little further elaboration, as they are based upon the areas that a couple counsellor would be expecting to explore or model in the

Stage Three – Action

  (a) Actions deriving from the models in Stage Two (b) (Figure 1.3) and requiring:
     (i) Challenge
     (ii) Reframing
     (iii) Behaviour modification
  (b) An understanding of the process of permanent change leading to the additional use of the following tools:
     (i) Communication exercises
     (ii) Genograms
     (iii) Sculpting
     (iv) Tools from TA

Figure 4.1 Detailed map of the Action stage of the RELATE Approach

sessions – ability to cope with ambivalence, security of arrangements, etc. These suggestions are summarised in Figure 4.2. We have not listed actual tasks since good tasks are context-specific. Usually these spring naturally from the counsellor's and clients' joint ingenuity. However, if a counsellor is seeking ideas for couple tasks, he may be helped by considering the many couple exercises included in *The RELATE Guide To Better Relationships* (Litvinoff 1994).

Action frequently depends upon the counsellor challenging the clients, helping them to look at matters differently or to begin to vary their behaviours, and so we shall first make some general considerations of challenging, reframing (a term describing the way a counsellor can encourage clients to see the same facts in a different way) and negotiating different behaviours.

CHALLENGING

We need to stress here, yet again, the importance of having the trust of the clients before challenging. The aim of challenging is to focus on discrepancies in thoughts, feelings and behaviours that become apparent during the Exploring and Understanding stages. Too early or clumsy an attempt will make the clients feel attacked or misunderstood and may bring the counselling to a premature end. Challenging underpins the Understanding of Stage Two and can provide the bridge to a desired change in the relationship. Initially, the counsellor can begin this process by:

- Summarising the themes and reflecting back what has been said to help clarify some of the issues that seem at odds with one another.
- Encouraging the clients to thoughtfully challenge each other.
- Encouraging the couple to question the strong family beliefs that have never been acknowledged by either of them.
- Introducing unacknowledged feelings. The counsellor may well become aware of a feeling that the clients might be denying. Simply sharing the feeling in the room – assuming that the counsellor judges it to be close enough to the clients' consciousness to be meaningful to them – can help clients gain new insights. Chapter 6 details how the phenomenon of counter-transference can be a key to discovering such feelings.
- Pointing out the discrepancies between verbal and non-verbal language between the couple. Neither partner may be aware of behaving in such a manner. Clients may say that they are angry but smile as they say it or, conversely, verbalise something benign in a hectoring tone.

The relationship between the counsellor and client can be used to look at possible blocks that may also reflect the client relationship. This is known

Actions for Different Models of Understanding

Projection and Splitting Model

- Model coping with ambivalence.
- Encourage open communication.
- Contain destructive arguments.
- Allow clients to become conscious of the denied parts of themselves.
- Demonstrate the possibility of not being drawn into conflict.

Attachment Model

- Examine the couple's expectations around bonding.
- Consciously address the effect of past losses and separation.
- Use behavioural tasks to improve partings and meetings.
- Create more realistic scenarios around rejection.
- Uncover and mourn past unacknowledged losses.
- Model offering security in the arrangement of sessions.

Triangular Relationship Model

- Address trust issues.
- Look at the ultimate disappointment of enacting the *Oedipal* fantasy.
- Examine past experiences of triangular relationships.
- Normalise the feared exclusion.
- Model and facilitate non-exclusive triangles.

Systems Model

- Find ways of identifying systems using stones, models, drawings.
- Examine the beliefs of different systems.
- Assess the clients' roles and look for conflict.
- Facilitate definition of preferred system.
- Establish it is rarely an 'in-or-out' choice – rather a reordering of priorities.
- Strengthen boundaries of preferred systems.
- Loosen boundaries of secondary systems.

Life-stage Model

- Recognise the existence of a difficult stage.
- Examine the tasks and conflicts of the stage.
- Compare history of similar transitions.
- Address anxieties aroused by change.

Figure 4.2 Actions for different models of understanding

as *immediacy*. For example, when a counsellor experiences an anxious client as very overpowering, she might say, 'Although I can see you are trying hard to explain your situation to me, I have a feeling of being very shut out at the moment'. This may well give the client the chance to realise that the effect of his anxious behaviour is to cause antagonism rather than to help the situation. Since it is happening in the room, it can clarify what is happening in an immediate sense and may give clients insights that were previously hidden or unknown.

The challenging we have described so far has looked at what the clients bring into the relationship, how they operate interactively with each other and with the counsellor. It is also possible to challenge clients' patterns of thinking – about themselves or about others. This is a way of helping people who, maybe because of a tendency to split things into good and bad or to make a catastrophe out of rejection, think in a self-defeating or negative way. We are familiar with the glass of water which can be viewed accurately as half-full or half-empty, depending on a positive or negative interpretation. Feelings or experiences can be viewed in exactly the same way. For instance, the young man whose underlying belief is that he must do well sees failure to succeed as terrible. It marks him out as an unacceptable person. He is dreading asking his girlfriend to marry him in case she refuses him. This belief is so overwhelming it is hindering their relationship and the commitment that he wants to make. If she should refuse, how could he cope with the rejection? The counsellor in this case would try to ascertain whether this belief is based on reality or fantasy. She may ask, 'What is the worse you feel can happen?' and challenge his conclusion that failure would be terrible, rather than just very sad. Alternatively, she may urge him to adopt a more positive belief, such as, 'We have a good relationship which we both enjoy. I have no evidence that my girlfriend is less committed to it than I am. She may be as ready to marry as I am'.

Couples may carry this kind of self-defeating thinking further into their intimate relationship. Not only will they believe that they must do well as individuals but also that other people and life in general must treat them well. Conflict and anger erupt when these expectations are thwarted. This can set up maladapted thinking and behaviour to avoid disappointment. For example, a woman may have experienced a series of rejections in earlier relationships. If these are linked to childhood rejections, the feelings aroused may be seen as intolerable, even though she survived perfectly well. One way of approaching this case might be to explore the past losses, as described under the attachment model. In addition, the dysfunctional thinking, 'I can't survive on my own; I can't bear being left,' could be gently challenged by making a comparison with the reality of what has happened and is likely to happen in the future.

STAGE THREE – ACTION

Challenging a particular example of behaviour can be a catalyst for understanding past patterns and therefore change.

> John was verbally abusive to his partner. 'I was really angry when she came in late and I told her so in no uncertain terms.' The counsellor asked him if he could remember what he thought when she came in, before he started shouting. After a lot of consideration and discussion, he recognised that his intervening thought had been, 'I'm sure she'll ignore what I say'. So he shouted and swore to try and make his point forcefully ... and she walked straight out again. By exploring his incorrect belief of 'people tend to ignore me', which was his childhood experience, and replacing it with 'I can make people take notice of what I am saying if I don't frighten them', he learned to modify his behaviour.

REFRAMING

As relationships develop and become established, the original couple fit can become very uncomfortable. Roles within the partnership have to be adaptable to fit the social and family changes. Behaviour that was previously enjoyed is now perceived to be unacceptable. This is very relevant to the life-stage model. We will look at a small part of a casework example.

> Greg and Mary met when they were teenagers. Both were very academic at school, but Greg was able to play in a band until all hours and still pass his exams with flying colours. Mary had equally good results but had to plan and revise in a much more organised way. Both went to university and continued their relationship there very successfully. They were the golden couple, even when Greg decided to switch courses. Midway through this course he decided to drop out of university altogether and concentrate on his music career. He seemed to butterfly from one thing to another in a such a carefree way, easily making good friends on the way. He was generous to a fault and Mary truly loved him.
>
> Mary graduated and then trained as a pharmacist. Greg had become a successful musician. Once Mary was established in her work, she felt that they should marry and have a baby. Greg did not initiate this move, but was perfectly happy to go along with it. Their relationship was harmonious and he saw no reason why it would not continue to be so. His motto in life seemed to be, 'Just let it happen'. Mary basked in Greg's easy ways and was very happy to organise the domestic part of their lives. Greg admired her ability to sort things out, hold down a good job, and take a very active interest in his music. They were a good partnership.
>
> Problems arose when they had their first child. Greg carried on as before but with a new son to adore. Mary still coped magnificently, returning to work after only a few weeks and organising the child care. On the surface the relationship appeared to have adapted well to the birth of the baby. However, Mary was full of resentment: 'How could he behave as though we were a young couple with no commitments?' He carried on with their lives as

usual, even expecting Mary and the baby to come on tour with the band. Greg noticed the change in Mary. He began to dread going home. The well-organised household now seemed a chain around his neck. Mary complained bitterly about his lack of responsibility toward the 'family'. The man who had been so carefree and generous now seemed irresponsible to her. The woman who seemed to be so well organised and able to him, had now become a complainer and a drudge. The behaviour itself had changed little, but the attitude and perception of it had changed enormously.

The counsellor reminded the couple of the positive interpretations they used to place upon each others' behaviour, and urged them to still consider things in the same light. By seeing Greg's 'irresponsibility' as 'carefreeness' again, Mary was more able to value it and to question it in a more respectful way. In addition, Greg felt more able to consider behaving differently when he did not feel his whole attitude to life was under attack. Similarly, by seeing Mary's 'fussing' as 'good organisation' again, Greg was able to give her room to make the same shift. Once this was established the counsellor encouraged the couple to reframe the demands they were making of each other as requests and statements of preference – so,'You shouldn't make such a fuss about the mess' became 'I appreciate you like the place tidy, but I'd rather clear up later'. Similarly, Mary would reframe 'You're completely irresponsible about money and should learn to grow up' with 'I'd like us to sit down tonight and plan our spending – I find it hard to be as carefree as you'. Within this reframing the couple were able resume an even-tempered dialogue, and so to begin to discuss the life-stage change of becoming a family.

BEHAVIOUR MODIFICATION

Modifying behaviour can be an effective initial intervention where there is a poor interaction between partners and where it is impossible to come to a good understanding. If there is sufficient motivation for change, the couple can implement new strategies and then return to examine the feelings the new situation produces. Change in behaviour itself arouses different feelings that then may lead to insights and understanding. The following guidelines are helpful when considering behavioural modification:

- The behaviour to be changed must be specific.
- The change must be capable of being observed.
- The change must fit the context to the clients' environment.
- The change must be within the clients own resources.
- The aim is to reduce conflictual behaviour and reinforce desirable behaviour.

STAGE THREE – ACTION

- Each partner should be asked to do an equal amount.

During the counselling, the counsellor may agree with the clients what changes in behaviour they would like to see. Collaboration at this stage is essential. The simple idea of keeping a joint diary for Martin and Dionne in the last chapter required them both to take responsibility for recording their plans so that they knew when they could expect to see each other. It was a novel idea for them both. It lessened Dionne's need to take responsibility for Martin and allowed him to see how leaving everything to chance limited the relationship. The keeping of the diary was a specific task so that the attachment issues it raised could then be addressed more directly, and the clients were motivated to begin to take action.

One of the dangers of making a request is that it may become a bartering process. Each partner has to agree to the task and look at it in terms of cost and pay-off to self as well as the partner. It becomes convoluted when one deliberately demands behaviour that he knows cannot or will not be met. Never going to the pub again is unrealistic, but the amount of time spent there may be talked through. Meetings with difficult members of the family cannot be totally avoided, but how the couple set up these meetings could be renegotiated.

The skill of the counsellor is to draw the clients back from broad abstract ideas of how they want their partner to change, to smaller realistic ideas. These have to be placed in the context of their normal environment. For example, a young couple felt that they both needed some quiet time together without the constant demands of their young children. An expensive hotel with babysitting facilities was out of the question financially. They discussed other options that might be possible with the counsellor. By the next session it had been agreed that the client's brother and wife would have the children to stay so that the couple could go and stay in a friend's caravan. All the cousins got on well and it had been agreed that the two couples would mind each other's children occasionally in order that the other couple could have a break. The resources were there but it took a kick-start from the counselling in order to put it into practice.

These tasks may appear simple on the surface but will require the counsellor's patience and encouragement. Clients are often disappointed because they have expected too much in too short a time. The couple that managed to get away for the weekend put all their energies into that task, so that they did not think through how they were going to use the time together. However, the success of the task in freeing up time for them together meant that there was now a context for addressing the intimacy problems which troubled them. There will be many fallbacks and disappointments and the counsellor will need to place them on a firm base of reality. In many ways the behaviour modification is an experiment, and the results are interesting and helpful irrespective of whether it succeeds or fails.

Let look at an example of behavioural tasks that Kemal and Mona were able to negotiate.

> The counsellor had worked with Kemal and Mona for some weeks after they presented with general rowing and poor communication. Using the attachment model, they were aware that their worst moments of tension were around when they parted in the morning or, especially, met again in the evening. Kemal worked as a bus driver in a large city. It was tiring work. He requested that he should have some time to unwind – a little peace – when he first arrived home after work. Mona immediately responded that she too was exhausted, being cooped up all day with the children, and where was she going to get her peace? They both had the same needs at the same time, and their reciprocal behaviour reinforced the unmet needs. Kemal was more specific and asked for half an hour's quiet time, and then he would do something for Mona. It was agreed that he would bathe the children while Mona made their supper. This would also have the effect of getting the children to bed at a more reasonable hour, and thus give them both more peace. A change was achieved in which both Kemal and Mona had gained for themselves, and not at a cost to each other.
>
> The tension between them lessened – but only slightly and there was a constant tendency to return to previous problems. However, the partial success of the task had begun to free the couple to look for other solutions. Kemal suggested that some of Mona's tiredness at the end of the day was a result of her being cooped up all day with the children. She thought that on bright days the children might like to walk down to the bus-station to meet Kemal. He was initially reluctant, since he liked to keep family and work separate, but agreed to a trial. The children expended masses of energy on the walk, and far from being unwelcome at the bus-station, they were greeted enthusiastically by Kemal's colleagues. Kemal came to love seeing them all waiting for him. It was very different from being crawled over as soon as he opened the front door. This was the beginning of a more profound change. Mona was refreshed by the walk rather than resentful about her tiredness. Kemal enjoyed being seen with his family at work, rather than being overwhelmed by them when he was tired. Working hard for his family became more worthwhile. The change in behaviour for individual gain had moved on to mutual benefits for the couple and had led to a different pattern of attachment within the family.

Behavioural modification will be defeated if there are underlying emotional conflicts. For instance, if there is an unacknowledged power struggle going on between a couple, the agreed behavioural tasks will be constantly undermined by both partners' incessant attempts to gain the upper hand.

The above example shows the limits that behavioural tasks need to transcend if they are to work, and why the RELATE Approach is not primarily a behavioural one. The problems that couples bring to counselling are

STAGE THREE – ACTION

rarely specific enough to allow for a simple change in a behaviour pattern to resolve them and RELATE counsellors are not trained to analyse conflict in behavioural terms. The techniques RELATE uses in the action stage are usually designed to encourage clients to adopt a different way of approaching a situation and coping with problems. The reasons for this will become clearer as we consider the nature of change.

CHANGE

Having agreed and understood problem areas, it is often clear to the clients that some form of change is necessary. The concept of change in a couple is usually very subjective. Each partner would prefer to hang on to the notion that it is the other partner who needs to change. This may be expressed very openly – especially in clients to whom the splitting and projection model applies, and who therefore tend to displace problematic feelings elsewhere. Most of our clients will have strongly-held views as to where the change should occur, but change cannot occur in a vacuum just because it is desired.

Change is a process with many facets, but can be considered in two broad categories – first-order and second-order. First-order change is one that occurs in a given system while the system itself remains unchanged; second-order change is one that changes the system itself.

The stereotypical picture of the nagging wife and withdrawn husband can demonstrate the two orders of change. The couple may have identified this interaction as the one they want to change. During the exploring stage, the counsellor will have started to build up the picture of their relationship and noted the level of their engagement and understanding of it. The couple, after some reflection, believe that if the wife reduces her nagging, her husband may put down his newspaper and listen to her. It had already been established that she did not feel heard and her husband had agreed that after the first few words, he switched off. 'Nagging' and 'listening' can be interpreted broadly and subjectively, but the couple knew what they understood by the words. Once this has been identified as the focus for change, an attempt at a first-order change can be made. There will be less *nagging* and more *listening*. However, if the change stops here and there is no improvement in the overall method of communication (i.e. the system), there is likely to be a fall-back to old ways of communicating and behaving. She relapses to her nagging and he returns to withdrawing behind his paper.

In the understanding phase, work may have been done to trace the roots of the problem. Both partners may have become aware of the history of this interaction. They may be more in touch with the fears which cause one to be insistent about communication and the other to withdraw. Perhaps the interaction has its roots in past attachment problems. As these are discussed in the room, the counsellor will urge the couple to experiment with different ways of communicating – encouraging the husband to be less guarded about allowing free communication to take place and the wife less concerned about her husband's need to withdraw. An interaction will take place, rather than an attack and withdrawal. It is this interaction that will be the key to a second-order change. If the couple experience enough positive exchanges, they will hopefully promote more understanding. Conversation will have moved from their current stalemate to a connection with each other. Building on these foundations will hopefully move them from mere interaction to a more intimate, deep relationship. This would then be a second-order change, where the system itself has changed. The nagging/withdrawing system has become obsolete and a new one has replaced it.

As in this example, first-order changes tend to involve doing more or less of the same thing but in a better way. The second-order change actually alters the 'rules' of the relationship where there are rewards for both partners. It is a development of the couple as a dynamic.

Another way of encouraging significant change – and the one most commonly used within the RELATE Approach – is to get the couple to take action together in the counselling room in examining the dynamic of their relationship, possibly linking it to some form of representation. This has several advantages:

- Firstly, the couple are involved in creating a view of the relationship which is uniquely theirs. This means they are much more likely to own the outcome.
- Secondly, the couple are improving their communication skills as they work together on the action.
- Thirdly, the counselling is given an active task to focus on, rather than just further exploration and understanding.
- Finally, the view of the relationship which is gained is usually of lasting value.

We explore below some such options. The first is communication work – then we look at the use of genograms, sculpts and a tool derived from Transactional Analysis in this connection.

COMMUNICATION WORK

Couples often perpetuate their problems by having dysfunctional methods of communication that do not allow the real issues to be addressed.

STAGE THREE – ACTION

The nagging/ignoring interaction described previously is a good example. Good communication allows couples to understand each other's feelings and needs, and gives them a sense of togetherness. Without this communication each partner can become isolated within the relationship and has to look to other means or people to satisfy their quest for intimacy. Effective communication is also needed to help couples through difficulties and misunderstandings in order to return to more intimate levels. Humans are innately good communicators. The counsellor's task is to unlock the skills when they have become blocked.

We first learn how to communicate in our family of origin. How we learn and what we learn is reflective of how the family interacts. Each family member has individual characteristics, but how these are responded to generally influences our communication skills. In some families feelings are made very explicit; in others, feelings may be expected to be kept under control and not expressed. Each family will evolve its own code of expectations. This code will become the individual's norms, the way he or she assumes that most people operate.

Later, communication skills are adapted and amplified by life experiences, through education, the workplace and social interaction. Defences will be built up against feelings, thoughts and behaviours that are uncomfortable. This process is subtle. Some people are more aware of their feelings and are comfortable with placing a high emphasis on their individual needs. Others are more comfortable with cultural, social or family rules to influence their thinking and more willing to sublimate or bury their own individual needs. Most people are a diverse mixture. In a couple relationship, each party brings his or her own very different history and communication experience, and there is great scope for misunderstanding.

Communication is the exchange of messages. These may be verbal, but we also use body language, facial expressions and eye contact. In a couple relationship, there is a real need to connect with each other. Partners must learn new communication skills and modify old patterns if they are to communicate successfully in the new relationship.

Problems frequently arise when there is a contradiction in verbal and non-verbal messages. A person who says he is very interested in the conversation but continually looks over the other party's shoulder is sending a very mixed message. The words are conveying an interaction, but all this is being undermined by the non-verbal behaviour. The exchange gets muddled as the other partner tries to claw back the attention. What should be a direct communication becomes something else. It may evoke memories of being ignored as a child, and this affects how the conversation is continued. This will in turn elicit responses designed to counteract uncomfortable feelings, and a self-perpetuating spiral of poor contact has begun. The words that are being said no longer reflect what is being felt. The counsellor needs to observe the posture to help the clients to focus on what they are doing and explore it: 'I notice that whenever you talk about your children, you clench your fists tightly'. Often you can encourage the client to repeat the gesture consciously but with the eyes shut and explain the feelings or memories associated with it. Conversely, the exercise can be done repeating the words but with a different gesture: 'When you were saying that you didn't feel John cared for you, you turned away and spoke in a quiet, child-like voice. Do you think you could say it to him directly in your normal voice?'

For some people direct eye contact shows interest, but for others it may be invasive. It will vary from individual to individual. Some people lean forward and touch during a conversation, while others may find this intrusive. Non-verbal behaviour is experienced very subjectively. Other peoples' behaviour is thus interpreted from an individual stance and endowed with their own meaning. Words are usually more accurate and precise. Clear communication needs both words and action. How something is said is as important as what is said.

In order to be precise in our spoken communication we need to be aware of our own feelings, and be able to describe them. There is also a possible gender difference here, as well as our own unique experiences. Whether it is nature or nurture, many men grow up believing that it is acceptable only to be strong and silent, while women are encouraged to demonstrate their emotions.

Most people will recognise that they do in fact experience the whole range of emotions, but that their conditioning will edit out the ones that they find unacceptable. Skynner and Cleese (1983) describe it beautifully as being put 'behind the screen'. This process is allied to the Splitting and Projection model described in the previous chapter, but also belongs here as an example of how a couple can further complicate communication. The unacceptable feelings are projected onto the partner and therefore are difficult to access and discuss. Unacceptable feelings can also be avoided by burying them. This process is effective to a degree, but puts stresses on the relationship, and inhibits deeper discussion.

> Elsa is a typical example She came from a very disruptive and violent family. Both parents fought like cat and dog and she and her sister learned to keep out of the way while verbal and physical abuse was meted out downstairs. Her experience left her feeling that anger was synonymous with a great deal of destruction. It was natural for her to bury negative feelings, however trivial. She had edited anger out of her life in the belief that it was the anger that caused the problem rather than the dysfunctional way of dealing with it.

STAGE THREE – ACTION

> Whenever her partner irritated her, she withdrew and became very depressed. She had put anger behind the screen but the feelings had reverberated through, making her feel depressed. Elsa's first move must be to recognise these feelings and take the risk of discussing them with her partner. She has to separate the destructive responses she has had in her original family and create a more constructive communication pattern with her partner.

However, accurately putting your feelings into words is only part of the communication between the couple. There is as much editing in the listening. This also has its roots in the families of origin. It is very easy to make assumptions about what people are trying to say – and then cease to listen after the first few words. Couples frequently say brusquely of each other, 'I heard what you just said, but I know what you really mean is...' Acceptance of each other's different opinions and thought processes is part of the intimate couple. Couples can get very confused with difference. This again might be linked with their individual pasts. In a family where difference between family members was not tolerated, difference with a partner may be very threatening. Difference may be seen as creating a win-or-lose situation, where one idea has to defeat the other. Recognising each other's truth paves the way for good communication in a couple relationship. Otherwise, the exchanges degenerate into a battle, rather than a true reflection of each others' feelings.

The counsellor using the RELATE Approach is a highly skilled listener. She will be listening to the overtly expressed content of the problems, but also noting how they are communicated to the partner. One of the simple but effective tasks to set clients with poor communication is the use of 'I' statements as opposed to 'You' statements. In the stereotypical case of the nagging wife, she would say, 'You always...' or 'You never...' The husband would experience this as attacking and cease to listen after a few words. If the statements are accompanied by angry body language and a hectoring tone of voice, the husband may well counter-attack with his own 'you' statements. There is no exchange of information, just a set of angry and hurt feelings. These miscommunications can go on for years with the resentment building up for both partners. George and May in Chapter 3, the 'cat and dog' couple, give an example of how this form of communication was maintained over 30 years.

> George and May both wanted the other to do all the changing, and thought they could then be as happy as other couples. The therapeutic alliance had begun in the room. There was a less charged atmosphere, and they had both started to trust the counsellor. She had sensed that both partners yearned to be cared for and even to please one another. In order for this couple to initiate the smallest change something had to be done to stop the trading of insults and the belittling of each other. The counsellor realised there were probably many emotional reasons for their behaviour and, from what they had told her, she

had already surmised that they both came from emotionally harsh backgrounds. What was the best approach to try and help them understand?

May was bemoaning the fact that they never went out. The counsellor asked if she had ever suggested this to George. There was no point as far as May was concerned, because he could never be bothered. The counsellor asked if they could rerun this scenario, actually discussing the problem together. She deliberately got them to turn their chairs to face one another. Initially May started, 'I know you won't agree to this but...' The counsellor gently urged her to simply say 'I would like...' George responded by turning to the counsellor and saying, 'What she doesn't realise is...' The counsellor urged him rather to acknowledge what May had said, and then reply directly to her. Slowly the conversation started. The counsellor moved her chair aside so that neither could turn to her. A completely different atmosphere entered the room as two people who had long since given up on expressing their own hopes and desires began hesitatingly to speak personally again. It took most of the session, but what was established was that May would like to go out for a meal occasionally because she was often very tired after a day's work and it would save her cooking. George agreed that it would be quite nice to go out. They used to do so in their early days before the children were born. He admitted that when he said he 'couldn't be bothered' in the past, he actually had thought that he would be subject to the 'same old taunts about his table manners'. This last remark nearly put them back into a heated exchange, but the counsellor intervened and got May simply to acknowledge the remark and say she had never meant to taunt him. George then owned that he often felt daunted by eating out because he saw other people as 'posher' than him. This exercise allowed them to accurately express what they would like, rather than carp and blame each other to disguise their real feelings.

Over the next two sessions they continued the exercise and began to address their own uncertain feelings about wanting to be with each other. The exercise sounds simplistic but it was certainly a change. George and May had to think about what they wanted, and then to put it into words without diminishing the other. If they could build on this they could perhaps move on to a second-order change.

As we have already seen, past experiences can cloud clear communication. Socially, many people only half-listen – ready to respond with their own experiences rather than to the words of the person talking. Truly attending to a partner, without thinking of individual agendas, is very enriching for both parties. It is the skill of empathy, and needs to be regularly practised between the couple. In George and May's case, lack of empathy had caused unnecessary misunderstandings and these had been interpreted as a lack of caring.

Between the next few sessions, George and May began building trust by really listening and understanding each other. This was achieved by setting aside a limited time each day when they agreed that they would take turns in talking and listening without making assumptions. They did this by reflecting back to the other their understanding of what was being said. It was slow and tedious at first, and they frequently fell back into their old

STAGE THREE – ACTION

ways. However, they were now able to recognise the pattern, and could put into practice the basic skills they had learnt in the counselling room. As time went by, this skill became a part of them both so that instead of having to set aside time for talking and listening exercises, they found that they did it automatically in less formalised settings. Washing up and driving together became less of a battleground and more of an honest exchange of feelings – both good and bad.

Clear communication also challenges the collusion that so often exists between couples. The couple will find it difficult to project unwanted feelings onto the partner if they are actively owning their own feelings. By setting these communication tasks, the couple have to actually set aside time to be together.

Poor communicating is very common when the clients are angry. In the circumstances in which they find themselves, this is natural and understandable, but strategies to limit the effects can be devised in the safer environment of the counselling room. The couple need to see the destructive nature of blaming and attacking their partner, and to explore the real reason for the argument. Anger so often masks other feelings, or is an accumulation of past hurts and disagreements. Defining the issue and agreeing to discuss it is an important first step. If the situation feels unmanageable it is wise to postpone the discussion and agree to meet later. This is not avoiding the conflict, but allowing each partner time to reflect on what the argument is about and how they want to express it. This reflection time is not to rehearse and brood in order to win. It is time to clarify thoughts and feelings. If the partner is part of the conflict he or she will also be part of the solution. All this will be carefully discussed with the couple, and a check-list for them to follow will improve the chances of a more fruitful discussion at the next meeting, along the following lines:

- Remain seated and maintain eye contact.
- Know why you are arguing.
- Listen and check that you have heard before replying.
- Say an understanding thing before launching into a response.
- Don't make counter-accusations or justifications.
- Keep to 'I' rather than 'you' statements.
- Admit mistakes and misunderstandings.
- Stick to the subject in hand.
- If the question has not been resolved after 30 minutes, agree to differ and return to it in a couple of days.

There are often common problems that lead to arguments. Once the heat of the discussion has dispersed it may be easier to see the thread of old issues that catch the couple unaware. One discussion is not going to resolve differences, but it is the beginning of change. The change is not only in how the couple communicate, but how they change the structure of dealing with anger. Resolving arguments and practising various communication exercises requires them to be together, in the same room. The agreed task may have originally been intended to improve communication, but the greater effect can either enhance or highlight problems with the couples' expectations of intimacy.

GENOGRAMS

When a couple first begins a committed relationship, one of the prime motivations is a yearning for intimacy. At the beginning each person may have a belief that their partner will have a deep knowledge and understanding of them, and an ability to fit automatically with their expectations. This vision may be loaded with unrealistic expectations.

The unrealistic expectations may have been generated in the families of origin. During the exploration stage the counsellor may commence a genogram that he draws up between sessions. This is a graphic representation, rather like a joint family tree, which covers all the relationships that have been important during the life of each partner. As the story unfolds he will be noting the patterns of interaction between important members of this family; how close individuals are and where there has been conflict in the past.

When looking at each family of origin, he will look at how the individual clients see themselves within the family, using their words and expressions. Triangular patterns may emerge, showing difficulties the clients may have with sharing. The position in the family in relation to other brothers and sisters can be significant. How clients' mothers and fathers viewed each other, whether they were both around and available to the client may well affect how the client views the world in the present. Roles that individual members of the family have taken on at various times can be recorded. The genogram can show the systems within the family and the systems outside the family. How did events affect the family? Did family members take up certain positions and how did the client fit in with all this?

When the clients have a shared family of their own, this too goes on the genogram. How does each partner relate to their children? Are patterns evident in the present family which reflect those which took place in the past? What are the roles allocated to men and women, how do they express different emotions? Similarly, significant past relationships can be included. Because the genogram has each person's age at the present moment on it (or in the case of those who have died a notation about relative ages), the counsellor can see if a present pattern reflects a past one.

STAGE THREE – ACTION

When described in this way, the fear could be that the result will be an unusable mass of unrelated data. However, this rarely happens. Usually, surprisingly clear patterns emerge and these patterns illustrate clearly the processes which have been described in the previous chapter.

Genograms are powerful tools. The use of the genogram can be divided into two distinct categories:

- As a history-taking exercise for the counsellor to help form an assessment of the problem.
- As an intervention to be drawn with the clients together to help them begin to view their history differently.

It would be both foolish and potentially harmful to launch drawing up a genogram with clients where the counsellor only has a sketchy understanding of her clients' history. However, once a degree of understanding has been achieved, work together on a genogram drawn on a sheet of flipchart paper and brought repeatedly to sessions can be an excellent way of exploring the repeated patterns which had previously been outside the conscious knowledge of the clients.

Let us look at a couple of examples of a genogram. Figure 4.3 shows Dionne and Martin, a young couple with attachment problems first introduced in Chapter 3.

> Exploring the genogram led Martin to recall how he was the baby of the family. He has two older brothers who, he thinks, have quite a close relationship and two younger brothers. The family lived in the West Indies until Martin was five, when they moved to England. Martin remembered this very clearly. He had broken his leg and it was decided that he would stay with his grandmother. This would allow his leg to heal and give the family time to get schools sorted for the older boys. He would be sent for. Time passed. His grandmother was kind but old, and found the young energetic Martin a handful. She let him have free rein and rarely followed up his check-up appointments at the hospital. Martin hated these visits, and would hide until his grandmother gave up. His leg healed in the slightly bent fashion that he still has to this day.
>
> He did not see his parents again until he was 10 years old. His grandmother had died and he was shipped to England. He was terrified that he would not recognise his parents, and gripped their photograph tightly in his hand when they met him. He had also acquired two younger brothers. He knew of them from letters and photos, but it was a real shock to meet them in the flesh. He never really felt integrated in the family, always a visitor, somebody on the outside looking in.
>
> Dionne came from a seemingly very different background. Her parents worked long hours, and she and her siblings were expected to help around the house. Dionne was the eldest and made herself indispensable to the

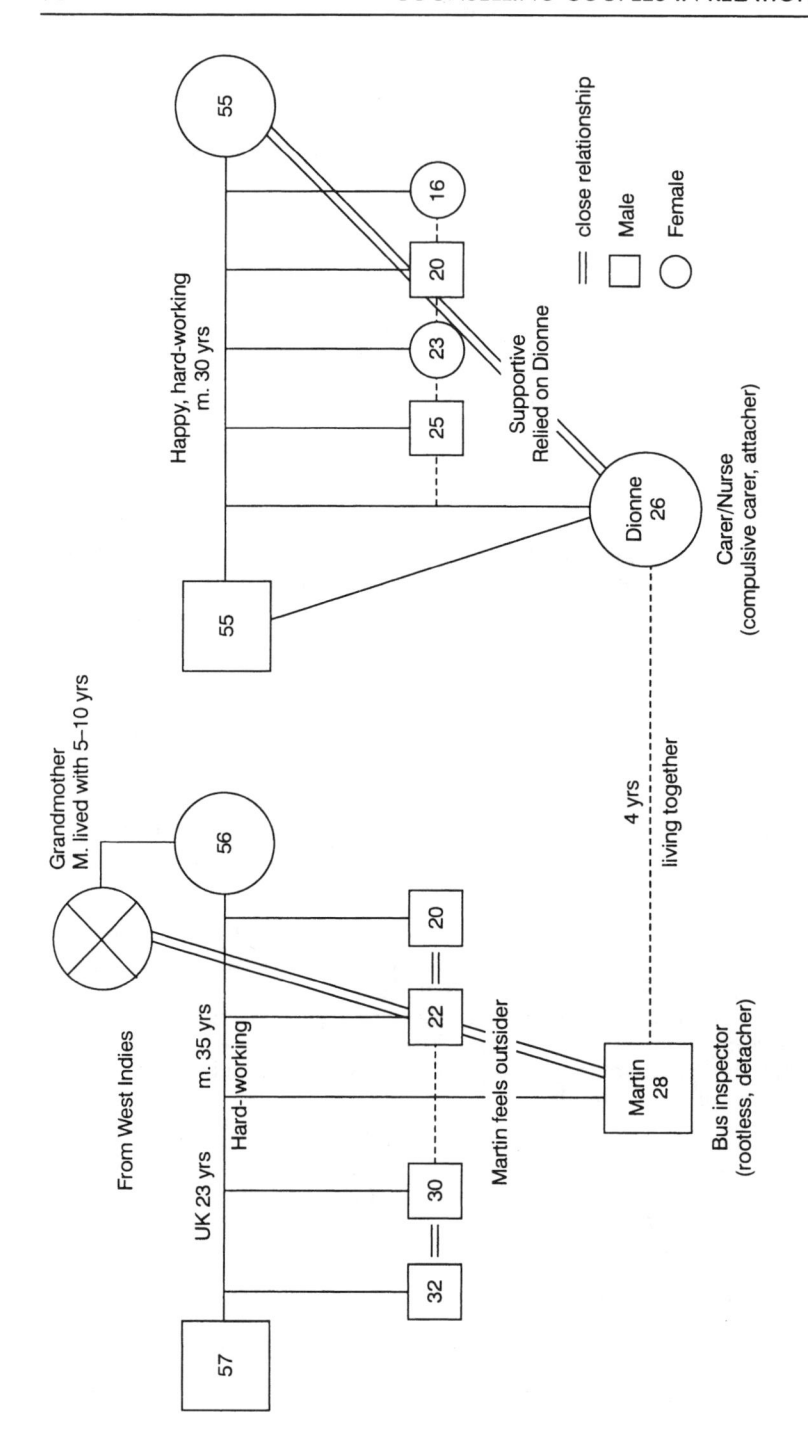

Figure 4.3 Genogram: Martin and Dionne

family. She was always an 'old head on young shoulders'. Her role in the family was one of great responsibility, and she had liked it that way. Unlike Martin she had been very involved in her family, and still was.

As their family histories unfolded, they were plotted on the genogram by the counsellor. This allowed her to encourage Martin and Dionne to see very clearly what differing expectations they both had of a close relationship. Martin had had a special relationship with his grandmother, but this was severed when she died. He remembered how frightened he was when it became obvious that he would not be joining his family immediately. He coped with it all by being very independent. Dionne, on the other hand, liked to be in the centre of things. It made her feel wanted and needed. If she was not organising everything and making sure all was well, her feeling of self-worth was diminished.

The couple began to understand their differences. Dionne needed to hold onto Martin, and Martin was quite happy to be hung on to. The problems occurred when the level of this 'fit' became too intense. Rationally, Dionne knew that Martin was not running away, and he knew that she was not going to smother him, but his past experience had taught him that there was danger in allowing closeness. His family had left and his grandmother, who had always been there for him when they left, had died. Dionne's experience of closeness was that you had to be highly visible and doing things to be loved and noticed. So, despite their different experiences, Martin and Dionne were in effect sharing the same confusion. They were both fearful of being left, and had devised different strategies to block the uncomfortable feelings that they were left with. Martin distanced himself and Dionne pursued him to bring him back into the fold. The rest of this case management was focused around behavioural and communication tasks once the couple understood the reasons why and how they attached themselves to one another.

Trust and a safe atmosphere have first to be established, for a genogram not only notes the family members but also the patterns that have been established, and the individual relationships within the family. The genogram should never be allowed to spring surprises on the clients. For instance, where there is a long history of violence, too early an intervention can overwhelm the client. It could give the impression that such a system could not possibly be changed, and will unnecessarily raise anxiety. When trust has been established some of this history will have been acknowledged and therefore there will not be a surprise element. This allows much more exploration of the underlying issues rather than known, but unpleasant, memories. Martin and Dionne's genogram highlighted their very different expectations of closeness. Let us now look at George and May's genogram (Figure 4.4) and see how their history influenced their marriage. In the last Chapter the counsellor working with them felt that the splitting and projecting approach might enable them to start changing the way they reacted to one another. Having changed their communication pattern somewhat, she got them to work together on drawing up a genogram to illustrate their past.

May came from a working-class background where there was a clear work ethic. Her mother was bright but had to leave school at 14 to contribute to family finances. Her father was proud and authoritarian. He believed that a woman's place was in the home. He strongly discouraged her mother from taking any employment. May's older sister had done well at school and had studied medicine. Mother was so proud of her and poured all her love and devotion into her. The parents' marriage seemed a cold and distant affair. As May described her background, George was visibly moved. He had heard the facts before, but had never realised the depth of feelings that accompanied them.

George had come from a very large family that was chaotic. Father was either at work or in the pub. Mother always had a baby in her arms, either one of her own or one of the numerous children that they fostered. He described his childhood as free but 'you had to just tag along'. George only ever got attention by behaving badly and getting into trouble at school. He did not remember ever receiving encouragement, and is uncomfortable when anybody praises him. May only ever got attention in her family by helping around the house. She was overshadowed by her sister at school. To please people, both George and May had to adapt their behaviour. Being themselves was never 'good enough'. In their adult lives this had been translated unhealthily. George's criticism of May's ability as a wife and housekeeper hit deeper than he could imagine. Her retaliation about his 'loutish' ways put him in mind of his unhappy schooldays, when he was always in trouble. Rather than think through what they were saying to one another, it was easier to trade insults.

The picture that the genogram highlighted encouraged them to explore themselves both as individuals and as a couple. In terms of the splitting and projection approach, this couple had not been able to integrate the good and the bad – they had been given little affection and so had seen only the bad in themselves and in each other. The knowledge of this helped them understand how they maintained the status quo. They were able to return to the communication exercises to discuss what they would like to do next. After 12 weeks of using both these tools the couple felt that they now needed time to consolidate what they were learning about each other. It was enough for now.

At the final interview the couple felt they had more understanding of each other and how they got into escalating rows. The 'cat and dog' fit was still there, and always would be, but it was now more contained. The counsellor could see many more strands to work with but respected the clients' wishes. They had made a first-order change, both in how they communicated and in their perception of each other's needs. On the occasions that one or other actually owned their own doubts, there was potential for a real breakthrough to a second-order change. George saying that he was uneasy in 'posh' places is a good example, and one May was able to respond to kindly. She had similar feeling of inadequacy when they vis-

STAGE THREE – ACTION

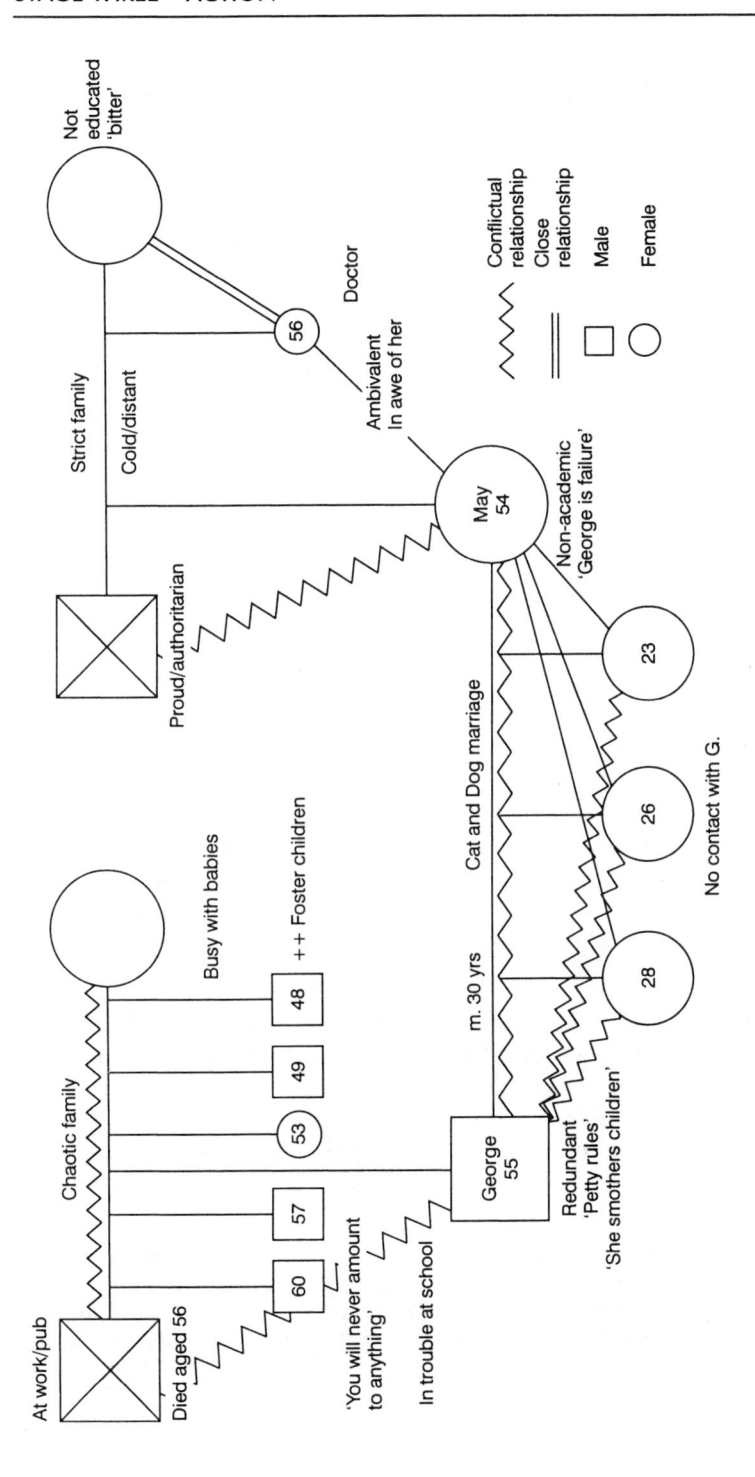

Figure 4.4 Genogram: George and May

ited her sister and family. They understood that each was solely responsible for the way they felt, and did not blame the other. In terms of the splitting and projection approach, they had taken back the projections, which allowed them to communicate further and deeper.

The interventions described so far require clients to have an ability to express themselves verbally. In the genogram they have to describe the patterns of interaction between family members and in their couple relationship, even if it is the graphics that give them the push to more insight of their situation. Some clients have difficulty talking about feelings in this graphic way. We need to use a physical representation of their different relationships to understand the dynamic.

SCULPTING WITH STONES, COINS, BUTTONS AND FIGURES

Pebbles and stones collected from a beach, varnished to accentuate their colours, are excellent for this exercise. The clients are asked to pick out stones that will represent people that they feel have an influence on them, either now or in the past. Once again, this should only be attempted when the counsellor has established the trust of the clients. It is important that the exercise does not appear to be some sort of game where they don't know the rules. In addition, the counsellor must also have given careful consideration to the possible problems. If the couple are still somewhat entrenched in some sort of power game, one partner may alter the 'sculpt' to directly negate the other. The ingratiating partner may alter the 'sculpt' to please. This can be managed, either by each partner observing in silence, or by placing the couple back to back as they arrange the stones.

The counsellor sets the sculpt in a contained but relaxed way. The stones are tactile and allow the clients to reflect on what they want to say about the significant figures that they represent. Time is taken to place the stones at the distances and patterns that mean something to the client. This adds a third dimension to the flat graphics of a genogram, and will help many couples to see each other's world in a different way, and also how their partnership fits into the larger world.

> Gita and Sunil came to counselling because Gita believed that Sunil put his work before her and the family. They were both highly articulate and explained the situation succinctly and appeared to be able to relate this to processes which sprang from the past. However, the counselling had got bogged down on the work issue. They had used the communication exercises, but had just managed to say the same things to one another, albeit in a different way. The basic premise had not shifted.

STAGE THREE – ACTION

They did the sculpting exercise sitting on the floor, back to back. Gita had placed herself and the children in a circle, with Sunil and a large black stone representing his work on the outside of the family. Sunil had selected many more stones to represent not only Gita and their children, but also her large extended family. He placed himself at a distance from the family. The counsellor then asked each one in turn to remove or change one stone, and talk through the reason. Gita instantly moved the 'work' stone. This seemed fine until she began to realise that it left the family vulnerable. Sunil and Gita had arrived in Britain as refugees from Uganda at the height of the political turmoil in that country. They had to all pull together in their respective families and start a new life from nothing. Family and the ability to provide for them were values that were deeply embedded in them both as they grew up. This mutual understanding was an important part of their original attraction to each other. It was too convenient to use work itself as a scapegoat for the couple's problems. Sunil's work provided the family with financial security. There was still a gulf between them as a couple. What the sculpt clearly demonstrated was that Sunil remained outside the family because Gita was surrounded so closely by the children. There had to be other moves to allow Sunil into this tight network that she had made for herself. Sunil was uncertain of what to move, as there seemed to be such linked forces against him. Yet he had deliberately placed himself at a distance, and after thinking tried to move his stone closer to the one representing Gita. Sunil's attitude to work had originally been seen as the root of the problem for this couple, but after this exercise a different focus had been highlighted. The counselling could continue to examine their roles within the system that the stones had demonstrated to them. They had to look at what it would mean to alter the status quo by making smaller changes, and thereby bring about a change to the system.

This couple were articulate and preferred to use this one insight as a base to start rethinking their relationship. For other couples like Michael and Soulla, introduced in some detail in the previous chapter, the sculpt of stones dramatically illustrated how entrenched they were in family systems.

Soulla elected to start using the stones. She selected a pebble that had varying hues and some points. She had been attracted to Michael because he was interesting and less 'obvious' than the other boys at school. The points signified that he stood up for her in the face of her parents' discouragement of their relationship. She selected a smooth white stone for herself. Soulla was not quite sure why and Michael wondered if it represented how her parents saw her, very compliant. Soulla's parents lived through and for their family. Disappointments about her not marrying a Cypriot could be forgiven as long as she visited home regularly. They wanted to know everything about her, and sometimes she felt consumed by their emotional dependence. She built up various stones around her to represent her family, explaining what she was thinking as she went along. A picture built up of a close family with all the family members deeply committed to one another. At this point the stones were all equidistant.

As Soulla sat deep in thought, she frowned. She remembered that the previous week her parents were hurt that she had to cancel one of her visits.

One of the pupils she had responsibility for was having trouble settling in class, and she had promised to talk it through with the family. Soulla selected a handful of small pebbles to represent the school students she supervised and placed them near her. There was not enough room for them to be close to her. Without thinking, she pushed the stone that represented Michael to one side, and did not notice Michael's sudden intake of breath. She mused on how difficult it was to give time to everyone. Her sister, Maria, and Soulla could do no wrong so long as they were part of the family, but anything outside the family was considered much less important and open to criticism, which was why she could not bring herself to move these stones. The counsellor noted that the result was that Michael was now not included as part of the family, displaced by her school work.

Michael was very subdued as he built up the varying stones around the regular one he had chosen for himself. His family was very insular, with business as the focus. There were groups of stones clustered around him. Just like Soulla, he included work in the sculpt. The store managers were in as close contact with him, as was Soulla. As he spoke he became more tense. He had been hurt when Soulla had moved him so casually away from her, but now he was feeling totally consumed by his family and business. He could hardly separate the two.

The visual groupings of this sculpt clearly demonstrated how little space, literally, there was for intimacy in their relationship. It also showed that Michael's family had no boundary between work and home, and yet a rigid boundary between this and the outside world. There was a clear space between the outside world that Soulla inhabited and his family and business. There seemed to be no contact between the families other than through the young couple. Soulla's family lived through Soulla and her sister. Soulla was very reluctantly shared with Michael, let alone her school children. The work could now be progressed by looking at the helpful and unhelpful systems in which they were both entrenched. They could discuss how they could change within the different systems. In doing this, they could be proactive, rather than reactive as they had been in the past.

Coins can be used in a similar way. They are less tactile but each coin has a designated value. It is a good exercise to focus on how people value themselves and members of their family. A good looking actor who appeared to be brimming with confidence selected a small copper coin to represent himself, while his small quiet wife selected a pound coin for herself. She had felt loved and valued at her parent's home. The actor came from a family where there were many separations between his parents until his mother's death when he was 11. This seemed totally at odds with the way they presented themselves to the world. It helped the couple to see each others' truth and start the accurate listening that is so often absent when relationships are in difficulty.

Buttons can be used because they vary in hue, pattern and size. Clients can use their imaginations much in the same way as with stones, although the buttons are less tactile. Some counsellors use model figures. These may

STAGE THREE – ACTION

be more limiting to the clients' use of imagination and visualisation, but they can help clients who think quite literally and who need more obvious similarities between themselves and the figures.

TECHNIQUES DRAWN FROM TRANSACTIONAL ANALYSIS

Although drawn from a different school of counselling, Transactional Analysis (TA) has certain tools that the RELATE method has found particularly helpful. Ego State Models were first formulated by Eric Berne and used in Transactional Analysis. However, they are equally relevant to many of the RELATE models, and can give clients a memorable image with which to internalise these models and to monitor their interaction in the future. Berne's ideas tap into clients' abilities to create images and word pictures of their relationships and to find patterns in their behaviour. They then have the option to give up those that are destructive and reinforce the patterns that are beneficial. The RELATE Approach uses some of these ideas to help our clients build up a picture of their relationship. It is a descriptive tool that plots the behaviour and communication patterns between the couple.

Briefly, there are three aspects of self, namely *Parent, Adult* and *Child* (Figure 4.5). The Parent aspect of self is derived from what the client has observed as a child. This experience is used to form a set of values and rules, a structure for living. It is subjective and it is subdivided to record the nurturing aspect and the controlling aspect of parenthood.

The Adult aspect of self is the rational, problem-solving part of the personality.

The Child aspect of self is the emotional part we are born with. It is experienced as a state of feelings and needs, and is subdivided to record the 'free' spontaneous behaviour of childhood or the more learned, adapted way of the child's interaction.

People in healthy relationships move between these states freely, adapting to the environment and situation that they are in. Negotiating to buy a house requires a strong Adult state, while running along the beach in a carefree way would be described as being in a free Child state. Stopping your child running across the road would require you to be a controlling Parent, baking a cake for him when he returns from school shows the nurturing Parent. Adapted Child behaviour is contrived, behaving in a certain way in order to get what you want.

Parent

```
        Controlling | Nurturing
        'Should/ought' | 'Good, well done'
```

Parent Ego State (taught concept of life)

Set of values and rules expressed in either a controlling or a nurturing way

Adult

```
        'How? Why? When?'
```

Adult Ego State (thought concept of life)

Rational, problem-solving aspect of self

Child

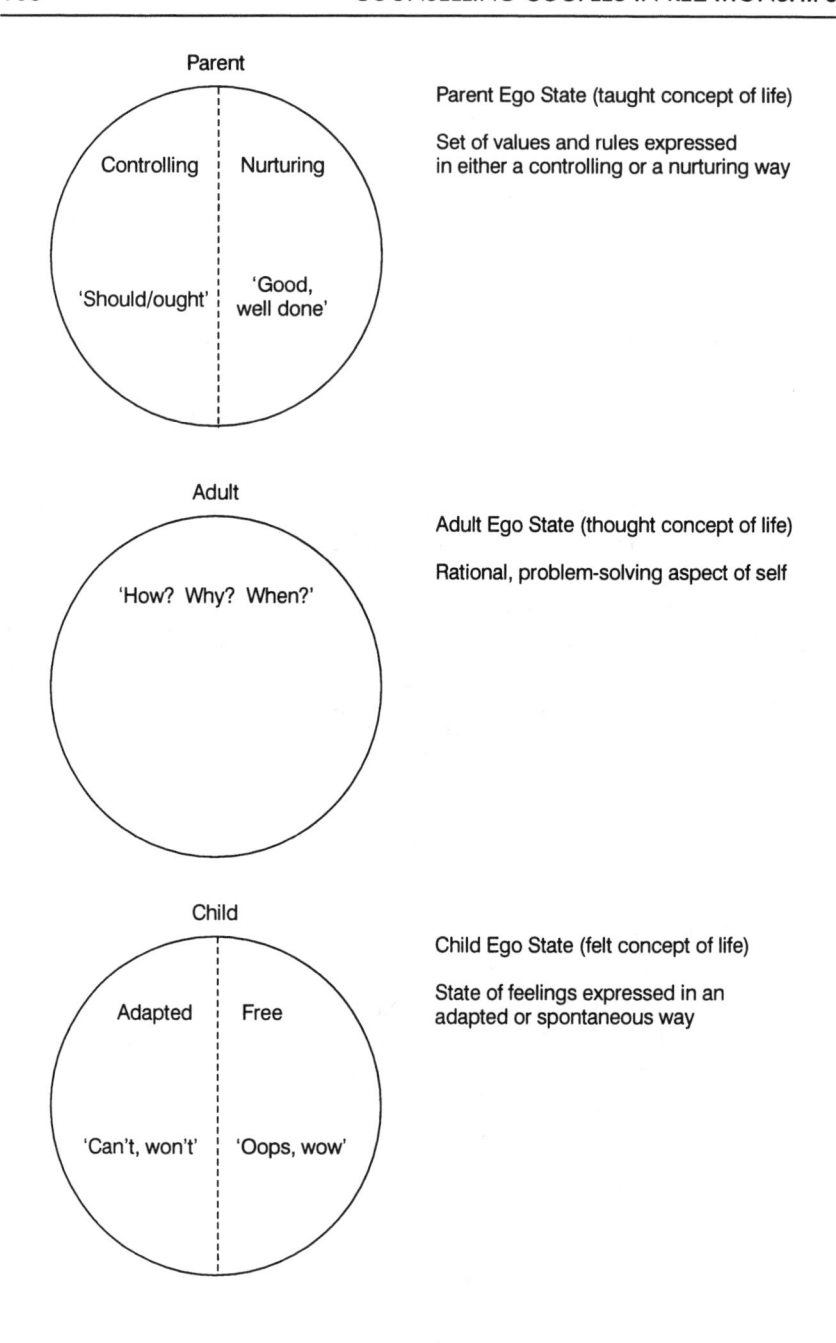

```
        Adapted | Free
        'Can't, won't' | 'Oops, wow'
```

Child Ego State (felt concept of life)

State of feelings expressed in an adapted or spontaneous way

Figure 4.5 Three aspects of self: parent, adult, child

STAGE THREE – ACTION 107

In couples, clients can get stuck in certain aspects of self that are reinforced and colluded with by their partners. Often clients continue to act in a way which was appropriate and necessary for them when they were a child, or else act in a 'parentified' way, treating their partner as though they were not adult also. Figure 4.6 demonstrates this in a visual way. The interaction between a couple being acted out in a parent-to-child way is shown in the first diagram; the adult-to-adult interaction that is required to recognise and remedy this by the second.

Communication is best when it is direct – the adult in one partner to the adult in the other, for example. It is more problematic when one partner talks as a parent to the child in the other. It is at its worst when both partners speak across each other and there is no true communication.

Clients can make immediate sense of this model. Images of parental and childlike behaviour seem to come promptly to most people, and the clear delineation of the fact that the purpose of couple work is to encourage adult behaviour is a helpful representation of the desired outcome of the work.

> Darren and Susan had recognised that much of the conflict over Susan's nephew, Keith, came from their own relationships with their parents. By looking at the ego state model, both agreed that parenting was an important area for both of them; both felt most at ease and fulfilled when they were

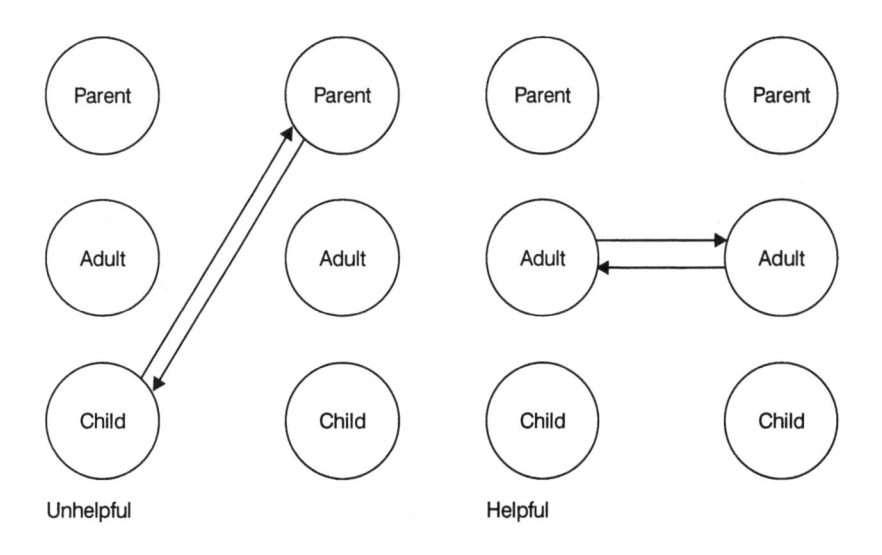

Figure 4.6 Communication between the couple on the Transactional Analysis model

guiding others. Darren readily recognised that he preferred a controlling stance – indeed, that was why he had disapproved of the way Susan indulged their own son. Susan could see that she thoroughly enjoyed looking after people.

'Is that how you communicate with each other?' the counsellor asked.

'I always feel that Darren is very ready to give me a lecture about how to lead my life,' said Susan. 'However, I have been a bit irresponsible at times, so I suppose that in a way I ask for it.'

'How about you, Darren?'

'Well, I am strict, but I'm not sure its a bad thing', he replied.

'Nobody's saying it is,' said the counsellor, 'But it's not the only way to be.'

Little further progress was made and the subject was not pursued. However, the next week Darren opened the session by saying that they had had a bit of a breakthrough over their disagreement over Keith.

'Susan and I sat and talked about what we could do for him, and we decided he could stop with us if he behaved around the house and didn't expect us to come and bail him out when he got picked up by the law. It didn't help him much – he got nicked after a couple of days. We didn't turn out to the station though; we let him get on with it. He got himself released after a night in the cells and came back to us. He said one of the coppers gave him a lecture about how lucky he was to have a place to go. The important thing was, Sue and I didn't argue with each other or get involved. I just made him a cup of tea and we let him get on with phoning the Law Centre.'

When asked how this had come about, both said they had talked after the previous session and agreed they would try to be a bit more 'adult' together about Keith. Once they had resolved that, it seemed easier to do than they had imagined.

This continued to be discussed in the counselling. The couple looked at how rigidly they had split the nurturing and controlling roles over their own children and redressed the balance.

'It's much better,' said Susan, a few weeks later. 'The only thing is, all this being adult is a bit serious.'

'Not a lot of 'free child' time together? No time for fun?' asked the counsellor.

'Is that the running on the beach bit?' said Darren, 'It's winter and I'm a bit old for that.'

In fact, they went bowling, getting in touch with a little fun and shortly afterwards resumed their sexual relationship. The spontaneous feelings of the free child state are a vital ingredient for good sex.

Healthy, strong relationships move between the aspects of self as and when required, responding to internal and external pressures. Trouble appears when the interaction becomes stuck in a repetitive exchange. People need to put appropriate energy into Parent, Adult and Child, just

STAGE THREE – ACTION

as grass needs nutrients, sun and water to grow. Growth will be stunted if any of these is withdrawn for too long and a relationship will be equally limited if any of the parts of self are neglected.

Ego state models are graphically simple and can help clients see the collusive behaviour that tends to hinder any real change. They are a useful intervention for all the approaches, especially when the exploring and understanding stages appear to be getting repetitive. The clients bring what are to them 'different' problems but are in fact the same couple dynamic being acted out in different ways. The ego state model can allow the couple to stand outside their relationship for a brief moment to view it from a different perspective.

A similar approach could have been used with Martin and Dionne to model how he tended to be careless about engagements in a child-like way, while she tended to mother him – agreeing to use the diary represented an adult interaction for them both. Emma and Jane may well have benefited from looking at this model to clarify how they both tended to behave like appealing children in the hope that a powerful parent figure would come along.

This concludes the consideration of action that can be taken with clients. Much of the enjoyment of working with couples using the RELATE Approach comes from the pleasure of joint problem-solving work – and the use of techniques which involve stones and flip-charts makes a welcome change from the more static techniques of the earlier stages. Frequently the Action Stage of counselling is one full of humour, and the relationship between the clients and the counsellor becomes much more equal as the clients again regain full control over their own life circumstances.

However, it is important to state again that the purpose of the action is to allow the couple to bring about a more permanent change by changing the attitudes and awareness of a situation, rather than just to find a single solution to a problem. Therefore, the counsellor needs to take time to explore what has become different which has allowed the change to work. If couples have internalised how the change was made and why it helped they will be better placed to make more changes for themselves when new problems arise. If they have just benefited from the counsellor's problem-solving skills they will still have problems when a new challenge appears in the future.

5

SEX AND COUPLES

Sexual love is undoubtedly one of the chief things in life...
　　　　　　　　　　　　　　　　　　　　　　　　Sigmund Freud

A large proportion of couples who seek help about their relationship problems will also experience difficulties in their sexual partnership. The sexual relationship may be the cause of the problems they are experiencing or a reflection of their intimate emotional relationship. One partner may believe that the only problem is on the sexual side, while the other may feel that the emotional problems far outweigh the physical difficulties in the relationship. Often, looking at how they interact sexually can help the counsellor identify the areas of general difficulty. For example, mechanical unintimate sex may be what one partner prefers for a sense of well-being. This may be linked to a fear of intimacy in other areas of the relationship. We will be looking at general sex problems in this chapter, analysing the difficulties around aspects of the sexual relationship to help the couple understand more general relationship problems.

We have already discussed the presenting problem in Chapter 2 when discussing how clients are initially assessed. Psychosexual Therapy (PST) is the treatment of choice in RELATE when clients present with specific sexual dysfunctions. It becomes less clear when there has been a sexual relationship between the couple that is now no longer satisfactory to one or both partners. Where should the counselling focus? Is the relationship problem a result of the unsatisfactory sex or the sex problems a reflection of the underlying emotional conflict between them? Experience has shown us that the wrong choice of counselling leaves clients feeling helpless, with no hope of change. Focusing on the physical aspect of the relationship with no acknowledgement of the emotional side is as debilitating as ignoring the sexual side to concentrate on the psychological interaction.

Clients who present with sexual problems and who appear to have a committed relationship are sent to a psychosexual therapist for an initial assessment. This takes the form of very clear questioning of the sexual problem. It is from this interview that a decision is made as to whether the

SEX AND COUPLES

clients are taken into more detailed assessment with a view to sex therapy or directed to other counselling or, possibly, medical investigations. It is important that potential physical, organic causes of sexual problems are not overlooked. Some drugs have medical side effects that contribute to or exacerbate sexual dysfunctions. The questioning highlights underlying problems that may better be dealt with initially in couple counselling. The therapist must make the decision where the root of the problem lies. Psychosexual Therapy is primarily a behavioural programme that deals with emotional blocks that emerge during the counselling. Counselling couples with sexual difficulties concentrates on the psychological blocks rather than the physiological difficulties that the couple are experiencing. The skill of the counsellor is to judge where the balance of difficulty lies in order to direct the clients to the best type of counselling.

SEXUAL DYSFUNCTIONS

The counsellor practising the RELATE Approach must have a working knowledge of sexual dysfunctions in order to decide what work is appropriate. Masters and Johnson categorised the dysfunctions first in the early 1960s. We list them below:

Male:
- *Erectile failure.* This is the inability of the man to maintain an erection sufficient to allow penetration of his partner. It may have always been a problem and would be categorised as a *primary erectile dysfunction,* or may be of more recent onset and described as a *secondary erectile dysfunction.*
- *Premature ejaculation (PE).* This is the persistent inability to maintain reasonable control over the timing of ejaculation during intercourse, or that ejaculation occurs before it is intended.
- *Retarded ejaculation (RE).* This is the inability to ejaculate. It includes a range of problems, varying from never ejaculating, to where intercourse has to be excessively long for it to occur. We also include in this category men who are able to ejaculate when masturbating alone but are unable to do so in the presence of their partner.

Female:
- *Vaginismus.* This is an involuntary spasm of the muscles surrounding the entry of the vagina, making penetration impossible.
- *Dyspareunia.* Penetration is possible but painful.
- *Orgasmic dysfunction.* Women who have never achieved an orgasm have a *primary orgasmic dysfunction.* Women who experience orgasms sometimes but not at other times during sexual activity have a *random*

orgasmic dysfunction. Masturbatory or *coital orgasmic dysfunctions* are the failure to achieve orgasm through masturbation or intercourse.

Any of these problems can lead to difficulties in the couple relationship that may be openly expressed and clearly stated to the counsellor. The physical problems may lead to a lack or complete loss of interest in any sexual activity with the partner. The sexual desire may be present for one or both partners, but the problems will inhibit their desire to initiate sex. Couples that present their problem as sexual where one or both have 'gone off it' have the choice of the more behaviourally focused Psychosexual Therapy or sexual counselling using the RELATE Approach.

SEXUAL COUNSELLING

The three-stage model of Exploration, Understanding and Action is as important a way of assessing clients with sexual difficulties as it is for those with general relationship problems. Jack Anon, a Clinical Psychologist working at the University of Honolulu, devised an amplified version of the model to describe various levels of help with sexual difficulties without resorting to the more intensive levels of therapy. PLISSIT is the acronym of this model and integrates well with the general model of our counselling approach of Exploring, Understanding and Action.

P = Permission (Exploration)
LI = Limited Information (Understanding)
SS = Specific Suggestions (Action)
IT = Intensive Therapy (PST)

Permission

At the exploring stage of sexual counselling it is vital that time is spent building up the therapeutic relationship with the clients. The clients have to feel safe enough to be able to discuss their sexual concerns and behaviour. As the story unfolds, the counsellor will obtain a clear picture of their sexual relationship, of both the behaviour and the feelings attached to the behaviour. Some of these feelings will be rooted in the past of their original family and expectations. Some will be attached to more recent experiences that have not been resolved or only partially addressed. There are many myths attached to sexual activity that persist despite the vast amounts of information available. The *permission*-giving role of the counsellor is vital to explore and recognise the impact of the myths and taboos.

SEX AND COUPLES

We list below some of the common myths that are held by both men and women. Counsellors will recognise some of their own myths in this list and despite being more informed and enlightened than their clients, need to be continually aware of the uncomfortable feelings that disclosure and discussion can evoke. This is particularly relevant when working with gay and lesbian couples who, after recognising their own sexuality, may experience problems of acceptance with family and friends. They do not want to experience this again in the counselling. It should be remembered that the couple who have decided to come to a mainstream organisation like RELATE have done so by choice, rather than go to an organisation that specialises in gay or lesbian sexuality. For some couples it may become clear after initial assessment that a more specialised agency would be more appropriate, but any defensive stance taken by the counsellor will negate or hinder the permission-giving part of the exploration.

- Sex should be natural and spontaneous – asking for it spoils it.
- Men are always ready for sex.
- Women must wait for men to initiate.
- All gay men are promiscuous.
- A large penis stimulates more than a small one.
- Men must take charge of sex.
- Having sex means having intercourse.
- Good sex always ends in orgasm.
- Good sex means the man always must have an erection.
- Most gay and lesbian partners adopt an active or passive position in their sexual relationship.
- Don't show affection to a man, he will expect sex.
- Performance is what counts for men.
- There is something wrong with a man who has a lower sex drive than his partner.
- You must orgasm together.
- Men should know all about sex.
- Women expect men to know about sex.

Exploring the statements that clients make about their sex life can bring some of these taboos to light and make sense of why their sexual relationship is failing. Some of their earliest sexual memories may be having an impact on them now. One female client used to bath with her brother and they discovered that his penis would harden when they touched it. Mother was appalled and very angry when they showed her, and they were smacked and never allowed to see each other naked again. Just talking through this incident made the couple realise that she was reluctant to touch her husband on some occasions. Her family were ill at ease with nakedness and although the woman had since had good sexual experiences, the feelings of not being able to touch could still reverberate through from the past.

People need permission to explore their own sexuality without feeling pressurised. What feels good and what does not is entirely individual and has to be separated from the oughts and shoulds that have been acquired from the past or expected by their partners. It is an invaluable first level of help for each client to say how he or she feels about his or her sex life, the failures and needs. When assumptions are made and expectations dashed in the sexual arena, the disappointment is often translated immediately to personal rejection. The splitting and projecting dynamic of couple relationships can be as well embedded in the sexual side of the relationship as in the emotional side.

Limited Information

Information about sex is readily available but it can be misunderstood in the simplest way by the myths and taboos we have mentioned. It is not only the content that has to be absorbed but also the way the information is processed. Not many people have been able to ask for clear, honest sexual information and received an equally honest response. In sexual counselling this is what is encouraged between the couple. The counsellor will check how much the clients do know during the exploration stage. This is not an interrogation, but the half-truths and misinformation will emerge and can be gently challenged. Thus, the counsellor herself must have a good working knowledge of the anatomy and physiology of sexuality. Generally counsellors use straightforward anatomical terms, as this will allow the clients access to other sources of information. However, the counsellor should be sensitive to the effect of this on clients. Information should be limited to what the clients need to know to understand their own special sexuality. If a counsellor works with a couple of different sexuality, care must be taken that the clients do not feel that they have to educate the counsellor. The counsellor will need to establish the clients' preferences, where their difficulties occur between them, the causal factors contributing to those difficulties and how this is dealt with in the relationship.

Specific Suggestions

Some clients may need more than permission and information. They may benefit from suggestions about how they can make changes in attitudes and behaviour as a result of their new understanding. It may start with exploring their own body in order to examine their own self-image. It may be touching and talking exercises or rethinking positions for intercourse. The tasks are better discussed in session so that they are manageable and achievable. It is vital that the counsellor appreciates the difference between behavioural tasks in sexual therapy and sexual counselling. PST is a treatment plan to remove a specific dysfunction, while sexual counselling facilitates the sexual communication and understanding between the couple.

Intensive Therapy

This should not be attempted by the counsellor unless qualified in PST. Inappropriate task-setting will have the same negative results as in general couple counselling. The couple will feel further failure and be less inclined to start again. If simple task-setting that the clients have set themselves with the counsellor's help is in difficulty, the management of the case should be looked at. It may require further exploration of more underlying emotional issues or a referral to PST.

> Robert and Jill came to counselling to 'deal with Jill's problem'. We first introduced them in Chapter 3 as the couple who had attachment problems, where Jill took on the patient role and Robert acted as the carer in their marital relationship. The precipitating factor to bringing them into counselling was that Robert was threatening to leave the marriage unless sex was resumed. There had been no intercourse or sexual activity for 18 months, although they had both enjoyed sexual intimacy in the early part of their marriage. At the reception interview they both agreed that it was Jill who had withdrawn from the sexual side and connected it with the experiences she had had in her family when she was a child. At the age of 13 she had returned home from school unexpectedly to find her father and their neighbour in bed together. Although she had been asked to keep this a secret she had not done so and the resulting disagreement had led the family to separate.
>
> Jill came alone to the first session. The counsellor started exploring Jill's early development and background to see what she wanted to share with Robert. Emotional trust is the cornerstone of physical intimacy and yet Jill seemed loath for Robert to be present during this exploration. He knew all about the facts of her past, she said. The counsellor had noted how smart and articulate Jill was. When she talked about her very deprived background, she appeared totally rational about it. The counsellor reflected that perhaps Robert felt that she had processed it all and put it behind her in the same way she was presenting it in counselling. Jill looked thoughtful and said she would talk it over with Robert. The counsellor was left with a paradox. The presenting problem of Jill's past causing the sexual problems, appeared not to be the priority problem. It seemed to be a convenient peg on which to hang the intimacy difficulties of the couple.
>
> Robert accompanied Jill to the second session, rather bewildered that he needed to be there. However, Jill was able to speak in more depth about the mixed feelings that the discovery aroused in her. She felt angry with her father for putting her in such an awkward position. Yet as she talked she also

got in touch with anger against her mother for 'not being able to keep her father faithful'. She also talked about how 'dangerous' a thing sex was. This gave Robert some insight. Jill would get very angry if he playfully touched her. He realised that although he accepted this, he did feel personally rejected and felt she was 'over-reacting'. Further exploration revealed that Jill felt responsible for the subsequent break-up of her parents' marriage. The discovery had appeared to trigger Father leaving home with her brother. After this, the family endured great financial hardship, with Jill feeling that she had to keep everything that was left, together. She had little contact with her father during the intervening years. By education and hard work she had been successful, but underlying this was the fear that if she made one wrong move, her whole world could turn upside-down. Her way of dealing with this was to try to keep strong emotions under control as much as possible.

Robert, on the other hand, came from a safe, secure service background and knew none of these insecurities. He believed that men looked after women, initiated sex and should know what they were doing. He was tough and strong and his only problem was that his wife denied him sex, which he could not understand. The counsellor asked him to say more about what he understood about his needs. It transpired that intercourse was his main way of getting loved. His family were never openly affectionate. The idea of just being loving without intercourse was alien to him. Masturbation and foreplay were not 'real sex', he stated firmly, even though when Jill had an orgasm it was usually before or after intercourse.

Over the next few sessions, the couple looked at their own sexual desires and fears, what felt good and what did not. Jill wanted less concentration on intercourse, which seemed difficult to Robert even though there had been none for 18 months. However, they agreed to this, which had the effect of freeing Jill to feeling sexual again and for Robert to experience intimacy in a different way. Simultaneously they were also looking at how they related to each other in emotional terms. Jill no longer saw loss of control in such a threatening way. Robert no longer had to be the strong man who was emotionally distant. They became less polarised in the roles that they had adopted.

The final obstacle was the resumption of intercourse. It was the ultimate control that Jill was using, just as Robert was using the threat of leaving of the marriage. More work had to be done on the attachment issues so that they could gain more insight into the disappointments and anger that sometimes turned their relationship into a power struggle. The relationship was on a much stronger footing, with their joint communication on a much more accurate emotional and sexual understanding. Jill had got back her sexual feelings and was having orgasms when they did pleasuring exercises that they had discussed in the counselling. Her fear of losing control was receding and Robert was enjoying their new-found intimacy and felt less angry and rejected. Just as the counsellor was wondering how to help them surmount the final hurdle, they announced that they had in fact 'disobeyed' the previous week and resumed intercourse as a natural progression from foreplay, which was pleasurable for them both. Their new understanding of each other's needs and fears had been separated from what ought to happen and the anger they both expressed as part of their disappointment.

There are a number of points to be drawn from this case study. The counsellor focused on the problem that Robert and Jill presented without colluding with them that Jill was the 'patient'. She formed a trusting enough relationship with them so that they could see that it was a joint problem. By exploring their sexual and their emotional expectations, the couple could see how the misunderstandings became embedded in the intimate relationship and finally acted out in their sexual relationship. Loss of face and control was a big issue for Jill, which distanced her further. Timing was another important factor. Although Robert understood what Jill was going through and had stopped feeling personally rejected, there was no immediate solution to what he saw as the bottom-line problem. By the time Jill was beginning to feel sexual about herself, he had cut himself off. The skill of the counsellor was to help them formulate a new understanding in which they could participate together. Jill had to 'catch up' with Robert on the physical level but he had to do so on the emotional level. The successful outcome was due to their commitment and dedication. The management of the case was an ever-evolving balance between their emotional and sexual difficulties.

UNDERSTANDING SEXUAL RESPONSE

We have looked at some of the common myths about sex. Ignorance of the anatomy and physiology of sexual activity is quite common. This will become evident during the exploration stage but it is important not to make assumptions about how much clients do know. Lack of knowledge and assumptions of their partner's anatomy and physiology is more often a causal factor. It is this interpersonal knowledge that needs to be understood in the counselling.

Figure 5.1. shows the five stages of sexual arousal for both men and women in relationships. Figure 5.1a demonstrates the patterns in a mutually satisfying sexual relationship. The intensity of the relationship is underpinned by good emotional communication that allows the stages of arousal to emerge freely. Figure 5.1b illustrates the sexual patterns that may arise between partners where anger, resentment and fear may be issues in their emotional relationship.

The Stages of Arousal

Desire

The anticipation and heightened awareness of the partner starts the desire stage. The pupils of the eyes dilate, the pulse rate increases and there is a

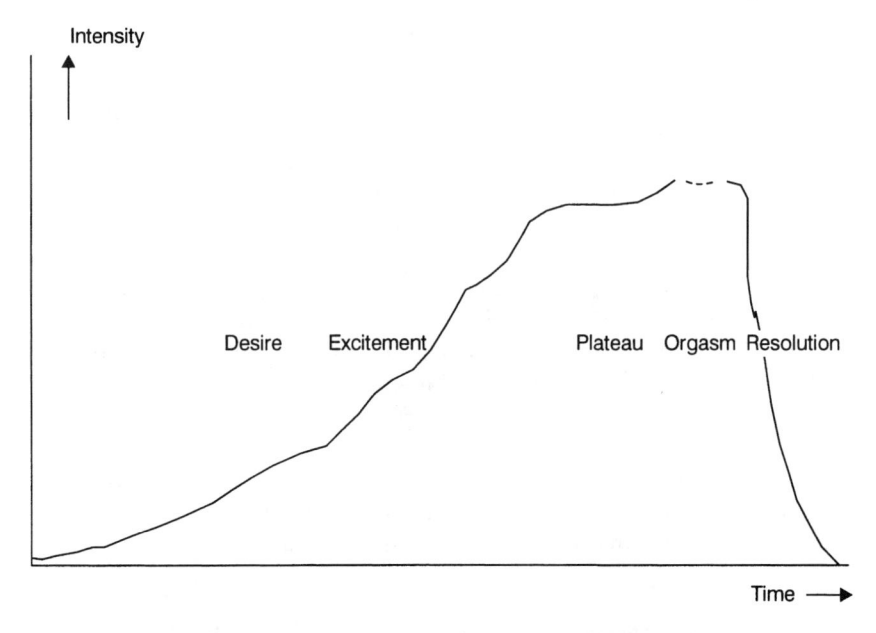

Figure 5.1a Responses in a loving sexual relationship

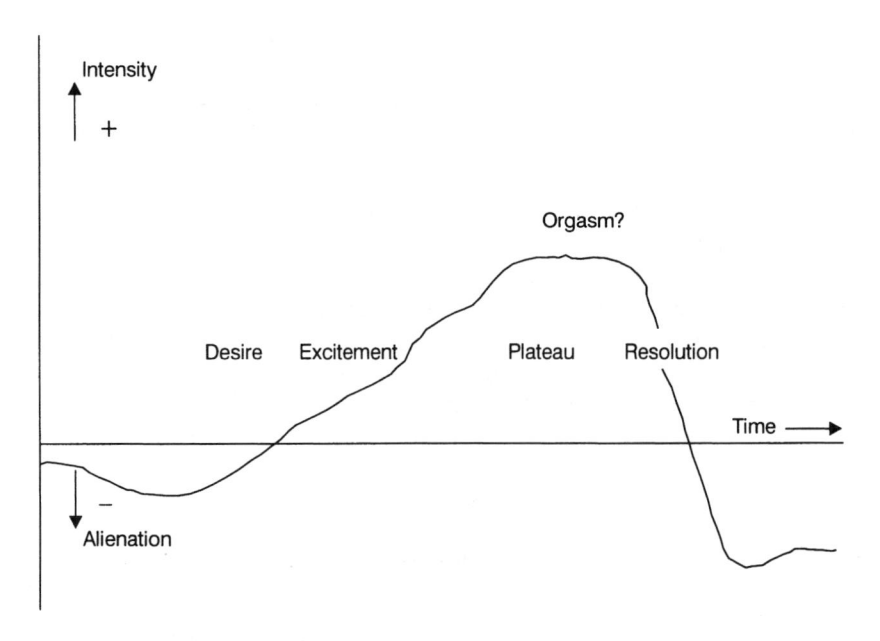

Figure 5.1b Responses in a conflictual sexual relationship

SEX AND COUPLES

stirring feeling in the body. Sexual thoughts and being attracted by the partner can be shown verbally and by touching and stroking to move onto the sexual foreplay of the excitement stage. Desire can be frequently experienced, depending on mood and circumstances, and is reversible if either of these change.

Excitement

This develops as a result of a combination of real and imagined emotional exchanges between the couple. These emotional exchanges will contain both conscious and unconscious elements, prompted by the foreplay that each partner is offered by the other. Physically, the sensory stimulation of foreplay increases the blood flow to the pelvic area. The male penis will start to fill with blood and become bigger, firmer and erect. The penis in the aroused state varies less in size than in the flaccid state. Small penises swell proportionally more than large penises. The walls of the vagina in the female become moist to allow for easier penetration. This lubrication takes place very early in the desire stage in women and is not necessarily an indication that intercourse should be initiated immediately. The clitoris will swell and emerge from the clitoral hood. Her nipples will become erect. The difference between men and women at this stage is the timing. Men in general can move quite quickly to the next stage or revert back to the unaroused state. Women can remain at this state throughout the sexual act, never progressing to the next stage and taking a longer time than the men to revert back to the unaroused state. This explains why women generally need more time at this foreplay stage. The clitoris may have to be massaged by the woman herself or by the partner, either manually or orally. As the intensity of this stage builds up both physically and emotionally, many of the partners' defences will be abandoned. It gives the couple the opportunity to learn and discover about themselves in the spirit of giving and taking.

Plateau

At this stage the testicles in the man are tight and elevated. The urethra dilates to help the passage of the seminal fluid. The foreskin folds back in uncircumcised men. In women the outer and inner lips of the labia open to make for easier access to the vagina and clitoris. The vagina becomes fully expanded and balloons out at the top to hold the seminal fluid. The lining of the bottom third swells in a way that narrows the entrance of the vagina to provide a tighter grip on the main shaft of the penis, whatever its size. The clitoris withdraws under the clitoral hood. The opening out of the vagina means that the sensitive glans of the penis receives less stimulation. However large the penis is, the stimulation reduces for the woman because the sensitive clitoris retreats and the vagina expands. This knowledge can help clients understand why the whole sexual play and not just the penetration can lead to a more fulfilling sexual relationship. If there are distractions or interruptions, this stage can be reversed in both men and women or used to move back to the excitement stage for more prolonged love-making. Emotionally, this plateau carries with it the inevitability of 'letting go'. Trust and being in tune with the partner will allow this feeling of loss of control to lead to orgasm.

Orgasm

The mutual pleasuring experience of excitement and achievement of the plateau gives way to the personal, almost self-absorbed stage of orgasm. There are two stages of orgasm for men. The vas deferens contract in the testicles and the man will recognise the quickening sensations that will take him to the point where he will be unable to stop ejaculation. This is impossible at the second stage, where ejaculation is inevitable. The man will feel contractions in the whole of the length of his penis, accompanied by intense pleasurable feelings. The woman has only one stage of orgasm. The vagina contracts and she will experience deep and intense feelings. Unlike the man, she may experience further orgasms within seconds or minutes. Orgasm is rarely simultaneous, although it is one of the most common expectations. Many women experience their orgasm in sexual stimulation outside penetration.

Resolution

After orgasm all the changes in the genital area reverse back to their unexcited state. There is a refractory period for men where they cannot be aroused again. This is short in young men but longer as the man matures. Women can be aroused again but if there has been no orgasm, the resolution stage takes longer and can sometimes be painful as the congested blood takes longer to disperse. Emotionally, this stage of resolution is an opportunity to offer each other reassurance and underline the mutual commitment to one another. It consolidates the bond between the lovers and themselves as individuals within that bond.

The stages of arousal are a complex combination of the emotional and physical communication between two people. Every union is unique as people evolve and develop as individuals and as a couple. The sexual act can provide a source of feeling varying from deep, mutual fulfilment to one of bitterness, frustration and alienation. Sometimes the sexual relationship will support the emotional relationship and sometimes the emotional relationship has to prop up the problems in the sexual partnership. However, neither will survive mutual exclusion for long. There are many factors that influence sexual harmony through a long relationship and we need to explore these with the clients.

PHYSICAL INFLUENCES

Many couples who have enjoyed a good sexual relationship expect it to continue despite the many stages and influences that can impact on them at any time. Pregnancy is an obvious example. Nobody knows how they are going to truly feel, emotionally or physically. There are many myths and concerns about sex during pregnancy and these need to be explored if problems arise at this important time. The couple may have planned this much-wanted baby together, but may find that they are very stretched emotionally when it actually comes to fruition. The woman may become very wrapped up with herself and her unborn child, leaving her partner feeling very excluded. The man may feel that not only is he losing his partner but he is going to have to be responsible for the family. He may find his partner physically unattractive as the pregnancy advances or concerned that he may harm the baby if they make love. She may feel rejected by this and withdraw further. None of these fears may be expressed and there may be feelings of guilt in even thinking about them. Thus, the shared joyful plan of having a family may be severely undermined by reality and further complicated by what they 'should' and 'ought' to feel.

Anxiety about contracting HIV and other sexual diseases may arise when an affair has been discovered. This is particularly relevant for male homosexuals if they have not practised safe sex, but the incidence of infection is rising in the heterosexual community and may need to be discussed where appropriate.

Age affects both the physical and emotional sides of the sexual relationship. In mid-life many men may need more direct stimulation to gain or maintain an erection and their ejaculation may be less forceful. The walls of the vagina in women become thinner and less moist. Young men can be aroused quickly and have a short refractory period. They can make love often, but as they mature this becomes physically impossible. Fears of performance and being able to satisfy their partner can contribute to sexual difficulties. It can become a vicious circle, where the individual personalises the problems, seeing himself as no longer attractive to his partner. Couples may worry about their body image as they age or if they have to have surgery. Surgery can leave obvious scarring and disfigurement that may affect either partner. It can also leave emotional scars that are less easy to acknowledge. The removal of the womb means that a woman's child-bearing years are over. As a couple they may have not intended to ever have any more children, but the hysterectomy takes away that choice. If the woman's sense of self is tied to her ability to have children, this operation will be very traumatic. Physical disability, long-term or as a result of an accident, will need careful exploration and assessment. Drugs that have to be taken for physical problems can have side effects that affect sexual performance. In men they can affect their ability to sustain an erection and in women they can affect the moistening of the vagina. Piles in the rectum will affect anal penetration if this is one of the couples' sexual preferences. Bodies become older and less supple and so some sexual positions may have to be adapted or abandoned. As the years go by, stamina may be reduced and fatigue will set in quicker. This will vary from person to person and between the genders. In Western culture, many men are winding down in middle age while many women may be restarting careers. Redundancy and unemployment can severely affect sexual performance. Depression and alcohol may create physical and emotional sexual difficulties.

Physical situations can affect the sex life of couples. Their home life may be very constricted with a growing family or a parent coming to live with them. There may be little privacy in a physical or emotional sense because of a change of circumstances beyond their control. One partner may get many of the physical affectional needs met by the growing family, while the other may not.

EMOTIONAL INFLUENCES

Anxieties about the partner, self, family or the wider environment may affect one or other of the couple at any time. If there is an undercurrent of anger or resentment towards the partner, it will often be reflected in the withdrawal of sexual intimacy or cold mechanical sex as punishment. Affairs can have this effect on a relationship. The partner who has had the affair may have put it behind her and want to re-establish a good, intimate relationship. Her partner may be in emotional turmoil, dealing with the denial and secrecy and trust that has been lost. He may associate affairs with loss because his mother left home to live with her lover. This resentment may take the form of a power struggle, so that the winner and loser mentality overrides the giving and taking that is so essential for loving,

SEX AND COUPLES

fulfilling sexual communication. When affairs have finished and the feeling of trust begins to emerge, underlying fears may still sabotage the process. This happened in the following case of a homosexual couple.

> Roy and Keith came into counselling because their two-year relationship, although emotionally committed, was going through difficulties. Keith was having problems maintaining an erection and was frightened that Roy would ultimately leave him because of sexual frustration.
>
> Keith had been married for 12 years and had a nine year-old daughter. He and his wife had known each other as far back as junior school and had drifted into marriage. Keith had experienced a couple of brief homosexual affairs in his youth but had been terrified that his very traditional family and work would find out. He had always been good friends with Linda and when they both reached 30 and were unattached, they married. Sex was hopeless for them both and ceased after the birth of their daughter. This was a mutually agreed decision. They were and are good friends to this day. Keith buried all his sexual desires until he met Roy.
>
> Roy came from a very different environment. He knew that he was homosexual from his early teens and his family accepted it. His parents had both straight and gay friends and so did Roy. He had also been on the gay scene and had a few relationships, one of which had been serious. At 28 he was tiring of the single life and was very attracted to the more mature Keith, whom he met at work.
>
> The friendship blossomed. Roy was easy-going and loveable. The relationship became sexual, a heady affair in view of the fact that Keith had long suppressed his sexuality and Roy possessed none of the taboos and myths that had dogged Keith. They finally set up home together and Linda appeared to accept the situation. She wanted continuing support of their child and Keith increased his visits until he was staying over every weekend. Roy was lonely and drifted back to his old haunts, occasionally having a one-night stand with an ex-lover. It was this discovery that shattered Keith.
>
> Roy felt shut out of the special relationship that he perceived Keith had with Linda and their daughter. Keith was shattered by Roy's infidelity. Roy was not emotionally connected to his ex-lover and had viewed their occasional couplings as a release of tension rather than an act of unfaithfulness. The sessions concentrated on their expectations of monogamy. It became clear during the counselling that they both tended to separate intimacy and sexuality. Roy on one level trusted that Linda and Keith no longer had a sexual relationship but was fearful that their shared history excluded him. Keith knew about mechanical sex, which he had experienced with Linda, but he loved her as a friend and the mother of his child. He loved Roy emotionally and sexually and could not have conducted a physical affair outside their relationship. They had to pull these strands of understanding together before any trust could be established.

Traumatic sexual experiences from the past can influence the adult sexual relationship at any time. Sexual abuse from a parent or other trusted person has many repercussions in adult life. It breaks the most basic expectation of trust and leaves children with a great fear of intimacy, guilt and poor understanding of boundaries. If they dare to tell there is further guilt if it results in the break-up of the family. If they are not believed, they become isolated and fearful with no sense of worth. In some cases they cut themselves off emotionally from what is going on physically so that they literally bury the memory in order to survive. Inappropriate sexual interference or abuse from a person who is known and trusted, such as a family friend or teacher, leaves the child with similar feelings of poor self-worth and lack of trust. The anger and impotence of his or her situation can be carried through into his or her adult relationships, resulting in a fear of intimacy and fears of losing control.

Clients who have been forced to have sex against their will have a particular problem with separating this act from the loving sexual act. Rape is about power and control and not about making love. It is usually associated with violence. Both men and women can be victims of rape, although men report it far more rarely than women. However, the emotional impact is just as great for men and much more likely to be bottled up. The reporting of rape can further damage people as the whole thing has to be investigated, sometimes very insensitively. Pregnancies that have to be aborted, or babies that have to be adopted, can have emotional effects on the women and their sexuality. The sexual act is connected with these losses and becomes an integral part of it.

It is important in sexual counselling to check out whether there are any of these factors in the clients' history or recent past. They will not become the focus of the counselling but may give insight and understanding to the feelings that the clients are undergoing in their current sexual difficulties. The focus will be the impact that they have on the relationship. Exploration around these areas may reveal deep-seated problems that have not been worked with at any meaningful level. The client may need to be directed to specialised personal therapy should this be the case. When the accompanying fears can be better managed, the couple can return to look at their joint problem.

These factors that cause sexual problems between couples will emerge in the *permission* and *limited information* part of the counselling process. It is from this exploration and understanding that the counsellor will be able to link the problems with the couple interaction and make an assessment of how to manage the case.

Inhibited sexual desire (ISD) or loss of sexual desire (LSD) by one or both partners are probably the most commonly presented problems in sexual counselling. When anger, resentment, fear or bad memories arise during sexual activity, the partner experiencing these negative emotions may want to stop. It depends on the power of these emotions as to whether it stops completely or goes on in a more limited way. If the emotion to please is stronger than the resentful feelings, it may be possible to move on to the excitement phase but is unlikely that the letting go that is required for orgasm will be reached. Faking desire is not an uncommon feature in sexual relationships. It may be steeped in past myths, such as 'men are always ready for sex' or 'women must please men'. The relationship may be more peaceful if the more sexually active partner is satisfied and the less sexually active partner feels less guilty. Unfortunately, if this continues with one partner doing all the giving and the other doing all the taking, the original negative emotions are liable to become amplified. These may become overwhelming and will lead to a total loss of desire.

When the presenting sexual problem is connected to this initial stage of lovemaking, the counsellor needs to focus on how the couple approach each other both now and in the past when sex was more satisfying. When couples meet and are very attracted to each other they experience the heady, omnipotent sensations of falling in love. The splitting and projecting of emotions between the two will be at its most positive. Some of these projections will be total fantasy but there will be a collusion between the couple to keep everything perfect. Idealised images and expectations will be transferred to the partner, of which he or she is unaware. As the 'in love' stage matures to a less fantasised state, these projections have to be adapted or withdrawn in both the general and the sexual relationship. It is the letting go of these projected emotions and feelings that can lead to varying stages of disappointment. If the communication is good between the couple, they will find a more soundly based relationship that will ultimately be more fulfilling. However, the disappointment may develop into deep anger and bitterness that erodes both the sexual and emotional relationship. Let us look at Robert and Jill again and see how this affected their sexual lives.

> The counsellor asked Robert and Jill to describe how their early sexual relationship with each other developed. In the early years they were separated by their respective careers and thus only actually saw each other at the weekends. They both described their developing relationship as terribly close, with long conversations on the 'phone in the week. The anticipation of meeting was exciting and the physical desire sometimes overwhelming. Robert lived in the officers' mess during the week, enjoyed the service life and lived much as he had always done. He was proud of Jill, how she looked and conducted herself in the sometimes very formal social life that his job demanded. Jill loved it too because it confirmed the image that she wanted of herself and they both basked in being a successful young couple. She had moved a long way from her deprived background and sometimes felt quite shaky that it all might disappear. She did not voice these fears but doubled her efforts to always look good and play the part.

Thus, the desire stage of their sexual relationship was based on a mix of reality and fantasy. The separations forced on them by their work kept their desire and excitement high for each other. Robert always initiated sex, found intercourse very satisfying because it made him feel very close to Jill. He was not particularly interested in foreplay but knew that it was good for Jill. It emerged that he rarely talked about his feelings for her during sex or after. Their emotional communication was done on the 'phone in the early days, balanced with good sex and a busy social life at the weekend. He looked after Jill and she happily allowed herself to be cared for as she had a very responsible job during the week. She trusted Robert but sometimes, when she was feeling insecure about herself, she found orgasm difficult to achieve. She tended to fake an orgasm when this happened because she did not want him to think that it was his fault.

The sexual communication was thus beginning to falter. This was exacerbated when they started living together and no longer needed to 'phone each other. Robert was used to living in a detached way both in his family of origin and in his service life. He still took care of Jill in many ways but not in the open, affectionate way that she craved. Jill felt emotionally starved and began to fear that this wonderful marriage was going to slip away from her and it was all her fault. She did not mention it because of her fundamental belief that sex was a dangerous force which caused more trouble when addressed. She withdrew into herself and found sex unrewarding until finally she stopped making excuses and refused any sex. She felt angry and confused but was unable to express any of it to Robert. He was unaware of any of this but the lack of sex deprived him of his main attachment to Jill. This is when they made the connection that her childhood experience must be responsible for her current feelings and was the reason she came into counselling. This had had an effect on what she was feeling, but in reality it was the emotional and sexual communication between the two of them that was at fault.

The question 'How do they approach each other' is fundamental to exploring the desire stage of couple interaction. It can reveal how the partners feel about themselves and what they expect of their partner. It can point up the splitting and projecting of emotions that may reflect in the general relationship. Sex that is based on idealisation, as in the case example, will often result in loss of desire because of the disappointment. The core of the counselling work is to unravel the fantasy from the reality so that the negative feelings are talked about and correctly attributed.

The sexual communication continues to be equally important throughout the stages of arousal. As desire moves into the excitement and plateau stage, a new level of intimacy is achieved. It is the time for experimenting, finding out what each partner likes without being limited by myths and taboos. Clients who present with erectile difficulties or dyspareunia need to be very explicit at this stage as to what is good and what makes them fearful. Clients who have difficulty in sharing or giving and taking in their general relationship, may start to have difficulties at this time. Where there are issues of control, as in the case of Jill, real fears emerge of the possibility of letting go that is to follow.

Many assumptions can be made at this time of what is acceptable, influenced by the past and more recent experiences. Couples that are angry with each other can reach the excitement stage and may use the sexual experience to resolve their differences. However, if the anger persists it is more likely to be damaging to both the general and sexual relationship. The key question at this stage is, 'How do they collaborate?'

The collaboration between the partners that is so essential for desire, excitement and plateau stages now requires supreme trust to move into orgasm, the self-absorbed part of the sexual act. It represents the letting go of boundaries in the presence of the partner and, at its best, is extremely pleasurable both emotionally and physically. In conflictual relationships where there is no understanding of each others' needs, this stage can leave either partner feeling used and abused. The client who has a poor self-image will be further traumatised. Clients who have had their boundaries invaded by inappropriate sex in the past can have all their old fears resurrected. If these fears persist, the abused client may feel that he or she may disintegrate, both emotionally and physically. Their only defence is to shut down from orgasm.

The difference in timing of the sexual act should be underlined. Part of the giving and taking within the sexual relationship is understanding this difference. Individuals come to climax at varying times depending on mood and circumstances and this should be taken into account in a loving relationship. Premature or retarded ejaculation in men may be seen as a problem, but if the couple collaborate well in the excitement stage, this will be minimised. If it is not and the clients seem to have a good general relationship, they should be referred to PST. Many clients take it as a personal failure or rejection if orgasm is not achieved nearly simultaneously, rather than as a response to difference. The key question at this stage is, 'How do they care for each other?'

After orgasm comes the stage of resolution. It can reflect all that is wrong in the relationship or provide a space for deep intimacy. Each partner will need something different and the relationship has to return to looking at mutual needs. Disappointment and anger may be acted out by withdrawing emotionally and physically. However, during counselling it can be seen as an opportunity to express what those frustrations are, without blaming and carping or feeling guilty. The counsellor needs to ask the question, 'How do they grow together?' In the case example, Jill loved the postcoital intimacy, which she experienced as a time to talk about their feelings and emotions. Robert did little of the talking but was very happy to listen initially. However, as the relationship progressed, he found that orgasm was enough for his intimacy needs and tended to fall asleep almost immediately. He had no idea that Jill experienced this as a total rejection. The nature of the bonding between them became unravelled. Jill no longer felt cared for and started to lose her desire for the whole sexual communication. This meant that Robert did not get his needs met and thus the whole stability of the relationship went awry.

Figure 5.2. shows the underlying issues endemic in couples who experience specific sexual problems and how it is reflected in the emotional interaction.

MOVING THE WORK ON

Specific exploration of the clients' interpersonal experience will highlight where the problems are. Tasks can then be discussed in sessions that arise from this information. Each partner must listen to where the difficulty lies and at what stage in the encounter, it is liable to break down. Robert in the case example had to spend more time at the excitement stage to allow Jill to become more aroused. Her vagina would lubricate and relax, to allow intercourse to be pleasurable and pain-free. It would also help her attain the subsequent stages of arousal in order to reach an orgasm. Both partners must be explicit as to what they want and must both agree to the task. The responsibility of each partner is to give and take openly and not to barter. Demanding a behaviour that the other finds difficult or perverted is bound to fail. The task of the counsellor is to feed back her understand-

Sexual problem	Underlying Issue	Couple dynamic
ISD, LSD	*Desire* How do they approach each other?	Splitting, projections
Erectile failure, dyspareunia	*Excitement/plateau* How do they collaborate with each other?	Collusions, power struggle, intimacy
PE, RE, anorgasmia	*Orgasm* How do they care for each other?	Giving and taking taboos
Poor negative communication, premature separation	*Resolution* How do they grow together?	Reward, punishment, bonding

Figure 5.2 Relationship between sexual problems and emotional interaction

ing of what they both want and to underline that it will be further discussed in the next session. If the tasks work well, this can then lead onto further exploration and change. If the feedback is negative, then it requires more exploration. It may mean that the task was poorly or inappropriately set but it must be acknowledged, otherwise the sense of failure may become embedded in the relationship.

All feedback, whether it is negative or positive, is significant. It gives clues to the underlying dynamic of the relationship that can be further explored. Achievement needs to be acknowledged and reinforced, while the difficulties and blocks need to be examined. There can be no movement until the progress is assessed and evaluated. The clients need to be supported as they reinforce the positives and reframe the negatives.

To summarise, sexual difficulties arise from the anxiety present in the general relationship. These can range from conflicts and unresolved difficulties from the past that come through to the current partnership to straightforward 'performance' anxieties fuelled by poor information. Partners may be able to be respond physically, but if their emotional needs are not met the relationship is likely to be further alienated. The resolution part of the sex act can play an important role in resolving and integrating some of the couple issues. We have to look at the individual experiences of the sexual relationship and focus attention on the emotional responses that they evoke. Underlying issues may emerge from this that may reflect the problems that are going on in the general relationship. It is at this stage that it may be necessary to intervene in order to progress the work. This may take the form of sharing the emotion with the partner without personalising the difference and taking offence. Robert and Jill came to understand their different approaches by talking about them and not experiencing the differences as rejection. Where there are fears of control, progressive physical intimacy exercises may be suitable. These must be discussed in session to ensure, as in all task-setting, that power games are not being set up. The use of dedicated time to look at all the issues, to exchange information about expectations and needs, is as important in the sexual relationship as in the emotional one. Keith and Roy in the case example became very aware of this. The collusive relationships of splitting and projecting, triangulating, attaching, being involved in the family systems and life-stages, all play their part in the sexual relationship. Each intervention should be designed to fit the clients' needs with these dynamics in mind. Clients need to be encouraged to explore the processes that affect their ability to approach, collaborate, care and grow in their sexual relationship.

6

PROBLEMS IN THE WORK

> *Man needs difficulties; they are necessary for health.*
> Carl Jung

We have now described the basic range of the RELATE Approach, and illustrated how it applies to many aspects of the clients' couple life. There is, however, one important element which remains untouched, and this is the counsellor's use of his own feelings to clarify what is happening for the clients. We introduce this as a beginning to the Chapter on problems as it represents a powerful way of gaining deeper understanding when this does not arise from the open and spoken content of the work. Then we will consider the different types of problems commonly encountered and how these difficulties may be overcome.

USING COUNTER-TRANSFERENCE TO UNDERSTAND PROBLEMS

Counter-transference is a reaction of the counsellor to the client's transference. Sometimes it is a conscious reaction to the observed behaviour of the client and sometimes a unconscious reaction to the felt, and not consciously understood, behaviour of the client (Mattinson, 1975).

There have been many definitions of *counter-transference* that have evolved over the years and further adapted in other disciplines. The Mattinson definition is the base from which we work with couples. It is a valuable diagnostic tool, and may give insights into the more subtle aspects of what it feels like to be the client in the relationship, or indeed to what it feels like to be a significant other in the client's life. The key questions for the counsellor to ask are:

- How precisely do I feel when I am with these clients?
- Where might these feelings originate from?

Let us take a simple example:

Charles and Eleanor present for counselling. They are an attractive vivacious couple. Both have been involved in transient affairs and this is the concern they are presenting. The counsellor is aware during the session that she finds Charles sexually attractive. She is careful not to let this change her approach, but thinks deeply about it after the session.

Once the counsellor has decided what her feeling is – in this case one of sexual interest – there are several different ways in which it could have originated.

1. Objective Counter-transference

The first possibility is that this is simply the counsellor's straightforward reaction to Charles' overt presentation. If Charles is displaying some of the personality traits that commonly lead others to be attracted – good looks, physical congruence, sexual confidence, humour, kindness – the counsellor's reaction is easily understood. It may well give the counsellor a clue to how others feel about Charles – especially Eleanor and maybe other women with whom he has become involved. This is called '*objective counter-transference*' – what Winnicott describes as, 'The worker's love/hate reactions to the actual personality and behaviour of the client'. It is a largely conscious reaction. If the counsellor uses this information, it will probably be in a straightforward way to see if Charles is aware of his attractiveness, and if he is able to deal constructively with the reactions it provokes.

2. Concordant Counter-transference

Let us now assume the interaction is slightly more complex. Let us imagine Charles is not overtly attractive and so the counsellor is surprised at her feelings. There was little talk about sexuality in the session and the couple were quick to say that sex was only a small part of their relationship. Charles confessed his surprise at how his relationships with other women took on a sexual dimension, as he always first thought of them as friendships. Indeed, he seemed quite annoyed that matters took this turn, even though he seemed to meet them in potentially romantic settings which the counsellor would associate with the beginning of a liaison and did not back off when matters took a more intimate turn. The counsellor wondered whether Charles was not consciously aware of the sexual dimension of his actions, even though unconsciously it was what he wanted. In terms of the projection and splitting model he had *repressed* it. However, the nature of the intimacy of his meetings suggested sexual and romantic liaisons and maybe it was this suggestion that had led to a feeling of arousal in the counsellor. Therefore, what she felt was in effect reflecting Charles' own repressed feelings of sexual desire. This is called *'concordant counter-transference'*. The worker experiences a feeling the client has but is denying. It would lead the counsellor to try and help Charles become more conscious of his own denied desires in the situations he described, and look at the reasons that had led him to consciously deny these desires and find them unacceptable while unconsciously acting them out.

Concordant counter-transference is closely linked to the process of denial described in Chapter 3 and often leads to work on splitting and projection.

3. Complementary Counter-transference

In the third example, the counsellor soon realises that her feeling of sexual responsiveness did not spring from either of the areas described above. Rather, it was because Charles was subtly flirting with her. He had complimented her on her patience and confessed she was younger and more attractive than he had expected a counsellor to be. When talking about the couple's problems, he had implied that he was sure that the counsellor had no such problems, and that 'her husband was a lucky man'. All this had been done with a considerable degree of charm and subtlety and had made the counsellor feel attracted towards Charles. However, she was aware from the story the couple had told that this was how he acted towards all women – she didn't think he found her especially attractive. Neither did she feel that Charles indulged in this behaviour consciously – rather, it seemed an automatic response.

Thinking more deeply about why Charles behaved like this when she had heard his history, the counsellor realised that he had had a similar relationship with his mother. As an only child he had had to compete for his mother's affections with his father and had learned to behave in a similar way to his father. The counsellor realised that she had possibly been feeling similar to how Charles's mother felt, as he had carried this childhood manner of relating to his mother into a manner of relating to all women in his adult life. This is called a *'complementary counter-transference'*. The counsellor's feelings are elicited by the client's behaviour, and may well resemble the feelings of a significant person in the client's past. In this case, understanding of the counter-transference may lead the counsellor to feel that counselling based on an attachment model (to help Charles consider alternative ways of cementing relationships) or on the triangular relationship model (to understand the significance of triangles in Charles's life) might be helpful.

4. Worker Transference

In this final example, the counsellor realised that her feelings towards Charles arose not from anything Charles did, but because he reminded her strongly of a past boyfriend of whom she had been immensely fond, but who sadly had been killed in a car accident when they were engaged many years previously. This is called *'worker transference'*. It belongs only to the counsellor and she would need to be careful to set this aside when dealing with Charles. This is made particularly difficult because some of the previous causal factors which are relevant to the work may also be in effect, and would need to be identified separately.

Counter-transference is a most useful tool for the counsellor, enabling her to grasp quickly information that may otherwise take a lot of time and intuition to unearth. However, it is also a very subtle one, and like many of the aspects of the approach based on unconscious processes can be difficult to grasp. Objective counter-transference is the simplest response and needs little further elaboration. Concordant and complementary counter-transferences are more complex.

Counsellor self-awareness plays an important part in these dynamics, and is essential to set up the therapeutic alliance. Counsellors are prone to transference issues in their own life and environment which give rise to worker transference. If a client reminds the counsellor of a significant person in her past, the counsellor will transfer these feelings and apply them to the client and the session. There will be no genuine empathy in the counselling because of the incorrect attribution and engagement will cease. This worker transference can be negative or positive. Negative feelings toward the clients that belong to the worker totally sabotage any alliance. The counselling could easily have come to an abrupt end – initiated by either the clients or the counsellor. The ending would be rationalised by the clients to the effect that counselling was useless, which it may well have been. The counsellor could justify withdrawal by deciding that the clients were uncounsellable.

On the other hand, positive transference can be just as self-defeating. The counsellor may want to please the clients because of her own transference issues. She may experience great satisfaction and pride in the work. However, because she is concentrating on her own feelings of gratification, she may be reluctant to challenge clients or admit difficulties. Therefore the work will not move on.

The knowledge gained by the counter-transferential feelings can be used in different ways. We have indicated how it may allow counsellors to choose between models. Additionally, it may allow them to make interventions, if the feeling is fairly straightforward and may be accessible to the client.

If the feeling is a more problematic one, like our example where the counsellor senses because of her own sexual attraction that one of the clients might be seeking a sexual involvement without being aware of this, it is usually better not to share this openly with the clients, who might well be disconcerted or mystified. Instead the feeling is used as a basis for the counsellor to hypothesize that the clients have had to use their sexuality to hold onto relationships in the past. As we suggest in the case in point, this might indicate problems with attachments in the past or that the triangular relationship model may be relevant.

The most important requirement is that the counsellor does not simply act upon the counter-transferential feelings according to the natural inclinations listed above. The client will have experienced such a response many times in the past, and repeating this will not open up any new areas of self-knowledge, but will rather confirm the clients' existing and possibly problematic world view.

This section is only the briefest of introductions to an area that is central to the RELATE Approach, and which practitioners study in depth. One issue that has not been examined in depth here is that the feeling can be between the counsellor and one partner or between the counsellor and the couple, depending on whether the transference is a shared or individual one. However, it is hoped that the simplified examples offer a useful introduction to the importance of the phenomenon of counter-transference.

The remainder of this chapter deals with problems that may arise with clients with whom the counsellor would expect to be able to engage in this work. In the next chapter we look at how work is organised when it is being offered to clients who seek more help than couple counselling alone can provide.

The problems that can arise when dealing with couples apparently suitable for the RELATE Approach can be divided into four broad categories:

- Those which concern the clients' ability to attend the counselling – for example inability to attend with a partner or to attend regularly.
- Those which concern the clients' unwillingness to engage with the process – either at the beginning or at a specific stage. Under this heading we consider the general subject of *resistance* and *defences*.
- Difficulties in establishing a therapeutic alliance with the clients – whether because a counsellor cannot feel sufficient empathy or because the counsellor becomes drawn into some aspect of the clients' way of relating, instead of remaining in a neutral position.

- Difficulties in reaching a suitable depth of understanding – either because the theoretical framework imposes limitations, because cultural differences hinder full understanding or because the couple problem demands specialist knowledge.

1. CLIENTS CANNOT ATTEND THE COUNSELLING REGULARLY

The most common problem that faces a couple counsellor is when there is not regular joint attendance at the meeting. This may be because the other partner is unwilling to involve him or herself in the counselling or because circumstances such as work prevents him or her from attending. The counsellor's approach will differ depending on the situation.

1i Only One Client Is Willing to Attend

It would be incorrect to assume that couple counselling can only be done in the presence of both partners. Much useful work is carried out using the RELATE Approach when only one partner is willing to attend the counselling. There are, however, certain guidelines to consider.

It Is Important to Ensure that the Apparently Reluctant Partner Is Given an Opportunity to Attend the Work on Equal Terms

The counsellor should not accept unquestioningly that the unseen partner does not wish to attend. This often turns out not to be the case, but rather to be a wrong interpretation made by the partner who is attending. The counsellor can invite the unseen partner to join the counselling – either indirectly through the partner, or directly by writing. A counsellor can only write if she has the full permission of the client who is attending to do so, since the direction of the sessions will be modified. Assurance must be given to both clients that any individual session remains confidential. However, we find permission is usually given and writing frequently results in a joint contract being established. The fact that counsellors using the RELATE Approach are willing to take these active steps to engage an absent partner often raises surprise amongst those used to other disciplines. However, we find that such an approach has several distinct advantages.

Firstly, it firmly establishes that the purpose of the counselling will be to attend to the couple relationship rather than to either of the individuals in the relationship. It demonstrates that the counsellor considers that both partners' perceptions of the relationship are of equal value, and that the counsellor does not intend to champion one side against the other. Irrespective of whether the invitation results in the partner attending, such a demonstration is helpful in the formation of a clear counselling contract.

Additionally, partners in a troubled relationship frequently find it difficult to both agree on any course of action, and this includes coming to counselling. It can be helpful if the counsellor takes this decision out of the arena of dispute.

Finally, the counsellor gains the chance of deciding how an absent partner is best introduced to the counselling process. The absent individual may well fear that he or she will have been prejudged, especially if there have been several sessions with his or her partner alone. Some of these fears can be allayed by a carefully written letter that makes it plain that the individual is being contacted to give him or her an opportunity to express his or her views and then play a full part in the counselling. In addition, it is frequently helpful for the counsellor to propose a single initial session alone with the unseen partner to allow him or her to establish a working relationship. Further attention is given to ways of establishing counsellor neutrality with a couple later in this chapter.

Before concluding this section it is important to underline that there are certain circumstances where it is inadvisable to seek to invite an absent partner. The most critical situation is when there is a suggestion that significant violence exists in the relationship – either between the partners or towards a third party, usually a child. This is dealt with in more detail in the next chapter, but a counsellor needs to be confident that she is not putting a client in danger or preventing an important disclosure being made by inviting a partner to join the work. Counsellors should also be aware that they may be manipulated by the attending client to contact the absent partner on the attending client's behalf. It would be intrusive to the absentee partner if it was clear that he or she has left the relationship and ceased all contact.

Additionally, a counsellor can be tempted to invite a partner to join the counselling when she is unsure of the proposed focus of the work, in the hope that a direction will become clearer. Unfortunately, the effect is the opposite, as it is harder to clarify an agenda for the work with two ambivalent people than it is with one. If there is a clear disinclination on the part of the client who has attended so far to agree to a couple focus, further exploration is needed before inviting a partner to attend. Discussion around the possibility of inviting an absent partner into the counselling frequently results in the clarification of the expectations of the work.

Take Steps to Ensure the Absent Partner's Perceptions Are Given Space in the Counselling

Merely because one partner in a relationship does not attend, does not mean that his or her perceptions of the situation are not available to the work. Clients are often able to summarise their partner's opinions vividly in answer to a question such as, 'How do you think your partner would respond to the criticism you have just made of him?' When clients do not know why their partners act in a particular way, they can be asked to solicit their partner's opinion and report this back in the following sessions. Sometimes clients can repeat a partner's response with convincing authenticity and the process of enquiring begins a dialogue between the couple that was previously missing.

The couple counsellor's task in such interchanges is to remember and assemble the different details about the absent partner, just as she does about the history of the client before her. A picture of the partner can be built up which offers a basis for helping the present client explore the realities and conflicts in the relationship and to plan different methods of relating.

Avoid Colluding with a Client's Projections

Initially the counsellor will accept the presenting client's description of his or her absent partner. These descriptions will be taken at face value, and the client will be supported in responding appropriately.

However, should this approach not help the client make any changes in the relationship, the counsellor may consider whether there is a distinct projective identification between the partners, as described in Chapter 3. When such an identification occurs, each partner genuinely believes in his or her vision of the whole; however, this vision is founded only on a partial appreciation of his or her own and the partner's feelings. The counsellor will not aid the withdrawal of these projections and the resolution of the situation unless she is able to challenge this incomplete view; indeed, if she accepts it and thus validates it, she may well contribute to maintaining the couple's problematic fit. The counsellor will need to use sensitivity and ingenuity to find a way of understanding the fit with only one partner present, and then to challenge it without seeming to be unreasonably prejudiced. It is not an easy task, but it is possible and most helpful to the client. A particularly useful approach is to begin to examine whether both partners take equal responsibility for expressing the full range of emotions – anger, sadness, happiness, sexual feelings, etc. – in the relationship. Where an imbalance is detected, the client who is present can reflect on his or her predisposition either to express all of a certain feeling or to express little of it. If the attending client becomes more able to cope with all feelings equally – in other words, to move from a split position to an more integrated one – the projective pattern of the relationship will change.

Retain the Distinction between Couple and Individual Work

In many counselling situations there is a tension between a couple's desire to work on the relationship and both partners' wish for the counsellor's attention to focus more on them as an individual. Where both partners are present, there is a natural corrective tendency that counterbalances each individual's natural desire to concentrate on his or her own world to the exclusion of the shared world. When only one partner is attending, however, much of this counter-balance is lost. Although the authors have no criticism of individual work *per se*, it is markedly different from couple work in terms of likely direction and outcome. It requires different approaches, support systems and safeguards. In the interest of clear client contracts it is important that the counsellor is able to define the type of work she is engaged in with a particular client. Therefore, counsellors need to pay attention to this distinction when working with partners alone, and need to raise the question with the individual when the focus of the work seems to be becoming indistinct.

1ii Circumstances Prevent One Partner Attending

Often the other partner is absent not because of disinclination, but for reasons connected with work. Shift workers, those who work abroad or offshore and those who serve with the armed forces or work with the merchant navy frequently fall into this category.

In these cases the counsellor should start the work at a time that is convenient to both partners, so that the initial problem is explored in the presence of both and a scheme of work can be agreed upon. Then a decision can be made about whether work is to proceed in the period when one partner is absent. If it is, a method can be devised that the absent partner is kept in contact with the progress of the work – by his or her partner telephoning or writing, for example.

1iii Neither Partner Can Attend Regularly

Traditionally, counselling is offered at the same time each week, and such a method is administratively simple and gives a rhythm to the work which appears greatly to aid its progress. However, a significant number of couples are unable to make such a commitment, even if sessions are offered in the evenings or at weekends.

When dealing with couples in such circumstances, there is a need for clear non-judgemental dialogue between the couple and the counsellor. On the one hand it is unhelpful to treat the clients' difficulties as if they were merely symptoms of a lack of commitment – rather, they need to be explored sympathetically. The couple may well have the commitment to make a slightly different approach work. On the other hand, distinct problems do seem to arise when counsellors attempt to use the RELATE Approach over a different time-scale to that for which it was designed. If there is regularly a longer gap than one week between the sessions, there is a tendency for the same ground to be covered repeatedly. If more than one session a week is offered, the work loses its connection to the outside world and becomes over-introspective. If session times vary markedly, both counsellor and clients can expend more energy on ensuring that they remember when the sessions occur and on being prepared for them than they expend on the actual counselling process. Flexibility of this kind must be very carefully managed and is not always practically possible in some centres.

Where after due discussion of the drawbacks such a contract is agreed, the counsellor can give consideration to maintaining the weekly rhythm of counselling. Tasks to be performed during the intervening time are a useful tool – often certain aspects of the clients' history can be explored and genograms drawn by the couple themselves and then reported to the counsellor. Similarly, clients can spend a fixed time together alone every few days discussing uncontroversial subjects, so that the improved communication which arises in the counselling room is brought into being by another method. Plans can be made for structured use should a series of sessions occurring at a shorter interval than a week be agreed – for example the sessions could be used to explore different aspects of the history of the problem.

It is important that a distinction is drawn between when clients cannot attend because of definite external constraints and when clients cannot attend due to some inner unwillingness to take part in the process. The latter case is an indication of *resistance*, and this is explored further in the following section.

2. CLIENTS DO NOT ENGAGE WITH THE PROCESS OF COUNSELLING

Clients using the RELATE Approach can find some parts of the process more difficult and more threatening than others, and this resistance may show in a variety of ways – missing sessions or not attending on time, failing to carry out certain tasks, regularly returning to issues that have already been explored.

In considering this subject, it is helpful first to remind ourselves of the three-stage model which underlies the RELATE Approach. This model consists of exploration, understanding and action. There is much evidence from the related field of adult learning to suggest that most individuals are stronger in some areas than others, and from counselling research to suggest that the preferences may be linked to gender or culture.

Exploration will not suit those who favour a pragmatic or active learning style (see Honey and Mumford, 1992, for a further exploration of this area of research). Evidence collected by RELATE about the different expectations of men and women (RELATE, 1995) suggest that in general RELATE's male clients are less comfortable with the need to explore before solutions can be found. Windy Dryden (1993) details research which suggests that many within our culture find this aspect difficult. This subject has been touched upon in the Introduction.

However, a phase of exploration of the clients' history and of the history of the relationship is usually needed if the counselling is to progress. Often resistance can be overcome if the reason for this exploration is explained in reassuring terms – 'Our past leads each of us to find some things easier and others harder – discussing that here might help us'. Similarly, unhelpful fantasies can be dispelled, especially any fear of psychological determinism – 'It is not my intention to attribute all your problems to some specific occurrence in the past, or to suggest that you can't now change the way you were brought up to act'. Finally, ways of carrying out the exploration can be found which fit with the couple's own preferences, for example, by linking present events to the past. If clients have difficulty in remembering the past, this should not be necessarily interpreted as resistance – there is a natural human tendency to forget what was routinely unhappy or uneventful; this trait can show particularly with clients who have a history of poor attachment.

Other clients can resist any move from exploration to understanding or from understanding to action. One explanation is that certain clients, particularly female ones (RELATE, 1995), are more comfortable with the exploration stage. Again, the counsellor needs to address the discomfort, to dispel groundless fears and to facilitate the work sympathetically.

Another common explanation for this resistance is that the earlier stage is not complete – the client is not happy that the counsellor has fully explored the subject or that the shared understanding is adequate and so is resisting moving forward. The counsellor needs to return to the earlier

PROBLEMS IN THE WORK

stages when this resistance occurs and to take care that the basic processes have been fully used and that assumptions have not been made. *'Yes, but'* is a particularly noticeable way in which clients demonstrate that they feel they are being rushed to a conclusion that is not theirs. In this case it is important that the counsellor pauses to check that the emotions that are associated with the area under exploration are fully understood and owned. An important tool the RELATE Approach favours in these circumstances is the Triangle of Conflict (Figure 6.1), derived from a concept first articulated by David Malan (1979).

The triangle illustrates that above the surface can be seen an active defence – in the case we are discussing this is a refusal to move to the action stage of the counselling. This defence is linked to an anxiety, which can often be guessed at – a fear of having one's opinions disregarded, perhaps. However, beneath this simple linking will be a hidden feeling – undoubtedly linked to a time when such a similar event occurred in the client's past. While this feeling remains undisclosed, it will often strengthen the defensive behaviour without either the client, the client's partner or the counsellor fully understanding why this is happening.

Each client has a hidden feeling attached to any resistance, and these feelings can often be unexpected and individual. A common example can be in work with partners who are survivors of childhood sexual abuse. The counsellor may be able to see that the client is now showing a defence against entering an intimate relationship – possibly by missing sessions and resisting tasks which would otherwise cement the relationship. The

Defence *Anxiety*

Withdraw from any change   My opinion is disregarded

CONSCIOUS

HIDDEN

Underlying feeling

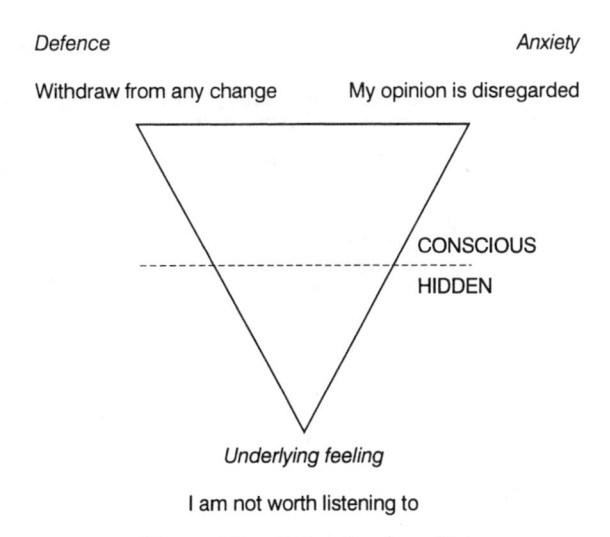

I am not worth listening to

Figure 6.1a   Triangle of conflict

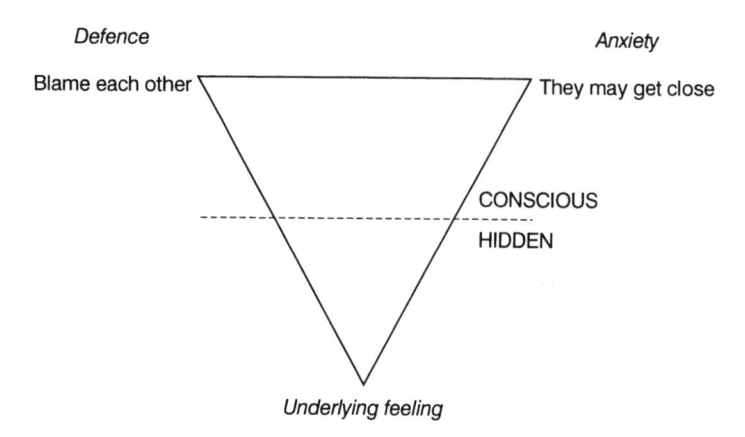

```
        Defence                              Anxiety
    Blame each other                    They may get close

                            CONSCIOUS
                            ─────────
                             HIDDEN

                     Underlying feeling
          I will not be loved by anyone who knows me well
```
Figure 6.1b   George and May

counsellor may correctly surmise that the client is anxious about intimacy, which is regarded as dangerous, and the client may agree. Yet what is the hidden feeling about intimacy? The counsellor could easily assume that it is a feeling of distaste and be working from that basis. Yet the client may not share this feeling at all – her feelings may be that intimacy represented a linking with a powerful other which was both frightening and fulfilling and in which she was relieved of any responsibility in an otherwise care-

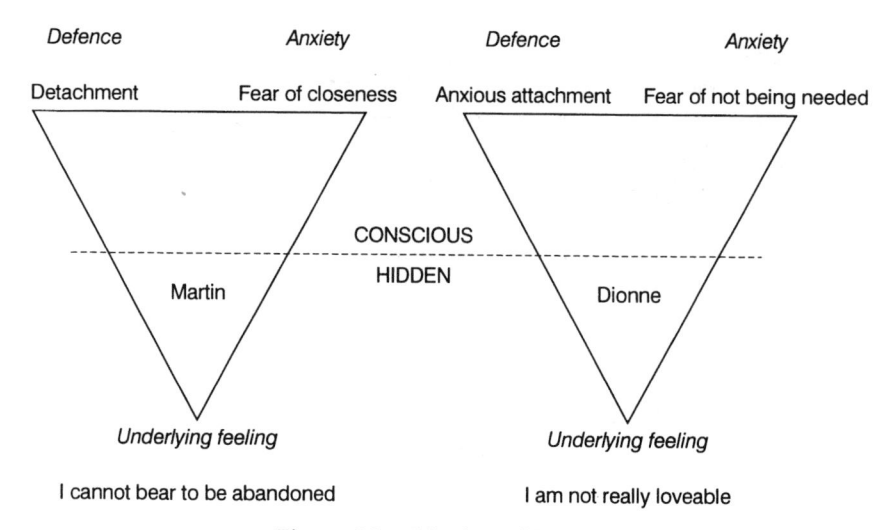

```
   Defence        Anxiety              Defence              Anxiety
 Detachment   Fear of closeness   Anxious attachment   Fear of not being needed

                            CONSCIOUS
              ─────────────────────────────────────
                             HIDDEN
         Martin                              Dionne

     Underlying feeling              Underlying feeling
  I cannot bear to be abandoned     I am not really loveable
```
Figure 6.1c   Martin and Dionne

filled childhood. Therefore, while the counsellor might be working on the assumption that the client avoids intimacy as she finds it distasteful, and so be trying to help the client find it more desirable, the client may well be avoiding intimacy because she links it with overpowering fulfilment, so is fearful that she will lose her individuality and direction if she yields to it again. Sensitive work using the Triangle of Conflict to uncover the hidden feeling would allow this to emerge in the counselling and so would allow the work to fit more closely with the client's particular resistance.

This triangle can also be used to highlight the shared anxieties and underlying feelings that may have formed the initial recognition and attraction of the clients to each other. The defences the couple form individually may be the same or be acted out in a different way to protect themselves from hurt. George and May are the 'cat and dog' couple that we have worked with throughout this book. In Figure 6.1b they both defended themselves by blaming and carping about the other. Their shared anxiety was that if they did not blame each other, it might be discovered how awful they really believed they were. Past experiences underlined this, where they both felt failures in comparison with others. The underlying feeling was that they both yearned to be loved for themselves, unconditionally, without having to compete with others who were 'better'.

Figure 6.1c shows the triangles that illuminate Martin and Dionne, the couple case study that centres on attachment themes, which we have used on a number of occasions. Martin's anxiety was that if he allowed closeness he might be abandoned, as had happened when he was young. He had developed this defence of being detached so that he did not have to face this anxiety. Dionne had the worry that she might not be needed and so had made herself indispensable to her family and others. Not being needed would leave her feeling abandoned, without any identity. She defended against this by close attachment behaviour. Thus, this couple used different defences to cope with similar fears. Anxieties like these are often exaggerated, rooted as they are in past experience that are probably not very relevant for now.

The counselling will hopefully put the feelings and anxieties into a more realistic framework but by looking at these triangles it is easy to see why couples unwittingly resist the very change that they are seeking.

3. COUNSELLOR FAILS TO ESTABLISH A SUITABLE THERAPEUTIC ALLIANCE

In the previous section we looked at difficulties which were due to the clients resisting the direction of the work which is suggested by the RELATE

Approach. A similar difficulty arises when one or both of the clients wish to actively pursue a direction that does not accord with the counsellor's expectations. In each of these cases a careful balance needs to be drawn. Counsellors do need to start the work largely from where the client has understanding, and so imposing a different agenda from the beginning is unhelpful. Concern is often felt by counsellors in the following situations:

- When they feel that clients' behaviour during counselling – whether inside or outside the counselling room – is at odds with the desired outcome of the counselling.
- When they feel that one of the clients is attempting to move the counsellor from a point of neutrality onto his or her side.
- When clients resist establishing a contract for the work in conjunction with the counsellor.

3i Counsellor Finds Clients' Behaviour in Counselling Difficult

It can be distressing to feel trapped in a room with a client or a couple who are behaving in an extreme way – with great anger, with overt sexuality or by being either uninterruptedly garrulous or else completely silent.

The situation can be made more difficult if the counsellor is unsure of the limits of her own authority or, in extreme circumstances, of her escape route. Many of these situations can be diffused if the counsellor is able to give a clear message to the clients about what is or is not expected and why this is the case. Engagement in the counselling process cannot happen unless these ground rules are laid.

Firstly, the counsellor should always know what the emergency procedure is, and be ready to use it if necessary. Usually the counsellor would leave the room in extreme circumstances – it is never advisable to attempt to physically intervene between clients. Most counselling centres will also have an emergency alarm system – counsellors should be fully aware of how it works and be ready to use it. The purpose of these preparations is not solely so that they can be used. A counsellor who is prepared for a difficult situation to arise and who is not worried about her own safety will be able to respond appropriately and directly to clients and take control of the situation. A counsellor who is nervous and unsure is more likely to come over as manipulative or evasive in her attempt to steer the clients away from extreme behaviour, and so runs the risk of aggravating the situation. Therefore, paradoxically, by preparing for an extreme situation a counsellor is likely to lessen her chance of experiencing one.

Anger

Clients will frequently get in touch with a deep sense of anger with their partner in counselling, and will wish to express it. Such expression can be a most helpful part of allowing hurt to be acknowledged and recognised. Sitting with an angry adult is almost always an uncomfortable and frightening experience, and counsellors would expect to find such a situation difficult – especially when it is an unfamiliar one. The urge to intervene too soon should be resisted in the hope that the clients themselves will prove able to take control of the situation, and will thus learn that anger is a survivable emotion that passes. However, the following guidelines may help counsellors draw boundaries when they are needed:

- No matter how angry they are, clients need to accept that the counsellor's role is to intervene and to direct the interchanges in the room where necessary – this may need to be clarified if events appear to have developed a momentum of their own.
- A client is always entitled to leave the counselling room if he or she wishes and to return on feeling calmer.
- Clients should remain seated and not pace the room or seek to physically intimidate (knowingly or otherwise) partner or counsellor.
- The expression of anger should not take undue precedence over the expression of other emotions.

We will look at guidelines for working where violence exists between partners in the next chapter.

Sexual Behaviour

Couple counsellors need to be able to talk about human sexual behaviour naturally and easily. Most clients will find the subject awkward, and few counsellors are totally at ease until they have a great amount of experience. Discussing sexual matters in detail can give rise to feelings of intimacy and arousal which can be disconcerting to counsellors and clients alike. We list some guidelines below:

- Counsellors using the RELATE Approach expect to deal with sexual matters only using discussion. Exercises and pleasuring tasks are carried out by the couple in the privacy of their own home. Any kind of intimate examination is the province of other professions.
- Counsellors need to be aware of the possible effects of discussing sexual issues with clients and take care not to give unintentionally confusing or mixed messages. In particular, counsellors should avoid dressing

or behaving in a way which unduly diverts the focus from the clients' sexual difficulties onto the counsellor as a sexual being.
- Transference of a sexual nature between the counsellor and the client is best discussed in a generalised way.
- Physical contact between counsellors using the RELATE Approach and the client is not helpful – in this connection, see the section on boundaries in Chapter 2.
- As with anger, the counsellor holds the right to direct and set boundaries on any discussion.

Other Behaviour

Some clients do prefer to remain almost silent and to listen, where others tend to speak more easily. A counsellor will respect these preferences and allow clients to follow their favoured behaviour where possible. However, counselling using the RELATE Approach is an interactive process which depends on the interchange of feelings and upon a commitment to open communication. Therefore, similar guidelines exist to those given above – the counsellor should not seek to modify the clients' behaviour solely to deal with her own discomfort. However, there are valid practical reasons to ensure that each client is given both chance and encouragement to speak and to listen.

Counsellors should be alert for behaviour which is indicative of mental illness – for example, a taciturnity which might suggest depression or a pressure of speech which may indicate a manic phase. These situations are dealt with in the next chapter.

3ii Behaviour outside Counselling Sessions

The most common cause of concern for counsellors is when a client coming to counselling for a couple problem is engaged in an ongoing relationship with a third party. Some counsellors who use the RELATE Approach establish a counselling contract which makes the discontinuing of the relationship a precondition to counselling. This is not the practice of the authors of this book. Although such a contract would serve to concentrate the client's thoughts and would demonstrate commitment to the primary relationship, it is our experience that to make such a request at too early a stage of the work is to appear to side with one of the partners against the other, and to force a difficult choice upon the other partner before he or she has explored the options. Additionally, such a stance can tempt the client to mislead both counsellor and partner as to what he or she is actually doing. It must be made clear that the counselling will concentrate on the primary relationship and not on the affair. In fact, affairs tend to dwindle away in the course of a successful piece of counselling in which both parties are fully engaged without the need of preconditions being made.

However, as we have stated, the RELATE Approach is designed for couples who wish in the longer term to form an exclusive relationship, and so it would be appropriate to explore this incompatibility with clients who appear to wish to make an additional sexual partner a permanent part of their relationship. There are time-scale differences in the short term, even when the affair has terminated. Both partners will be in a state of grief, one because of the betrayal and the other because of the loss of the intimate affair that may have been important. They will both be in very different positions regarding the processing of their joint grief and need acknowledgement that one has to come to terms with the loss of trust and the other the loss of the affair. There will be a temptation to justify their feelings and behaviour rather than understand each other.

Behaviour outside the counselling setting which may raise concern about continuing to engage the couple in counselling – for example, self-destructive action – is dealt with in the following chapter.

3iii Counsellor Cannot Find a Neutral Position between the Couple

In Chapter 3, we considered the case of Emma and Jane when looking at the Triangular Relationship model. We saw how both clients worked to form an individual relationship with the counsellor which excluded the other – even though neither had a clear idea of what she stood to gain from such a relationship.

Such a theoretical understanding lays behind the RELATE Approach's expectation that clients will on occasions seek to destabilise the triangular relationship which exists between the counsellor and the couple and to exclude their partner from the counselling.

Such actions can range from the comparatively easy to deal with, such as when one client seeks to favour his position over his partner's, to the far more complex and ethically difficult, such as when one partner seeks individual sessions in order to disclose secrets that make the continuation of the joint work far more difficult.

It is helpful if the counsellor makes it plain during the initial sessions that his intention is not to adjudicate between the clients or to favour one client over the other. Rather, the counsellor's role is to improve understanding and communication so that the relationship may prosper. Some counsellors also firmly state in the initial contracting that they intend only to work with the couple together, and decline to see either partner alone. Although helpful in clarifying the couple focus, this approach has distinct disadvantages. Firstly, it works to the disadvantage of clients who wish to do couple work but whose partner cannot or will not attend. Secondly, it denies the counsellor a role in helping a client who may choose to come alone for one or two session for valid reasons – most usually that he or she wishes to clarify his or her thinking on a particular subject before broaching it with his or her partner.

It is important that the counsellor maintains a position of neutrality between the couple and refuses to side with either partner. When a task is set, it is important that it is reciprocal – that both partners are asked to give and that both stand to gain. If a counsellor is concerned that he might be siding with either of the clients, this can be clarified with the couple. In the authors' experience, in a healthy counselling relationship each client feels that the counsellor is somewhat on the other partner's side! The critical point is that both partners should have the same sense of the counsellor's position, and should know that it is safe to raise the issue if they feel they are being sided against.

It is appropriate for a counsellor to resist a request for individual sessions if the purpose within the couple work is unclear. However, in some situations – for example, when there is an antagonistic relationship between the couple which seems to preclude any admission of vulnerability – individuals sessions can be helpful to allow each client to make some movement. In other settings they arise by chance, and can be used productively. Here are some guidelines to help counsellors successfully negotiate them:

- Be even-handed in offering individual sessions – even if the other partner does not take up the offer, it is important that neither client feels particularly favoured or excluded.
- Everything discussed in an individual session is confidential and cannot ethically be disclosed to the partner. However, it is reasonable to set the scene at the beginning by noting that the session is a chance for the client to examine him or herself in the relationship and to work on issues which can eventually be shared and aid the couple. Similarly, it is helpful to leave enough time at the end of the session to explore whether there is anything which cannot be communicated to the partner.
- Try to avoid letting individual sessions be used to discuss the absent partner.

Inevitably, despite these precautions, the counsellor will sometimes be presented with a fact in an individual session which cannot be freely disclosed in the joint sessions. Very occasionally this might be serious enough for the counsellor to feel so compromised that he is unable to continue with the joint work unless the client is willing to disclose this matter to his or her partner. However, more commonly the secret will be containable – such as the fact that one partner is involved in a relationship about which the other partner does not know. In these cases, it is helpful for the counsellor to explore whether the partner is seeking help in disclosing the situation. If the affair is over, disclosure may not be relevant – although careful thought will need to be given to what the couple need to re-establish their relationship and what the individual needs to deal with guilt or grief. If there is to be disclosure, exploring how it might be done is a comparatively simple matter – although the counsellor should not assume that what is rehearsed will necessarily happen. If the client does not wish the matter to be disclosed, it is important that the counsellor makes it plain that this confidential knowledge will not affect her demeanour in the joint sessions. Holding a secret is difficult and often the client will share it with the counsellor in the hope of relieving the tension that the secret brings to the couple relationship. However, if it is disclosed in confidence, the tension has not in fact been relieved in any real way, and it is important that the client is helped to realise this so that he or she may continue to explore how to resolve the uncomfortable situation.

4. FAILURE TO REACH ADEQUATE SHARED UNDERSTANDING

The theoretical framework we have outlined so far has proved to be a robust vehicle for working with a vast range of clients and has generated the most encouraging results. However, it clearly has its limitations, and counsellors using the RELATE Approach will encounter clients whose couple problems demand more specialist knowledge. Let us look at these issues in this final section of the chapter.

It is not reasonable for counsellors who see a full range of couples to burden themselves with the expectation that they can know in advance everything that they need to help their clients. Counselling is about communication and about working together to generate new solutions. Most counsellors who use the RELATE Approach have a general competence in all of the different theoretical models we have outlined, and choose to develop a deeper knowledge of one or two of them which gives a firm theoretical background to their general counselling. We have indicated in the bibliography where counsellors might seek further information.

An equally valuable source of further learning is through supervision.

RELATE offers both group and individual supervision. Group supervision gives counsellors a chance, when presenting a case, to learn from the different theoretical knowledge and the life experiences of a range of counsellors. Individual supervision also contributes greatly to the learning process.

However, despite these inputs, counsellors will still encounter clients whose cultural backgrounds or specific life circumstances demand more knowledge than the counsellor has. In general, the RELATE Approach does not support the assignation of particular clients to particular counsellors, except where counselling needs to take place in a language other than English, or where a specific strong transference means that counselling can only proceed with a counsellor of a certain gender. It is our experience that such an allocation is exceptionally difficult to bring about. Additionally, it can raise expectations in the clients about being intuitively understood rather than having to learn to communicate effectively, and can allow counsellors to continue to marginalise important learning which belongs in the mainstream of counsellor experience rather than with specialists.

In this situation the adage from school teaching that, 'It's OK for the teacher to learn the subject the night before the lesson, but not OK for her to learn it during the lesson' applies to the counsellor. Counsellors have many potential sources of information that they can use to raise their awareness of issues that confront them in the counselling room. It is not reasonable to expect clients from visible minority groups in our society to have to educate their counsellor on all the implications of major general issues faced by them – for example, as members of ethnic minorities, as gays or lesbians, as people with disabilities, or as couples dealing with such problems as infertility or sudden infant death. In addition, counsellors need sufficient knowledge to ask the right questions sensitively so that they can explore the clients' experience of their circumstances, rather than be inhibited by insensitive stereotyping. We live in an age of open communication. Much excellent information and many personal contacts are easily available to any counsellor wishing to broaden his knowledge. This would help him challenge his prejudices about the realities of life for those in the different sub-sections of our community. Counsellors who are unable to uncover the broad realities of life for a particular client group will need to examine the limitations of their personal and professional support networks.

This is not, however, to suggest that the couple counsellor should undertake work where specialist therapeutic skills are needed. Clients who present with mental health problems, addictions, problems of anger management, clear and specific problems with children or other specific needs or traumas often require specialist help alongside or instead of the RELATE Approach to couple counselling.

The next chapter considers this subject in detail.

7

CLIENTS REQUIRING WORK ELSEWHERE

It is the height of folly to want to be the only wise one.
                                                    La Rochefoucauld

RELATE has developed considerable experience in working with a broad range of clients in the time that it has had to develop its counselling approach. Research has shown that RELATE counsellors regularly engage with clients in considerable distress and that from this distress comes a resolution of couple problems.

However, RELATE's experience has also shown that despite the earnest attempts of its counsellors to extend the range of clients with whom couple work can be done as far as possible, there are client problems for which the RELATE Approach either does not offer a solution, or offers only a partial solution.

The concept of one approach only being a partial solution mirrors developments in areas of mental health care. These have moved thinking away from an 'either–or' approach when choosing between interventions, and instead note the strengths and weaknesses of different approaches in order to link them to clients' situations and form care plans. Therefore, workers using the RELATE Approach are becoming more commonly involved in working alongside other practitioners. Counsellors suggest that clients refer themselves to other agencies and receive clients who come on the advice of other agencies with whom they are involved. This is particularly true with the increasing number of counsellors who are attached to GP practices.

The need for a greater understanding of more specialist areas is shown by the fact that the training in the RELATE Approach now includes modules on dealing with: domestic violence; counselling and mental health; working with adult survivors of sexual abuse in the context of couple relationships; alcohol and couples; bereavement; and divorce counselling. All these modules help counsellors assess where the boundaries of the usefulness of the RELATE Approach lies and how the approach needs to be modified when working with certain clients.

Each of these areas is complex and little more than an indication of guidelines can be given here. However, although these are not enough to fully inform practice, we hope they will give readers a sense of how assessment is made and when the Approach varied. This exploration will be done under the following headings:

- Couples and domestic violence.
- Couple work in the presence of mental illness.
- Couple counselling with adult survivors of sexual abuse.
- Clients with other urgent therapeutic needs.

COUPLES AND DOMESTIC VIOLENCE

Over the last two or three years there has been a considerable amount of co-ordinated research and debate on the subject of domestic violence. As the extent and consequences of domestic violence have become more apparent, couple counselling agencies have needed to consider their position in detail and to make their guidelines more explicit for two ethical reasons. Firstly, working in a way which does not clearly address who is responsible for taking action to stop the violence could appear to condone it. Secondly, continuing to work without a definite plan in the presence of ongoing violence might prevent the couple seeking appropriate help to stop the violence. RELATE has been fully involved in this debate and has produced the following guidelines to inform those counselling using the RELATE Approach.

Where ongoing domestic violence exists, the first priority is to address what steps can be taken to end the violence. Counselling may be one, but so equally may individual therapy, separation and legal restraints. Social control is sometimes necessary to stop violence, as violence is a criminal act for which legal sanctions are appropriate. Counselling should not become a diversion from this. Therefore, it is important not to offer counselling if legal action is in process. In other cases a careful assessment is needed initially to ascertain the following points:

- Does the perpetrator take responsibility for the violence, and the survivor for his or her own safety?
- Does the perpetrator agree to no further violence?
- Do both want to come to counselling to end the violence?
- Do both wish to understand the violence – and to contribute to change?

- Do both respect the other's right to speak honestly?
- Is it clear that there is no neurological or psychological impairment that should be referred to a GP or psychiatrist?
- Is it clear that there is no serious alcohol or drug abuse that should be referred to the appropriate agency?

If the answer to all these questions is 'Yes', the RELATE Approach may well be helpful. Although some authorities would question whether a couple model can ever be the most appropriate, the fact that the clients have presented as a couple without coercion and expressed a wish to tackle the problem as a joint one makes the offering of a couple response appropriate. As a general rule, the less chronic the violence, the better the prognosis. In the work, the counsellor takes a clear position that violence is not an acceptable way of dealing with passionate feelings or disagreement.

Counselling is carried out in the recognition that the vast majority of perpetrators of damaging violence are men and their victims women, and that this gender inequality is often reinforced by both physical reality and some societal mores. This does not deny that there is violence initiated by women towards their partners which can be equally damaging, both emotionally and physically. When violence is first highlighted as the problem, no assumptions should automatically be made as to who is the perpetrator. RELATE's suggested approach to counselling couples who have experienced a history of violence, but who have been assessed as suitable for couple work, is similar to the general approach but has specific extra structured elements.

Firstly, communication through the counsellor rather than directly between the couple is encouraged. This is to minimise the risk of any violent interaction between the couple as they discuss their problems and plan physical separation when violence threatens. Successive sessions then concentrate on:

- Tracking actual arguments in detail.
- Considering how the couple behave when they are separate and when they are together.
- Looking at the couple's history with a view to understanding how issues of gender difference, power and control were handled.

The work can be very powerful, and it is important that when the counsellor is concentrating on one partner the other does not feel neglected, as this may recall previous life experiences of neglect. Therefore, the counsellor needs to acknowledge this possibility and allow it to be voiced if need be. Similar feelings of abandonment may well arise when the couple separate rather than become involved in violence, and these feelings need to be normalised.

Work is done with the perpetrator to emphasise that he has choice about whether to be violent or non-violent and has exercised this choice in the past. This allows him to acknowledge that violence is not an integral part of himself, and thus allows him to regain dignity and control. Similarly, emphasis is placed on challenging the notion of 'being provoked', emphasising that the perpetrator has the choice of whether to respond. Once the perpetrator has understood this, he is freed of the feeling that he must have control of his partner to have control of his own life. It is important that the effect of violence on the survivor is not underestimated by it being seen as just one of a number of presenting problems, since the effect of even a single violent episode is to severely undermine trust and to put deep fear into the relationship.

If the contract of no violence has not been established after four or five sessions, or if it cannot be sustained at a later point, then couple work using the RELATE Approach is not possible. The counsellor needs to try and make this ending not seem punitive, but to concentrate on ways of recommending that the clients approach a more specialised source of help, probably as individuals.

COUPLE WORK IN THE PRESENCE OF MENTAL ILLNESS

The last decade has seen a change in practice in the approach to mental illness in Britain. There has been a greater emphasis on care in the community and on moving away from the segregation of the mentally ill. Couple counsellors are being asked to play a greater part in this treatment, and older notions that the existence of mental illness somehow precluded clients from counselling have been challenged and modified.

Counselling has been particularly affected by this change since many branches of counselling grew as a response to the more prescriptive and labelling approach of certain mental health practices. This history has resulted in counselling offering a healthy challenge to many of the more depersonalising practices of psychiatry, and has helped to keep the person behind the illness in view. However, it has at times also led counsellors to take a somewhat simplistic view of mental health issues. To deny the reality and persistence of certain conditions is no more helpful to the clients than the labelling that was being avoided. In the RELATE Approach we have sought to address that split and to encourage a rapprochement between the two areas. There are many cases where no actual diagnosis has been made, and the attribution of illness by one partner to the other is a matter of opinion rather than medical fact. These cases need to be treated with caution, as often the problem can be a shared rather than an individual one. However, there are also many cases where one partner's symptoms clearly exist independently of the couple relationship. RELATE has evolved a set of principles to inform counsellors who wish to use the RELATE Approach with clients who have been diagnosed as suffering from mental illness.

Principles to Inform Work with Clients Who Suffer from Mental Illness

- Mental illness is a real phenomenon for which there exists formulated medical diagnostic and remedial practice. Counsellors using the RELATE Approach should work with due regard to this reality.
- Couple counselling using the RELATE Approach is unlikely to have a curative effect on mental illness apart from on mild reactive conditions. Such outcomes should not be promised or sought.
- The presence of mental illness does not necessarily preclude sufferers from using the RELATE Approach. Resolving such clients' couple problems and increasing their relationship skills is likely to be beneficial to their general mental well-being.
- Once the presence of an illness is noted and understood, great care needs to be taken to assess what work, if any, is possible and to ensure any work that is undertaken is appropriately focused and that it does not increase clients' distress by inducing confusion or anxiety.
- Care needs to be taken to ensure that clients with severe mental disturbance are recognised and if possible directed to an appropriate source of help.

Communication with other workers involved in caring for the clients is encouraged if the clients are in agreement, and often a couple counsellor can help the couple focus on how the diagnoses affect the couple relationship. The most commonly diagnosed mental illnesses are depression and anxiety. Counsellors should ensure that they are familiar with the symptoms of both conditions and are ready to advise sufferers to seek medical help where appropriate. When working with clients where these are a significant influence, counsellors need to be aware that extended exploration alone has not proved to be a useful tool, and indeed in certain circumstances can exacerbate the conditions. In the cases of psychotic illnesses, current research suggests that sufferers can be adversely affected by a high degree of expressed emotion, and thus a goal-orientated approach by the counsellor can be more helpful. Work that relies upon an interpretation of possible unconscious motives should be avoided, and contracts should be kept brief and purposeful. Generally it is suggested that counsellors consider a pragmatic approach which helps the clients move towards a couple adjustment that faces the realities of the conditions, along the lines set out below.

Couple Adjustment to Mental Illness

- The illness is understood by both partners – its symptoms, severity, duration and frequency.
- It is accepted that the sufferer is not to be blamed for being ill.
- It is accepted that the non-sufferer is not to be blamed for finding his or her partner's illness difficult.
- There is a joint commitment to making the relationship work in the presence of the illness.
- Healthy, reasonable and practical ways of acting which alleviate the negative effects of the illness are sought.
- Joint responsibility is taken for seeing these are implemented.
- General couple problems around accepting difference and compromising are not attributed to the illness alone.
- The affected partner is encouraged to express his or her particular needs and to have them met where reasonably possible.
- The non-affected partner is encouraged to express his or her particular frustrations and difficulties and to find support in dealing with these where reasonably possible.

The aim of this approach is to counteract the tendency for the affected partner to carry an over-large responsibility for the relationship problems, and to provide a framework in which the illness can most helpfully be supported.

COUPLE COUNSELLING WITH ADULT SURVIVORS OF SEXUAL ABUSE

As with domestic violence, recent research has revealed that sexual abuse has been a far more widespread phenomenon than was previously reckoned. Research has produced a wide range of figures, dependent on how abuse is defined and how the research is conducted. However, there seems to be a current general agreement to the suggestion that at least one in ten of the adult female population has suffered significant sexual abuse involving actual physical contact before the age of 14. Authoritative figures for male adults are even more difficult to substantiate, but point to a lesser but still significant number. This abuse can often result in impairment of the ability to form good relationships and can lead to inhibited or otherwise damaged sexual responses. Therefore, it is to be expected that many adult survivors of sexual abuse will present as clients for couple counselling, and frequently abuse is first disclosed in such a setting.

RELATE's experience has shown that the medium of couple counselling, sometimes with limited individual work, can be an excellent one for resolving these issues. In other cases, the individual trauma involved is too great to be dealt with within the confines of couple work, and needs more specialist individual work with therapists who are specifically trained and supported.

The following indicators have been evolved to help those using the RELATE Approach decide whether clients who are survivors of sexual abuse can be helped within a couple setting.

Indicators for Couple Counselling to Deal with Effects of Past Abuse

- Client has done previous work on the sexual abuse as an individual.
- Evidence of commitment to the relationship.
- Evidence that the couple are able to communicate with one another.
- Openness to discussion of the sexual abuse between the partners.
- A wish to let go of relationships formed on abusive dynamics.
- Evidence that any individual work within the couple contract could be very short-term i.e. less than six weeks.

Indicators against Couple Counselling to Deal with Effects of Past Abuse

- Sexual abuse has never be disclosed or worked with before.
- No committed relationship exists.
- Evidence of very strong defences against discussion of abuse.
- Need to keep the abuse secret.
- Other clear evidence that substantial individual work is needed.
- Chronic self-destructive behaviour.
- Current other traumatic events needing to be worked through.

CLIENTS REQUIRING WORK ELSEWHERE

The choice to disclose is a most important one for the client. It is helpful if it can be met with acceptance and belief, irrespective of whether the couple counsellor will be able to conduct longer term work with the client.

Work on sexual abuse in the RELATE Approach follows a common five-stage model used in many settings – sometimes described as the journey from being a victim to being a survivor.

1. Telling the story.
2. Working out who was to blame.
3. Expressing the feelings safely.
4. Making sense of what happened.
5. Returning to normal life.

However, in the couple setting there is the added complexity that this path will have to be negotiated by both partners, and that often the original fit of the couple – which could have been based upon one of them being in a victim role – then has to be renegotiated.

Counselling with survivors of sexual abuse requires a calm and thoughtful approach. The work can rouse many uncomfortable feelings in the counsellor – longing to repair the irreparable, deep discomfort with the sense of voyeurism and sexual arousal that can accompany the work, despair at the bleak picture of man's cruelty and indifference to suffering that the accounts of the survivors can paint. Where there is a decision to work, there needs to be a clarity about many issues concerning session boundaries and limits of confidentiality, since the work can result in pressure on these – for example, requests for out of session support or lengthened sessions, threats of self-harm; concerns when children are at risk of abuse in the present.

Two specific dynamics can arise in the counselling which have been the subject of debate and over which the counsellor needs to be especially vigilant.

The first is a relationship pattern which is particularly common where past sexual abuse has occurred. This type of relationship can also occur in many other counselling cases where clients might appear as victims, although it is dealt with at some length here. It was described in Transactional Analysis as the Drama Triangle. This triangle is shown in Figure 7.1. Once a relationship has been formed involving two or more of these roles, it becomes very difficult to move to any different roles apart from the three described.

Let us take an example. A counsellor may see a client who comes alone, with a distressing history of abuse which has been disclosed to no-one else.

```
        Rescuer              Persecutor


                   \           /
                    \         /
                     \       /
                      \     /
                       \   /
                        \ /
                       Victim
```

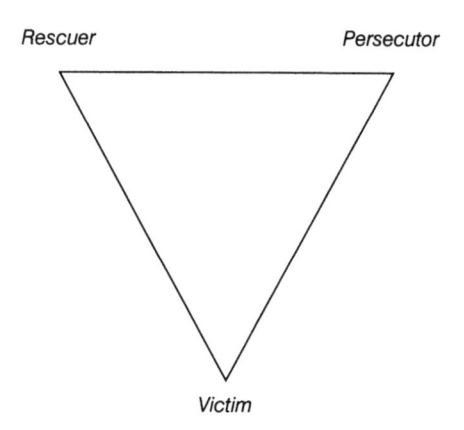

Figure 7.1   Drama triangle

The counsellor sees the client as one of society's victims, and sees herself as the chosen rescuer who can help this client, a feeling reinforced by the client's choice to disclose first to her and the positive outcomes of the first few sessions. In response to these feelings the counsellor allows herself to work in a different way with this client, extending sessions and agreeing to allow extra ones. She does not raise the question of asking the counsellor's husband to join the counselling as she usually would. However, far from being helped by this exclusive attention, the client is encouraged by the counsellor's actions to request more and more support. Soon the counsellor feels she has become the victim, being persecuted by this insistent client, and looks for someone to rescue her – possibly a supervisor who will help her lay down some boundaries. However, when this happens and the supervisor firmly recommends a return to normal counselling procedure, the client abruptly and angrily ends the counselling, feeling again a victim. The counsellor is left feeling she has persecuted her client and been unsympathetically treated by her supervisor. This dynamic can be even more complex and pervasive in couple counselling, where the counsellor can become caught trying to rescue one client from a seemingly persecuting partner, only to be accused of victimising that other partner.

Fortunately, Transactional Analysis not only provides a description of this problem, it also offers a solution (Figure 7.2). By superimposing the triangle upon the parent–adult–child model, it shows us that in this interaction both the persecutor and the rescuer are encouraging the victim to see herself as a child – helpless and in need of parental support, but vulnerable to parental persecution. However, no-one is behaving as an adult – which involves offering realistic choices within a fixed framework and accepting

CLIENTS REQUIRING WORK ELSEWHERE

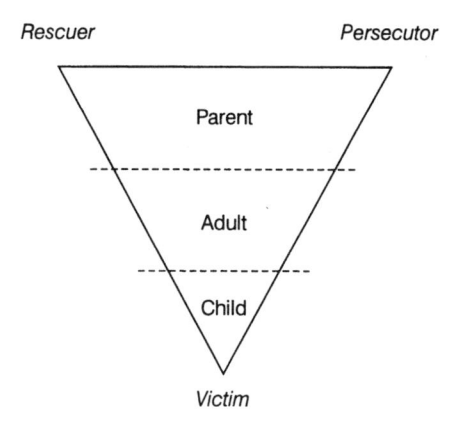

Figure 7.2 Drama triangle and ego states

that past hurts can certainly be explored, mourned and lived with but they can not ever be removed. It is this adult mode which is addressed by the RELATE Approach and many clients can work within this, once encouraged. A client who cannot do so needs a therapist of another discipline.

The second dynamic which seems particularly prevalent in abuse cases is one where the counsellor appears to impose her own agenda upon the client. This has surfaced into public debate around the question of False Memory Syndrome (FMS). Christiane Sanderson has noted in her comprehensive handbook on counselling survivors of sexual abuse (1995) that while the case for FMS remains totally unproved, some poor counselling practice has been highlighted by the debate. Counsellors can move away from the concerns which have brought clients to counselling, preferring rather to concentrate upon a diagnosis of abuse and then taking it upon themselves to urge particular actions upon clients. As we have noted in Chapter Two when discussing boundaries, a fundamental principle of the RELATE Approach is that close attention is always paid to the client's expressed needs, together with a full respect for her autonomy. An understanding of the limits of the couple counsellor's role underlies all the work, and it is particularly helpful to bear this in mind when working with adult survivors.

CLIENTS WITH OTHER URGENT THERAPEUTIC NEEDS

The most pressing cases under this heading are those where clients express the intention to attempt suicide; other difficulties are commonly encountered when a significant role is played by alcohol or when the presenting problem centres around a bereavement.

Clients Who Express Suicidal Thoughts

The clients may have a variety of reasons for expressing an intention to commit suicide in counselling – for example, as a clear indication of a definite plan, as a way of expressing a particular intensity of feeling that cannot otherwise be articulated, or in the hope of influencing the outcome of the sessions. However, there is no evidence that indicates a particular motive is less likely to result in successful suicide – individuals appear to attempt suicide for a variety of reasons, and even if they act on an impulse or from a desire to influence a situation rather than from a clear considered desire to kill themselves, they still run a very high risk of doing themselves serious actual damage.

Therefore, the RELATE Approach suggests that all hints about suicide should be taken most seriously, and that a similar procedure should be adopted in all cases when one is made.

Response to Threats of Suicide

- An overt threat is never ignored, but always taken seriously.
- Room is given for the client to explore his or her ambivalence, i.e. the drawbacks as well as the gains of this course of action: some probably exist because otherwise the client would have already taken action.
- Alternative means of expression of the feelings involved (which can often be of anger as well as of sadness) are sought.
- The client is offered the Samaritans' phone number and encouraged to guard against sudden self-harming urges.
- Tactics are sought to lessen particular exposures to preferred methods – for example, storing extra drugs at a friend's home, avoiding hazardous situations when upset.
- The client is urged to consider seeking medical help and permission is sought for the counsellor to liaise with the client's GP.
- The counsellor works to engage the client in a non-suicide pact. At best this is a promise from the client to do him- or herself no harm. This could be indefinite or, if that is not possible, for a fixed time (for example, during the initial counselling contract, until this marital problem is resolved, until the next session). At the minimum there should be a firmly expressed hope on the counsellor's part that the client will take care of him- or herself.

CLIENTS REQUIRING WORK ELSEWHERE

Once the session is over the counsellor will need to make prompt contact with a supervisor – both to allow them to share the deep ambivalent feelings that clients threatening suicide can engender and to consider whether further action, such as a disclosure, is necessary.

By taking these steps the counsellor is steering a path between two extremes. On the one hand, to ignore or to strongly react against such a significant and important statement by the client implies that either the counsellor does not take what the client says seriously, or else that whether the client lives or dies is a matter of indifference to the counsellor. On the other hand, to react with extreme urgency – for example, by the counsellor offering extra sessions or other panic measures – implies that the counsellor has no confidence in the client's coping and survival skills and also reinforces the belief that the client can get particular attention in the couple relationship by threatening to harm him- or herself. Overall it is the client's decision whether he or she wishes to continue to live. The counsellor does, however, have a short-term responsibility to competently guide the client – especially if there are indicators that the client is in a particularly acute state of crisis.

Counsellors should be especially vigilant and take particular care in directing the client to another source of help if the client appears to be:

- Currently suffering from severe depression.
- Currently in a psychotic state.
- Expressing a strong death wish.

Another indicator of urgency is the presence of more than one of the following:

- A previous suicide attempt.
- A definite choice of method (especially if that method is to hand).
- A suicide note written or contemplated.
- Isolation of the client from others.
- Previous psychosis in self and loved one.
- Recent emergence of the client from a severe depression.
- A lack of obvious secondary gain (e.g. revenge) than can be expressed otherwise.
- Obvious exhaustion of the client's coping resources.
- Frequent resort to alcohol.

There is not space in this introduction to the RELATE Approach to outline the symptoms of depression – however, all counsellors should be aware of them and should exercise particular vigilance when there is a suggestion of suicidal intent.

In the longer term, couple counselling cannot be carried out in the continued presence of acute suicidal intent. Accepting this intent will unrealistically limit what options can be explored in the counselling and will tend to normalise the denial of individual responsibility for survival, which is implicit in the linking by the client of his or her individual will to live to how well the couple relationship is functioning. Therefore, it must be dealt with first, either by work to create an unconditional agreement by the client not to harm him- or herself, or by work to stabilise the immediate situation and then to direct the client to another source of help for his or her distress. There are marked similarities between the approach to suicide risk and the approach to domestic violence – in both the use of a firm contract to contain the risk if counselling is to proceed, and in the attitude which is adopted if such a contract cannot be established. In this case it is important to make clear that the decision not to proceed is being based on what is realistically possible and available for the client, not on a desire to punish him or her or to deny help.

Clients Who Misuse Alcohol or Other Substances

The excessive consumption of alcohol very commonly accompanies a couple problem. In some cases help for the couple relationship enables the clients to moderate their drinking; in other cases, separate treatment for alcohol dependency improves the couple relationship. The situation is complicated by the variance of attitudes towards the consumption of alcohol between different social groups and the difficulty in establishing the precise drinking patterns. Severe dependency makes the client intractable and unable to engage with couple counselling.

If the couple present the misuse of alcohol as part of their problem, the counsellor will find the following indicators useful in making a decision whether to try and counsel the couple or to suggest that they seek help elsewhere. Where alcohol consumption is linked to other major areas which have been addressed in this chapter – for example violence or suicidal intent – it is advisable to address the most immediate issue first.

Indicators That a Couple Approach May Be Helpful

- Alcohol consumption is in a couple context (even if it is only done by one partner).
- Alcohol consumption seems a response to particular problematic couple situations (being alone together, caring for children, socialising, arguing, sexual contact).

- Alcohol consumption has changed in response to changes in the couple situation.
- There is a joint desire to address the patterns of drinking.
- There is ability to discuss drinking patterns openly.
- There is evidence that both partners can modify their consumption of alcohol if they so choose.
- Neither partner's use of alcohol (measured in units per week) constitutes a severe health risk.

Indicators That a Couple Approach May Not Be Helpful or May Need to Be Pursued Only in Conjunction with Other Specific Therapy

- Alcohol consumption leads to markedly changed behaviour.
- One or both partners are unable to take responsibility for their behaviour linked to their consumption of alcohol.
- One or both partners are unable to modify specific patterns of alcohol consumption significantly.
- Alcohol consumption is in response to factors outside the couple relationship, e.g. work stresses, outside social networks.
- The couple cannot reach broad agreement about the amount of alcohol each consumes.
- Alcohol consumption is not a subject which the couple can discuss together.
- Alcohol consumption has caused major problems outside the relationship (loss of work, repeated or major legal prosecution, etc.).
- Clients cannot undertake to attend counselling without having drunk alcohol immediately before.
- Either partner's consumption of alcohol (measured in units per week) is categorised as a severe health risk.

Understanding the precise role of alcohol in any particular relationship requires the counsellor to make full use of her skills of exploration – allowing clients to feel that they are being accepted and not judged. The counsellor will probably need to gain and record specific detailed information about drinking patterns and advance (and if necessary abandon) various hypotheses to explain the alcohol-related behaviour. The unit system of calculating and comparing consumption of different types and volumes of alcoholic drinks, which is now in general use, is a simple and handy tool for relating client's subjective impressions to an objective scale. .

Very similar guidelines would apply to misuse of drugs other than alcohol.

Clients Who Have Suffered Significant Bereavement or Other Losses

Many couple problems are linked to the fact that a significant past loss has remained unmourned by one or both partners. The loss may be connected with a death in one client's family of origin, with the death of a partner or child from a previous relationship, or with the death of a child of the current couple relationship through stillbirth, abortion or miscarriage. A couple of sessions devoted to acknowledging and discussing the significance of this loss, to the feelings of guilt and blame and to how the loss can be mourned may be enough. When more work is clearly needed, the counsellor needs to consider whether it is a realistic possibility to carry this out in the setting of the relationship. Possibly, sustained individual work by another worker who specialises in bereavement is needed.

Similar thoughts apply to the loss of contact with a person by means other than death, such as the permanent placement of a child elsewhere, family separation, denial of legal access, involvement in religious cults, etc. They can also apply to the loss of things other than another person – for example, the loss of a faculty or physical aspect of the self, such as disability, serious injury, physical misuse and disfiguring surgery. The losses caused by emigration, adoption, war and natural disasters are also most significant and need to have time devoted to how it has affected and been experienced by the couple. More is said about loss and endings in the next chapter.

As we end this chapter we are aware of the responsibility counsellors have to guide clients to the appropriate help that they need. It is important that counsellors are aware where couple counselling can help and where it will not. Working inappropriately is misguided and can stop the clients receiving the help that they need. It is not professionally responsible to take clients into inappropriate counselling merely because there is no other source of help available. The first few sessions can be a critical time for assessment so that counsellor and clients are clear about what is possible. Supervision is an important resource to clarify this assessment and, if appropriate, aid a sensitive referral. As the Code of Ethics and Practice for Counsellors states, 'Counsellors shall take all reasonable steps to monitor and develop their own competence and to work within the limits of that competence. This includes having appropriate and ongoing counselling supervision or consultative support' (BAC, 1996).

8

ENDINGS

A work is never completed ... it can only be one stage in a series of inner transformations.

Paul Valéry

Shakespeare's command in *Macbeth* to 'Stand not upon the order of your going, but go at once' is often good advice in everyday life – for example, cutting short protracted partings at railway stations, etc. However, RELATE counsellors are frequently confronted with situations which require a more studied and sympathetic approach.

We have been considering counselling as a vehicle for change. Clients may want these changes but they involve risks and losses as well as benefits and gains. The clients come to counselling with a knowledge that it is going to end and hoping that their goals will have been achieved by that end. However, there is a tension between wanting it to end and avoiding the finality of the ending when faced with it. One of the risks is that despite the endeavour of one partner to keep the relationship going, the other partner may decide to end the relationship. Similarly, one partner may engage with the counselling whilst the other may not. In this chapter we will explore the impact of endings and partings within the casework and the termination of the counselling relationship itself. There are many different endings, varying from the abrupt withdrawal of clients to a longer planned termination. This may reflect the clients' experience of endings or may be a reaction to the counselling process. Counsellors who have not resolved their own experiences of loss and attachment can further impede a satisfactory completion of the agreed work. Relationships are continually developing and changing in a satisfactory or unhealthy way and thus the question for both clients and counsellor is, 'When do we know when the counselling is finished?'

When the work is clearly not going to be concluded by the RELATE Approach we need to look at how the ending of counselling is going to be managed or adapted. Regular reviewing and checking out what the clients think monitors progress and blocks. However, if little has been achieved by 10 sessions or so, there are some possibilities to consider.

Some clients do appear to make consistent progress but it seems very slow. This may be due to their own individual learning patterns. It may be because they are deeply uncertain and need longer-term support to counteract some of the consistent negative messages they have received in the past. In such cases the RELATE Approach should be adapted to allow an appropriately longer time scale. This rarely takes longer than 26 sessions. It is important to keep this work client-centred to allow the learning to be consolidated by the clients, rather than allow them to be pulled along a path that they are not ready to negotiate. This longer commitment should not be confused with psychotherapy, with the counsellor taking a much more central position in the clients' lives. The focus will still be on the couple problems.

Some clients clearly do not progress but are committed to resolving their problems. Counsellors need to look at what is blocking the counselling. Chapters 6 and 7 describe common blocks and resistance. If there are no signs of such problems, the counsellor may wish to consider whether a different and more specialised approach – behavioural, systemic or psychotherapeutic – might be more helpful. Often clients who do not respond to RELATE's more client-centred and flexible approach can be helped by a different and more firmly defined discipline.

During the counselling it may become clear that the original presenting problem of couple difficulties has now moved to a decision that one or both the partners cannot come to terms with. The decision to separate is rarely a joint one made at the same time.

CLIENTS WISHING TO END A COUPLE RELATIONSHIP

It is difficult to differentiate between clients who have relationship problems and clients who wish to end their relationship, since the difference may only be a small one of degree. The couples in one group may easily become members of the other group, depending upon what emerges during the counselling. Often the boundary does not have to be drawn too precisely, since a large proportion of counsellors who work remedially to help couples resolve problems also work as divorce and separation counsellors. They help couples who feel they wish to separate explore this option and make a decision. If the decision is to separate, the clients will be encouraged to consider why the relationship has come to an end and how best to deal with the ending.

Divorce counselling does not fall within the confines of this particular book, and requires specific skills and knowledge that have not yet been touched upon. However, we will summarise the areas of importance to enable readers to consider how they should best approach couples wanting to end their relationship. This is done because couples in crisis are often balanced on the point of deciding whether to separate or to attempt to resolve their problems. RELATE's experience suggests that this is a critical time for the counselling work. Counsellors need a particular awareness of the dynamics that are present and skill at working with them if they are not to move into a position which ceases to be congruent with the clients – either because they are advocating saving the relationship when the clients have ceased to believe this is possible, or because they are introducing the question of endings when the clients are still struggling with the hope of retaining the relationship.

The four basic components a counsellor needs to work with couples at the point of separation are as follows:

1. The ability to take a strategic approach to couple separation.
2. An understanding of the emotional dynamics of the couple considering separation.
3. An ability to work with a couple at the point of deciding about separation.
4. A knowledge of the routes and resources available for a separating couple.

A Strategic Approach to Couple Separation

The early stages of the process of couple separation consist of the following stages:

- Disillusion.
- Erosion.
- Detachment.
- Physical separation.

Some of the first two processes will have taken place before the couple present for counselling. We have seen in the cases throughout this book, that couples frequently have wishes and fantasies about the partnership that end in disillusion. Relationships can be further strained by other circumstances that disappoint the couple, amplifying this disillusion. By the time they come to counselling the relationship is often in crisis. In many cases one or both clients may have definitely made their minds up to leave, in which case the outcome is decided. It takes two people to make a relationship, but only one to decide to break it. However, many others will be unsure.

The outcome will depend upon a number of factors, which include:

- The clients' original expectations of the relationship.
- How much the clients' goals have changed during the relationship.
- How much the clients have personally changed during the relationship.
- Whether these changes have placed the clients closer or further apart overall.
- How much goodwill has accrued during the relationship.
- How much resentment has built up during the relationship.
- What the individual circumstantial pressures are for and against separation.
- What the broader societal pressures are for and against separation.
- The strength of each client's hope that he or she might get his or her needs met in the relationship.
- The strength of each client's hope that he or she may get his or her needs met outside the relationship.
- Each client's capacity and willingness to accept disappointment.
- Each client's capacity and willingness to embrace change.
- The clients' ability to express themselves on these matters.
- The clients' ability to understand their partner's position on these matters.
- The clients' ability to find agreement with each other on any course of action.
- The counsellor's ability to help the couple discuss the issue of whether to separate productively.

These factors will not only have affected how much of the foundations of the relationship have been eroded, but also how much of that foundation existed in the first place. Exploring and understanding these issues defines what capacity there is to renegotiate the relationship.

In this complex situation the counsellor also brings a set of values. At one extreme a counsellor may believe separation always represents the less desirable option, and so helps the couple cherish and build on any hope that remains, no matter how small or how long it may take. At the other extreme another counsellor may feel that there is little point in working on a deeply eroded relationship, since the fulfilment of each individual is far more important than preserving a couple relationship. It is important that the counsellor is clear of her own values and does not get into a collusion with the partner that best reflects her personal constructs. As in all counselling, maintaining a neutral position and being aware of one's own values is essential.

RELATE statistics show that 25% of couples who have separated when they start RELATE counselling are reunited. Other research suggests that 30% of partners who wished to separate at the point of crisis, regret their decision within two years. Divorce and separation can have a harmful psychological and economic effect on the family. However, there is evidence that the structure of the family is changing in many industrialised countries, and that attempts to hold a couple together in the face of a considered determination to leave is at best pointless and at worst actively counter-productive.

Based on a consideration of these and other facts, RELATE advocates that counsellors offer joint work to couples who are considering separation. This should be long enough for each partner to consider the implication of his or her choice, so that any decision is an informed one based on realistic understanding. If both partners agree to engage with this work, it typically takes a period of about 6–10 weeks. This time is spent in looking at the history of the relationship and allowing both partners to explore their options and to hear their partner make a similar exploration. The time that can be spent in such a truly indeterminate state appears to be limited by the natural human desire to make a decision and to resolve painful conflicts in one direction or another. Once this consideration has been given and a decision is made, it is for the clients to choose the route they wish to take, without the counsellor urging any particular outcome.

The Emotional Dynamics of a Couple Considering Separation

When a couple are close to the point of separation, the atmosphere in the counselling room is particularly charged. Separation from a partner is one of the most stressful life events, and this is underlined by the fact that in the counselling room clients feel the most primitive of feelings, moving from one extreme to another. Such an atmosphere is not an easy one to work in, and the counsellor must guard against the temptation to prematurely limit the distressing disagreement. This commonly occurs in one of three ways:

- By the counsellor pushing the couple to decide to focus on only one of the options – either to separate or to remain together. Conflict can be lessened by doing this, but so is the chance of a full consideration of the choices.
- By the counsellor over-emphasising the view of only one client. Frequently one client sincerely wishes to save the relationship, while the other strongly wants to end it. This degree of conflict is distressing, but unless both clients feel that their opinion is being listened to, there is little chance of them also listening to their partner.

- By focusing totally on one issue to an exclusion of the others. Frequently this one issue is the welfare of the children. This is a vitally important issue, but in many ways it is dependent upon a clear decision being made about the future of the relationship. The future of each individual family member is an important *part* of this decision, but it is not the whole of it.

Working at the Point of Separation

Working with a couple at the point of making a decision about separation requires the counsellor to be able to firmly hold a central position. As with couples dealing with violence, communication often has to be through the counsellor rather than between the couple, with the counsellor ensuring each person is helped to articulate their feelings and to listen to their partner. Accusations about the other person's behaviour, attempts to allocate responsibility or listing of past faults are less helpful. When a decision – be it either to work on or to end the relationship – has been made, the couple can begin to explore how they will communicate together about the past. However, to make that vital decision they often need the counsellor's active help in ensuring that all the necessary opinions have been heard and registered but that the couple are not side-tracked into repeatedly revisiting old disagreements.

A particular counselling skill that is needed at this point is the ability to work productively with a *split agenda*. This requires the counsellor to be able to accept that each client may have a passionately held desire for a particular list of outcomes, yet this may not strike any common chord in his or her partner. Whereas at other points in couple counselling it may be more relevant to search for common ground and to seek the common threads in a disagreement, the decision about separation requires a true and accurate inventory to be drawn up of the differences between the couple. This inventory needs to address what their differences are, how great they are and whether either partner considers that there is room for compromise. Although it can be immensely difficult for the counsellor to help each client face the differences which separate them from their partner, only when each person can do so can there be any hope that a realistic and achievable decision about the future can be made.

Divorce and Separation Counselling

If the decision to work to rebuild the relationship is made, the counsellor is then able to employ the skills and knowledge which we have described previously. If the decision is made to separate the clients may wish to continue with couple counselling to explore some of the following issues:

- Understanding why the relationship existed and why it has come to an end.
- Understanding how the end of the relationship can be publicly marked and explained.
- Deciding how the couple will continue to relate together.
- Handling the actual separation.

For each individual there may be work to be done on the following issues:

- Reflecting on the ended relationship.
- Deciding how they wish to live now.
- Experimenting with how they intend to form relationships in the future.

There may be a need for mediation and conciliation work for the couple in the future, to allow them to decide on specific issues concerning family arrangements.

With each separating couple who wish to do further work these final sessions have to be planned with care. Some work can clearly be done together. However, the reality of separation is that the couple will begin to change independently of each other, and will cease to know each other so intimately. It is helpful if the counselling can reflect this reality, and thus help the acceptance and mourning of the ending – a mourning which should not be mistaken for a desire to reform the relationship.

The counsellor has been a joint asset of the couple and so it helps if future counselling arrangements can model an agreed division of this asset. At the ending of some relationships the issue of 'Who gets the counsellor?' can arise and no suitable answer can be found. The counsellor then needs to be sensitive to not undoing previous work by appearing to favour one partner over the other. Other couples are more accommodating in separation, and can allow room for the counsellor to work with one partner by mutual agreement. Work with a newly separated individual is sometimes largely about grief work, but is often also characterised by an emotional energy comparable to that of adolescence.

ENDING THE COUNSELLING

When the work has been achieved by the RELATE Approach, counselling should model a good ending. Ideally this is arrived at by joint planning of both counsellor and clients. We have looked at contracts and reviews in Chapter 2 because they play an important part in the planning of endings. Regular reviews highlight what has been achieved and what has been disappointing. Achievements are quickly integrated and become part of the norm for the couple. If they cannot remember them, they are more likely to dwell on what they have not achieved, which further undermines their ability to change anything. Contracts also serve the purpose of reminding clients that counselling is finite. This is not used as a threat but as a management tool to chart the progress and disappointments of the work.

We have already discussed how important it is to be able to integrate the good and the bad feelings about the first important attachment figure in our lives. If we are unable to attain this, we split off the unacceptable feelings and project them onto someone else. The ending process has a similar dynamic. If the counselling was not considered good enough, it may be that the clients prefer to blame the counselling rather than take the responsibility for the stagnation of the relationship. The splitting and projecting will have become part of the ending process and probably a reflection of the couple problems. This is likely to happen to 'Babes in the Woods' relationships where the bad is always projected outside the couple. The counsellor may have been idealised, someone who would save the relationship and is then denigrated for not doing so. George and May, first introduced in Chapter 3 as the 'cat and dog' couple, were able to look at their splitting and projecting and adapted their relationship to a more manageable level. Theirs would always be a fiery relationship but at the end of counselling they were able to see what they had achieved and had a framework to work with. This was a realistic ending to the counselling. Thus, an essential part of the ending where there is this type of interaction is not to get drawn into the conflict. Understanding the projections and helping the couple withdraw them will enable a healthy conclusion. In counselling terms the counsellor should become the 'good object' that is internalised by the clients and taken away with them.

The ending of counselling reflects much of the underlying dynamic that defines some of the couple problems. The counsellor who worked with George and May knew that the couple would not be able to tolerate the ambivalent feelings associated with endings. They finished abruptly on the concluding session rather than reflect on the ending. Similarly, Emma and Jane with their problems with triangular relationships did not want to linger over the termination of counselling. Neither were so threatened by the possibility of being excluded as they were at the beginning of counselling. However, the counsellor was aware that Emma might want a final session on her own. This did not happen as both Jane and Emma recognised that it was a pattern of behaviour that they could both revert to when feeling uncertain. Soulla and Michael had to be gently coached into an ending, reflecting how they still tended to be dependent on rules and systems. Darren and Susan, first introduced in Chapter 3, began to sum up the work that they had achieved but then rang and cancelled the final session as they felt sure the counsellor should see other clients who needed her more. This left the counsellor unsettled and wondering. During supervision she realised that both Darren and Susan saw themselves as rescuers, and although they may have learned a great deal in the counselling they were keen to consider others who were more needy than they were.

An essential part of ending counselling is to be able to take the criticism that the clients may level at the counsellor. It is disappointing when the change that has been longed for cannot happen. The counsellor may be equally discouraged by the outcome. It can be tempting to defend what has been achieved rather than stay with the sad feelings surrounding the changes that have not been possible. It is important that this is not colluded with. The disappointment is not the reason to leave but needs to be balanced with what been achieved and what opportunities may arise in the future. It will not help the clients if they leave angry with the counselling because the counsellor wants to avoid discussing the disappointments.

Integrating the 'good counsellor' can become very apparent in the counselling when it is moving towards the end of the contract. Clients often remark that they sometimes think in the middle of an exchange, what would the counsellor say about this? In other words, they are able to suspend what is happening and put themselves in the counsellor role. This is a valuable first step to integrating their own counsel. Endings have a particular significance for clients who have issues with attachment in their intimate relationships. It is a natural interaction for clients who have a history of wanting to please, to also behave in the same way with the counsellor. Dionne and Martin, first introduced in Chapter 3, demonstrated this in very clear ways in the counselling. The ending was likely to generate anxiety that reflected the couple dynamic.

> Dionne was the 'good client' who checked appointment times and always made sure that she arrived on time. Her anxiety was that the counselling would end suddenly, before she was ready. Martin had no such worries. The couple had both engaged with counselling and had improved their communication so that their partings and meetings were much better organised. Martin still remained the more detached of the two but Dionne no longer experienced it as personal rejection. A third six-week contract was agreed to review how they were experiencing the relationship now.
>
> Dionne realised that she felt much less distressed. Martin agreed. He had realised on some level that leading his rather lackadaisical existence contributed to her anger. He now knew that he did it partly because he was comfortable in his own company, but also to avoid her. When she 'got in a

state' he always wanted to run away. The genogram had highlighted their specific losses so that they had a greater understanding of themselves as individuals and how it affected the partnership. Their expectations and experiences of bonding were very different. They had started to value that difference, rather than see it as a threat. The counsellor felt that their relationship was on a much firmer footing. Martin agreed, but Dionne wanted to come to counselling once a month, just to 'check things were going OK'. She had stopped struggling so hard to hold onto her relationship with Martin as there was less of a need to. Instead she was trying to hold onto the counsellor, with whom she had formed a trusting relationship. It was Martin who recognised this. Dionne always hated to lose contact with anybody, even her patients at work. The remainder of the work centred around how she survived these partings and how to put the counsellor into a more realistic context. Dionne agreed to the ending, but always sent a Christmas card to the counsellor with the message, ' Just to remind you of us!'

There is no clear end point in counselling, which is why contracting and reviewing will facilitate an ending that can be arrived at. Understanding the relationship allows the couple to start changing some of the behaviours and attitudes that persist to undermine it. The counselling process encourages the change and looks at what might hinder that change. It looks at the successes and failures. People fail and revert to old ways of thinking and behaving. The difference is that if they have the understanding they can use the skills they have learned to accept the 'failure' and move on. Good counselling encourages the clients to believe that they can sustain the change that they have made and forgive themselves for the fallbacks.

RELATE's Approach does not allow for phased endings. Each contract should have a focus and as new understandings emerge, so the possibility of further work arises. Phased endings can muddle clients who are working towards autonomy. We believe that the counselling should be reviewed regularly and in depth so that clients are clear about what may lie ahead of them and what the possible fall-backs are. Offering clients a decreasing number of appointments over months would seem to undermine their ability to sustain change and understanding. It also may feed into the omnipotence of the counsellor that in some way they will not be able to manage without her. Thus, endings and how they are handled can be loaded with significance for both clients and counsellors. For every change, however much wanted, there has to be acknowledgement of some loss and the accompanying mourning.

MOURNING

We have seen that the loss of a person that one is attached to, whether it be bereavement or the end of a close relationship, results in a similar pattern of reaction. Bowlby originally studied children and their reaction to loss of their initial important attachment figure, but these experiences can be carried through to adult intimate relationships. Clients who have experience of a loss that has not been mourned will find any ending, whether it is their current relationship or the counselling itself, very painful. Mourning is not a time-limited crisis. It is a process of adjustment with periods of regression at certain times. People who have suffered loss may feel that they are recovering, only to find that they may be suddenly tipped back to feelings of primeval despair. Exploring the patterns of reaction does not short-cut the process in any way, but can reduce some of the anxiety. Knowing that these feelings are 'normal' and part of grieving puts them into a more manageable context.

Patterns of reaction:

- Shock, denial, disbelief.
- Alarm, panic, anxiety.
- Anger, protest.
- Sadness, grief, depression.
- Re-building, re-integration.

There are no rules about these patterns of reaction. People in mourning can experience all or some of these emotions at various times. However, for some, the feelings are too intense or frightening to endure and so they take flight into some defensive thinking or behaviour to avoid the feelings. These buried or avoided feelings can be resurrected when a new or impending loss is experienced. This loss will make the client redouble the effort to stop the pain and the whole cycle of avoidance is restarted. The counselling room should provide a safe place of containment to look at these patterns and explore the areas of concern. Some of the losses and incomplete grieving may stretch back to childhood experiences and some may be more recent. They often have a common factor in that the client cannot express one or more parts of the grief process. The avoidance of this takes all their energy so that they cannot address the underlying feelings. These feelings take on an intensity that is out of all proportion to reality. Any kind of intimacy is associated with the possibility of overwhelming loss. Let us look at a part of a case where this became the focus of the initial work and alerted the counsellor to possible problems at the end of counselling.

> Sarah's father died when she was 11. He had been in and out of hospital for some time. Her mother was completely tied up with his treatment and Sarah took on the role of housekeeper and parent to her younger brother for much of the time. Her father was nursed at home for the last two months of his life

and she helped with his caring. He told her that she was a marvellous little girl and not to be sad when he died. She must carry on looking after her mother and brother. Mother went into a deep depression after Father died and she suffered poor mental health from then on. When Sarah grew up she married Neil, who also suffered precarious mental health. Neil committed suicide two years before Sarah came into counselling and her friends were impressed by how well she had managed after his death. She had recently met Richard, who was a widower. His wife had died some five years previously and they had met at a local support group. He was being tremendously patient and understood that she did not want to be rushed, but it was clear that he wanted much more than a friendship. Sarah was very attracted to him both physically and emotionally and they had started a more committed intimate relationship. However, she had suffered two severe panic attacks, and her GP had referred her to RELATE because she felt they were allied to the loss of her husband.

Sarah presented herself as bright and cheerful and felt that her doctor was over-reacting. She had a full life balancing a job and looking after her children. Richard was not putting her under any pressure at the moment, and she was enjoying their relationship. He knew that she was coming to RELATE and had wanted to come with her. She had been surprised by this but felt strongly that she wanted to come alone. This counselling was to look at what might be behind the attacks and she failed to see what could be gained by Richard being there. The counsellor noted this strength of feeling but agreed that they would work together for the next four sessions alone to explore Sarah's feelings around the loss of her husband. The therapeutic alliance would have to be well established before the counsellor could raise the subject of Richard attending the sessions, and yet the counsellor felt that their new and increasingly intimate relationship had a vital role in how Sarah was feeling now. She knew that she risked colluding with Sarah, but she sensed that she would lose her if she referred to it again until later.

Sarah missed Neil terribly in the first few months but he had a long history of attempted suicide and she felt she could have done nothing to stop him. The counsellor liked Sarah and admired her determination. However, she felt curiously detached from her and even further distanced from her sad story. Was this the counsellor's own fear of acknowledging loss or was it a counter-transference in the room? This interaction was discussed in supervision. The counsellor was reminded that Sarah had said that Richard complained sometimes that she 'shut him out'. This was exactly how the counsellor felt and led to the detached feeling. Sarah appeared not to have even started the grieving process, starting right back in her childhood. Her father had told her not to be sad and that was what she had put her energies into. Sadness to her meant mental illness and loss of the family. She had buried all the feelings attendant on loss and had learned to put on a brave face. This false face kept her safe but also distant to those closely linked to her. She connected all sadness, anger, protest and despair with annihilation, rather than allow herself to experience them in a more realistic framework. Once the counsellor reached this empathetic understanding with Sarah, the work moved on with much more clarity. The counsellor allowed her the time and space to look at her losses so that she experienced the feelings without the accompanying fear of her very survival. The next focus of the work would be whether she could risk allowing Richard into the relationship without the fear that something out of her control would befall them. Sarah's experience of close relationships was that they were taken away from her. Great care had to be taken with the termination of this case.

The goals had been achieved in that Sarah had no repeat panic attacks and felt comfortable that she and Richard were developing a good relationship that satisfied them both. Initially she minimised any problem with the ending of counselling. She was fine now. The counsellor reminded her that this was how she had first presented at counselling and wondered what was different. They agreed to four sessions to see what could be different about this ending. They discussed how good it would be if Sarah could make the decision and take control of when it should finish. She suspected that she might not turn up for the last session and so it was agreed that she would phone and confirm the appointment. The last session went very well, reviewing and underlining what she had achieved since Neil had died. The counsellor had enjoyed working with her and wished her well for the future. She had no doubts that Sarah had the abilities to continue to have a good relationship with Richard. The counselling work was finished. Sarah had decided that 'it was enough for now'.

Endings and partings are integrally linked with the mourning process. Loss has to be acknowledged, giving plenty of time and space to listen to the story. Endings have a different impact on people, depending on how they have experienced them in the past. These patterns need to be explored in order to manage the end of a relationship, whether it is within the casework as part of the clients' history or as part of the present counselling. In general terms, the time set aside to terminate effectively is directly proportional to the duration of the counselling. The clients may become very attached to the counsellor with whom they work for a long time. There will be more information to review and more set-backs to acknowledge. Their dependency on the counselling process to explore new work will be stronger. Conversely, clients are likely to be less attached to counsellors with whom they have worked for only a short time. This is further underlined by the fact that in short contracts, the end of the counselling is in sight and clearly acknowledged at the beginning of the contract.

Counselling is like peeling an onion, layer by layer. The focus of the work emerges during the exploration stage and the contract will be agreed for the number of sessions that are deemed necessary. Further work may emerge during these initial sessions, which may be suitable to be addressed in current counselling or may have to be looked at later. This can be further complicated by the different time-scales individuals need to process understanding and the nature of the problem. For example, Sarah in the case study needed time to experience her new understanding of endings and loss and how she associated them with any intimate relationship. She had coped well with the termination of counselling and the end of the relationship with the counsellor with whom she had felt very close and trusting. She knew that the counsellor had a belief in her and her ability to cope with fall-backs to old destructive feelings. Counsellors who can model such good endings and have a genuine belief that their clients are ready to move on, greatly assist the ending process.

Thus, as each layer is uncovered, the counselling has to be planned as to whether a further contract is set immediately, or whether the clients need to take some time out and live in their adapted framework. These endings should be very clear, with the understanding that further work may be done in the future. This will be the clients' decision. However, some issues that may initially appear to be manageable, may be more embedded than originally thought. Obsessions such as alcohol abuse, eating disorders or violence may be causing problems for the couple. It is the degree of the problem that has to be monitored. If the problem dominates the couple relationship so that no work can be done, an appropriate referral should be made. This is not to deny that there is a relationship problem or to say that one partner is the cause of it. The couple have to be managing these obsessions to some degree before they can look at the relationship.

DIFFICULT ENDINGS

So far we have looked at good endings, where there is time and space to explore the achievements and disappointments in both the couple relationship and the counselling. However, clients can abruptly withdraw from counselling, and it is important to look at what might be the contributing factors to this. It is sometimes easier to label the clients as too defensive or guarded to take on the difficulty of counselling, rather than believe that the counselling was at fault.

Poor Therapeutic Alliance

Throughout this book we have emphasised the importance of engaging with the client. In couple counselling, this is further complicated by having to engage with both partners and the relationship that they bring. Our knowledge of the triangular relationship model informs us of the potential for rivalry for the counsellor's attention in the sessions. Counsellors can complain of being deskilled by clients. They can consider this an explanation of why the clients withdrew. However, we believe that although counsellors may have a preferred way of working, it is primarily the job of the counsellor to be adaptable enough to find a way of engaging with the clients. If one partner complains of not understanding or not being heard, the counsellor must acknowledge this and take responsibility. It may be a reflection of the couple relationship, but it may be a lack of the counsellor's skill. Unless it is addressed, that client will be lost.

Overwhelming Anger

Clients come to counselling for some kind of change. During the exploration part of the process, some clients realise that their old ways have been very limiting. The anger and hurt that this can engender may be too painful to continue. One couple had suffered a very difficult marriage for many years, exacerbated in latter years by the woman's secret drinking. It became very clear to the counsellor that no couple problem could be addressed while the woman continued to drink to distance herself from the painful feelings. This became the primary focus for the counselling because the need to drink was paramount. The wife came to see that she needed specialist help with this problem, before they could look at their joint troubles. On the final session, the woman raged at what lay ahead of her. Her dependence on alcohol had not started the conflict. She had turned to it to stave off the hurt and now it was going to be taken away from her. It may have limited her but she had survived. In a case like this, the anger is a defence against what is to come. It is better for the counsellor to understand this rather than counteract it in any way. The price of change may be too high. It may require clients to be more active than they believe they can possibly be. Some clients may recognise that they would prefer to stay in the unhealthy relationship that they are familiar with, rather than risk uncertainty and change.

Denial

Pretending that the counselling will continue and that no ending has been discussed is a common way to avoid endings. Martin, who tended towards detachment in all his relationships, never remembered when a contract was finishing. It was part of his underlying belief and thus an important part of the work. Clients like him can delay the ending work by absenteeism or turning up late. The counsellor had to draw attention to the delaying tactics, so that a more proactive, satisfactory end could be achieved.

Regression

This is another way of avoiding the end. If the clients have engaged well and trust their counsellor, they may have formed a strong bond. When these bonds are threatened the clients may regress to feelings of great anxiety and protest. They may slide back to being dependent on the counsellor, clinging together and finding new problems to work with. This should not be confused with genuinely new insights that might be worked with. The new problems may be different superficially but maintain the same underlying dynamic. The counsellor will need to identify what this is and help the clients look at when these problems are most likely to arise. Looking at where and when it is likely to happen gives the clients the confidence that they are equipped with the skills to handle future problems.

Flight

Just as some people gradually unwind from a relationship without discussion, so some clients will reduce their interaction with the counselling. They may appear bored and withdrawn so that finishing will be a relief rather than a celebration. They may find other means of support before technically finishing so that they can drop out early. Some clients may avoid the final session by taking flight into good health. They will reassure themselves and the counsellor that everything has been achieved. In reality they cannot bear to look at what they have not accomplished and what may lie ahead of them. It is unhelpful to counteract these beliefs; it is the clients' way of coping with the impending close of counselling.

Clients may withdraw abruptly from counselling for all or some of these reasons, despite having a good therapeutic relationship with the counsellor. We believe that a simple letter to acknowledge that the counselling has terminated and offer the hope that they may want to return in the future, constitutes a better ending than no further contact. Self-discovery is a process and later on they may feel embarrassed about leaving prematurely. The letter acknowledges their right to leave but allows an open door to return.

When reviewing what has been understood about a relationship, there can be a discrepancy between what the counsellor hoped and what the clients achieved. The counsellor may be assessing her own performance rather than keeping the client needs as a priority. The counsellor has to come to terms with what cannot be done in exactly the same way as the clients have to. Part of the process of counselling is for the counsellor to keep notes of the problems that have been identified to work with. This structure allows the clients to explore quite freely because the counsellor will keep the sustained focus of the work. These notes will help the counsellor evaluate what has been achieved. At the end of counselling the counsellor will have to check out what each partner is understanding

ENDINGS

about each other and the relationship. It is important to explore whether this understanding reduces the problems and gives the partners skills to handle future problems. Requiring this to be clearly expressed not only confirms it for the clients, it also helps the counsellor separate her own ambitions and hopes from those of the client. The counsellor may have to deal with her own feelings of rejection. The clients have engaged with her, may have become dependent on the counselling, but now no longer need her.

One of the interesting developments in counselling can be the subtle change of power. Initially, the counsellor is invested with all the knowledge and authority of how this relationship functions. When clients engage well with the process and gain their own insights to how they operate as a partnership, this balance of authority tips back towards the clients. During the final sessions the clients may feel that they have shared an enormous amount of intimate detail about themselves that they want to redress. It is not uncommon for leaving clients to suddenly show a great deal of interest in the counsellor personally. It is a desire to equalise and normalise the relationship. Counsellors may find this uncomfortable but it is a natural progression and should be recognised as such. Some clients may want to give the counsellor a gift as part of this equalising process and as a genuine sign of their appreciation of the work that has been done. It would seem churlish to us to refuse small gifts. However, gifts of large value or money should not be accepted personally but perhaps accepted on behalf of the organisation if appropriate and agreed with the clients. Some clients want to show their appreciation by working for the organisation in some voluntary capacity. This is a possibility but must be handled sensitively. What they may do and how long in the future needs to be discussed with the supervisor. It would not be appropriate if it is a disguised way of hanging onto their counsellor.

Some counsellors find it difficult to accept the limitations of the work. The unskilled counsellor may be tempted to try and cram in some of the unexplored work towards the end of counselling. This only confuses the clients and may burden them with an anxiety, which in truth belongs to the counsellor. Counsellors who have not resolved their own problems with endings, may allow the clients to coast rather than bring the work to some kind of conclusion. Self-awareness and supervision will minimise this risk. It is essential to know what kind of partings the practitioner is comfortable with. In their private lives, these can range from an informal, pragmatic good-bye around the kitchen table, to running alongside the moving train, hands outstretched, to keep contact until the last moment. Counsellors need to know to which end of the scale they belong so that they can separate their own experience of endings from those of the clients.

The ending of training of the counsellor will often highlight these personal experiences. It is similar to the end of counselling for the clients. Knowledge and skills have been taught and explored to aid understanding. Awareness and attitudes have been juggled with to expand emotional intelligence and insight. The over-riding anxiety for both the newly trained counsellor and the ending clients is, 'Do I know enough?', or the more angry, 'Is this all?' The answer is that the real work for clients relating together starts when the counselling is finished. The counselling is just a catalyst for change that the clients will make and hopefully continue to make for the rest of their lives. Similarly, the counsellor at the end of her training now has a basic knowledge of human relationships to hand, but will continue to develop her emotional intelligence, to enable the clients through experience and clinical practice. It is what makes the job endlessly fascinating. Counsellors who believe that they are 'expert' limit themselves and in turn limit their clients.

In conclusion, endings by definition require something to be left behind. This allows for new beginnings and opportunities. Just as the child has to integrate good and bad in order to separate from mother, so must the adult individual acknowledge the strengths and weaknesses of the relationship that they are leaving or rebuilding. This applies to both the intimate relationship of a couple partnership and the counselling interaction that has to come to an end. Dependence on the counselling for a time may have been appropriate while exploring the problems, but the clients should now have the skills to resolve the problems that they can change, and adapt to the ones that cannot be resolved. They will fail and falter on the way but will have the confidence to sustain the change. Their autonomy is a time for a little sadness and reflection for both clients and counsellor, but it is also a celebration.

BIBLIOGRAPHY

Beck, A. (1988). *Love Is Never Enough*. Penguin, Harmondsworth.
Berne, E. (1968. *Games People Play*. Penguin, Harmondsworth.
Bowlby, J. (1988). *A Secure Base*. Routledge & Kegan Paul, London.
Bowlby, J. (1979). *The Making and Breaking of Affectional Bonds*, Tavistock, London.
Brown, D. and Pedder J. (1979). *Introduction to Psychotherapy*. Routledge, London.
Burnham, J. (1986). *Family Therapy*. Routledge, London.
Cade, B. and O' Hanlon, W. (1993). *A Brief Guide to Brief Therapy*. W.W. Norton, London.
Casement, P. (1985). *On Learning from the Patient*. Routledge, London.
Casement, P. (1990). *Further Learning from the Patient*. Routledge, London.
Clulow, C. (1993). *Rethinking Marriage: Public and Private Perspectives*. Karnac, London.
Clulow, C. and Mattinson, J. (1989). *Marriage Inside Out*. Penguin, Harmondsworth.
Crowe, M. and Ridley, J. (1990). *Therapy with Couples*. Blackwell, Oxford.
Culley, S. (1991). *Integrative Counselling Skills in Action*. Sage, London.
d'Ardenne, P. and Mahtani, A. (1989). *Transcultural Counselling in Action*. Sage, London.
Dallos, R. (1991). *Family Belief Systems: Therapy and Change*. Open University Press, Milton Keynes.
Dicks, H. (1967). *Marital Tensions*. Karnac, London.
Dickson, A. (1985). *The Mirror Within*. Quartet, London.
Erikson, E. (1995). *Childhood and Society*. Penguin, Harmondsworth.
Freeman, D. (1990). *Couples in Conflict*. Open University Press, Milton Keynes.
Hooper, D. and Dryden, W. (1991). *Couple Therapy: A Handbook*. Open University Press, Milton Keynes.
Jacobs, M. (1986). *The Presenting Past*. Open University Press, Milton Keynes.
Jacobs, M. (1988). *Psychodynamic Counselling in Action*. Sage, London.
James, A. and Wilson, K. (1986). *Couples, Conflict and Change*. Tavistock, London.
Kaplan, H. S. (1995). *The New Sex Therapy*. Penguin, Harmondsworth.
Klein, J. (1987). *Our Need for Others and Its Roots in Infancy*. Tavistock, London.
Lerner, H.G. (1989). *Dance of Anger*. HarperCollins, London.
Lerner, H.G. (1992). *Dance of Intimacy*. HarperCollins, London.
Litvinoff, S. (1994). *The RELATE Guide to Better Relationships*. Vermilion, London.
Litvinoff, S. (1992). *The RELATE Guide to Sex in Loving Relationships*. Vermilion, London.

Malan, D. (1979). *Individual Psychotherapy and the Science of Psychodynamics.* Butterworth, Oxford.
Marlin, E. (1989). *Genograms.* Contemporary Books, Chicago, MA.
Masters, W. and Johnson, V. (1966). *Human Sexual Response.* Churchill Livingstone, Edinburgh.
Mattinson, J. (1975). *The Reflection Process in Casework Supervision.* Institute of Marital Studies, London.
Mattinson, J. and Sinclair, I. (1979). *Mate and Stalemate.* Institute of Marital Studies, London.
Mearns, D. and Dryden, W. (1990). *Experiences of Counselling in Action.* Sage, London.
Morley, R. (1984). *Intimate Strangers.* Family Welfare Association, RELATE, Rugby.
Nelson-Jones, R. (1997). *Practical Counselling and Helping Skills.* Cassell, London.
Parkes, C.M. et al. (1991). *Attachment Across the Life Cycle.* Routledge, London.
Pincus, L. (1960). *Marriage: Studies in Emotional Conflict and Growth.* Institute of Marital Studies, London.
Ruszczynski, S. (1993). *Psychotherapy with Couples.* Karnac, London.
Sanderson, T. (1994). *Making Gay Relationships Work.* Other Way, London.
Satir, V. (1967). *Conjoint Family Therapy.* Souvenir, London.
Scarf, M. (1987). *Intimate Partners.* Ballantine, New York.
Skynner, R. (1976). *One Flesh – Separate Persons.* Constable, London.
Skynner, R. and Cleese, J. (1985). *Families and How to Survive Them.* Methuen, London.
Stewart, I. (1994). *Transactional Analysis Counselling in Action.* Sage, London.
Storr, A. (1979). *The Art of Psychotherapy.* Butterworth-Heinemann, Oxford.
Tanner, D. (1991). *You Just Don't Understand: Women and Men in Conversation.* Virago, London.
Wallerstein, J. and Blakesee, S. (1989). *Second Chances. Men, Women and Children a Decade after Divorce.* Bantam, London.
Watzlawick, P. et al. (1994). *Change.* Norton, London.
Zilbergeld, B. (1979). *Men and Sex.* Fontana, London.

REFERENCES

BAC (British Association of Counselling) (1996). *Code of Ethics – Practice for Counsellors*. BAC, Rugby.
Butler, C. (1993). *Evaluation of Whittam Drop-In Counselling Service*. RELATE, Chelmsford.
Butler, C. (1995). *The Use of Consultancy Supervision to Enhance Management Effectiveness*. University of Greenwich, London.
Crowe, M. and Ridley J. (1996). *Therapy with Couples*. Blackwell, Oxford.
Dryden, W. (1993). *Thirty Ways to Improve Counselling*. School of Education, University of Durham.
Dryden, W. (1991). *The Relevance of Research in Counselling and Psychotherapy*, Vol 3. Whurr, London.
Erikson, E. (1995). *Childhood and Society*. Vintage, London
Honey, P. and Mumford, A. (1992). *Manual of Learning Styles*. Honey, London.
Hunt, P.A. (1985). *Clients' Responses to Marriage Counselling*. Research Report No.3, National Marriage Guidance Council, London.
Kundera, M. (1991). *Immortality*. Faber, London.
Litvinoff, S. (1994). *The RELATE Guide to Better Relationships*. Vermilion, London.
Malan, D. (1979). *Individual Psychotherapy and the Science of Psychodynamics*. Butterworth, London.
Mattinson, J. (1975). *The Reflection Process in Casework Supervision*. Institute of Marital Studies, London.
Mattinson, J. and Sinclair, I. (1979). *Mate and Stalemate*. Institute of Marital Studies, London.
McCarthy, P. et al. (1996). *Going to RELATE: The Short-term Effects*. RELATE Centre for Family Studies, University of Newcastle.
Nelson-Jones, R. (1993). *You Can Help*. Cassell, London.
RELATE (1995). *Client Evaluation of RELATE Counselling – Intermim Report*. RELATE Centre for Family Studies, University of Newcastle.
Sanderson, C. (1995). *Counselling Adult Survivors of Child Sexual Abuse*. Jessica Kingley Publications, London.
Schein, E.H. (1993). How can organisations learn faster? *Sloan Management Review*, **34**, 85.
Skynner, R. and Cleese, J. (1985). *Families and How to Survive Them*. Methuen, London.
Walker, J. (1995). *Client Evaluation of RELATE Counselling in the Midland Region*. RELATE Centre for Family Studies, University of Newcastle.

Winnicott, D.W. (1964). *The Child, the Family and the Outside World.* Penguin, Harmondsworth.

Zand, D.E. (1993). Managers and consulting. *Journal of Management Development* (USA), **12**, 51.

INDEX

Action, 19
   as a skill, 87
   stage 22, 81, 83
Affairs, 44, 47, 60
   counselling with, 145–6
Alcohol, 164–5
Ambivalence, 56
Anger, 144
   behaviour check-list, 95
Anxiety, 141
Assessment, 27–9
Attachment, 61–5
Autonomy, 3, 14
Awareness, 51

Behaviour, 19–20
  case example, 88
  guidelines, 86
  harming, 33
  modification, 20, 86–7
Bereavement, 166
Bonding, 63
Boundaries, 71, 145–7
  professional, 50

Case notes, 39–40
Challenging, 20, 82–5
Change, 89–90
  closed to, 33
Client
  base, 14
  categories, 46
Coercion, 3
Collusion, 55
Commitment, 31, 33, 47
Communication, 20–1, 90, 92–5, 107
Confidentiality, 31

Contracts, 47–9
Counselling
   access to, 7
   other/psychotherapeutic, 7–9
Counter-transference, 130–3
Couple
   defining the problem, 9–10
   nature of, 1–2

Defences, 141
Depression, 163
Discriminatory practice, 1, 141–3
Divorce, 3
   counselling, 168
   see also Separation
Drama Triangle, the, 160, 161

Empathy, 41–2
Endings, 23, 167–8
   casework example, 174–6
   difficult, 180–83
Equality, 12
Ethnic balance, 11
Exploration, 15
   initial, 34–9
   stage, 17

False Memory Syndrome, 161
Fidelity, *see* Affairs
Focus, 44
   see also Presenting problem
Funding, 13

Gay couples, 12
   casework example, 123
Gender, 43, 12
Genogram, 21, 96–7, 101
   casework examples, 98, 101

Health, physical and mental, 37–8
Homeostasis, 70
Homosexual couples, *see* Gay couples, Lesbian couples

Immediacy, 84
Intake, 27
  assessment, 28–9
  procedure, 16, 27
Intimacy, 142

Jealousy, 66
Joharri window, 41

Learning, interpersonal, 6–7
Legal action, 38, 153
Lesbian couples, 12
  casework example, 68
Life stages, 75–8
Listening, 42, 93
Loss, 166

Marital fit, 55
Mental illness, 9, 32, 155–7
Mourning, 176–9

Object Relations Theory, 61
Oedipal feelings, 65, 66
Other agencies, 38

Payment, 50–1
Person-centred counselling, 42
PLISSIT model, 112
Presenting problem, 35–6, 44–5
Problems, 22–3, 36
  gender attitudes, 43
  joint/individual, 10
  with the counselling, 134–5
Projective identification, 57
Psychodynamic, 8, 53
Psychosexual therapy (PST), 110
Psycho-social element, 75
Psychotherapy, 8–9, 17

Reframing, 20, 85–6
Referrals, 14
RELATE Approach, overall map, 26
Relationship, 14

clients without a, 32
focus, 34
Repression, 54
Resistance, 139–40
Review, 174

Safety
  of client, 14
  of counsellor, 144
Sculpting, 21, 102–4
Secrets, 149
Separation, 169–72
Sex abuse, 123
  counselling, 172–3
  indicators, 158
  work with, 159
Sex and couples
  casework examples, 115–6
  emotional influences, 122
  physical influences, 121
  sexual counselling, 124
  sexual dysfunctions, 111–12
  sexual problems and emotional interaction, 128
  sexual response, 117, 118
Split agenda, 46, 172
Splitting and projecting, 55–60
Suicide, 9, 22, 162–3
Supervision, 13, 14, 141
Systems, 70–4

Therapeutic alliance, 40
  problems with, 143–4
Three-stage model, 15
Transactional analysis (TA), 21, 105–8
Training, 13
Transference, 53–5
Triangle of conflict, 141–3
Triangular relationships, 65–70
Trust, 43
Unconscious, the, 18, 53
Understanding, 16
  model, 52–3, 79–80
  stage, 19, 52